HOW
AUSTRALIA
BECAME
BRITISH

ABOUT THE AUTHOR

Howard T. Fry is a historian specialising in the expansion of the British trade during the long eighteenth century. Having served in the Second World War in the army and RAF, he returned to academia, serving first as a schoolmaster and then taking his Ph.D from Cambridge with a thesis on Alexander Dalrymple. He established and taught a course on South-East Asian history for the University of North Queensland, spending two decades of his career in Australia; in 1984 he was awarded a Harold White Research Fellowship at the National Library of Australia.

HOW AUSTRALIA BECAME BRITISH

EMPIRE AND THE CHINA TRADE

HOWARD T. FRY

AMBERLEY

This book is dedicated to my beloved wife Georgiana, and to the memory to my dear late Australian cousin, Lisa Cameron.

I would like to express my deep appreciation for the help received from the following:

Jason Ng, whose careful typing at an early stage saved me from hours of work; Betty and Joseph Ng whose early help got the project started; George Reade who presented me with a DVD of Abbe Raynal's 6 volumes, History of the European Colonies in the West and East, *which has been of great use and will continue to be of great interest in the future; Madeleine Gill whose continuous help and tips in the use of my computer have been invaluable; and Ellis whose computer skills have been invaluable as the book approached publication.*

First published 2016

Amberley Publishing
The Hill, Stroud
Gloucestershire, GL5 4EP

www.amberley-books.com

Copyright © Howard T. Fry, 2016

The right of Howard T. Fry to be identified as the Author of this work has been asserted in accordance with the Copyrights, Designs and Patents Act 1988.

ISBN 978 1 4456 6498 9 (paperback)
ISBN 978 1 4456 6499 6 (ebook)

British Library Cataloguing in Publication Data.
A catalogue record for this book is available from the British Library.

Typesetting and Origination by Amberley Publishing.
Printed in the UK.

CONTENTS

INTRODUCTION

The opening chapter of this book deals with the memorable voyage of the *Pitt* East Indiaman, under the command of Commodore William Wilson, when new ways of reaching China were tried and found practicable for ships that had been delayed and were unable to make full use of the prevailing monsoon before it changed. In the case of the *Pitt*, not only had she been late in leaving England but she had also been delayed by sickness amongst the passengers en route. Ships like the *Pitt* were notoriously unhealthy to sail in but this had been made much worse by the fact that she was overcrowded. In addition to her 311 officers and men (and she was only designed for 250) she was also transporting an additional 164 soldiers. The voyage was taking place in the middle of the Seven Years' War, and the opportunity was being taken to send out to Fort St George, Madras these soldiers as reinforcement in anticipation of an early attack by French troops under the command of Lally. As a result, twenty-eight seamen and thirty soldiers had already died before reaching India, where another thirty-two were to be lost. Because of the great increase in the consumption of tea in England after 1784, the size of the East Indiamen ships was steadily increasing, and the *Pitt* was armed because she was expected to combine the role of merchantman and warship.

When an Indiaman suffered delays on its journey out, the standard practice was for the vessel to put into a friendly port and to stay there until the favourable monsoon returned; that might, of course, entail a stay of anything up to six months and was a very expensive procedure. Wilson knew that it was common for ships based in Madras, bound for the Malabar coast of India and for Persia during the south-west monsoon, to leave Madras on a south-easterly heading until they crossed the equator and reached the region where south-east trade winds blew. They then headed westwards until they were well beyond the meridian of their intended port, after which they headed back north across the equator, and so sailed before the monsoon to their destination. He decided to use the same principle to reach China and avoid the north-east monsoon in the China Sea. If he could prove that the theory was practicable, East-Indiamen in the future would be able to reach China at any time of the year with a great saving in time and money.

Wilson had proceeded as far as the south-western coast of north-western New Guinea when he found a strait – later called Pitt's Strait – to carry the *Pitt* into the Pacific Ocean. Henceforth he would continue towards Japan until he was able to alter course to a north-westerly heading that would bring her, after coasting the northern shore of the Philippines, to the port of Canton. After safely returning to England by the same route, he received the East India Company's Gold Medal from a grateful court of directors.

The *Pitt* had been too large and well-armed for the Dutch

to challenge, but when other smaller East-Indiamen tried Wilson's route, they were immediately stopped and the EIC was made to realise that the Dutch could yield to French blandishments if the EIC persisted in such incursions. As a result the Eastern Passage remained unexploited, save for a brief period during the 1786–70 Falkland Island Crisis, until the French Revolution and Napoleonic Wars, when its use became habitual.

In 1785 the boy Napoleon graduated from military academy and was posted to a training school for young officers where he continued his education, in the course of which he did much reading and was absorbed by the six-volume history of the European colonies in India and America by G-T, Abbé de Raynal, which was first published in 1770 and had gone through 30 editions by 1789; a new edition has recently recently been published in the USA. In this work he was able to read of the exploratory work of the Portuguese as they found their way from Portugal to India and the East Indies, amassing great riches in the process. He read how in due course they had been superseded by the Dutch and the Dutch East Indian empire. In view of the fact that the French East India Company was being re-established at the very time that he was reading this volume, it was no surprise that it fired his imagination and ambition.

Meanwhile, as the British had been concentrating upon improving their lines of communication with the east, they had been forced to recognise that the South China Sea presented an insuperable problem. All three member states of the Triple Alliance had been bitterly disappointed by the terms of the peace treaty, which had seen France gain nothing and Spain fail to recover Gibraltar; while the Dutch found the Austrian Netherlands in control of much of their European trade. Yet France was trying hard to reform the Triple Alliance and if she was successful, the South China Sea would become a dangerous place for the East India Company's shipping in time of war, since that sea's eastern shores were controlled by the Spanish Philippines, the southern shores formed part of the Dutch East Indies, and its western shores were rapidly coming under French strong influence. The French missionary Bishop Pigneau de Behanie was helping the Nguyen Dynasty regain political control of Cochin China (modern South Vietnam) in the wake of the Tay-son rebellion. In 1786 he set out for France where he had an audience with King Louis XVI and some of his senior advisers, and on 28 November 1787 a Franco-Cochin China 'treaty' was signed, though it was never to come into force. This and some effective military persistence, led by the bishop himself, gave the French great influence for a time on the western shore of the South China Sea. Its northern coast was China itself, then in a state of political chaos. All this left the South China Sea under the effective control of the potential Triple Alliance, which would mean that any English East-Indiamen damaged as a result of military action or stormy weather would have no friendly harbour to turn to.

The East India Company needed to find an alternative approach to Canton, at the very time that the English government was searching for a base for a convict settlement, and it was in April 1785 that the House of Commons set up a committee under the chairmanship of Lord Beauchamp to seek for a site. Matra and Sir Joseph Banks immediately urged that such a settlement should be located in New Holland and both were anxious that it should be in Botany Bay.

The year 1785 was promising to be a challenging one for the English East India Company, with its French counterpart revived and a new Franco-Dutch alliance being negotiated. The EIC needed a new harbour to replace those off-limits in South China Sea. Its ships were already regularly using the Eastern Passage, which approached China from the Pacific, and a Pacific base was needed to link up that Pacific Ocean approach to Canton. The obvious solution was the magnificent Botany Bay, discovered by Captain Cook in 1770. After experienced captains of East-Indiamen had given assurances that the hitherto unused section of this east-coast route to China would prove practical and safe, the government gave its approval and Botany Bay was established both as a penal settlement and an East India Company base. The ready availability of naval stores at Norfolk Island was of an importance that needs no emphasis.

Chapter One

THE DISCOVERY AND INCREASING USE OF THE EASTERN PASSAGE

When the *Pitt* East Indiaman dropped anchor off Fort St George, Madras, on 14 September 1758, it was evident that she could not reach Macao before the onset of the north-east monsoon, which sets in, in the South China Sea, during the month of October. In such circumstances, it was the normal practice for a ship to put in at some safe port en route and to remain there for some six months awaiting the return of the favourable south-west monsoon. For Commodore William Wilson, however, who was in command of the *Pitt*, such an expensive delay was unacceptable, and he decided to make an audacious experiment. He would test the practicability of a new route to China, and sailing by way of Batavia,[1] the south coast of Celebes, and through what was to become known as Pitt's Strait between the islands of Battanta and Salawatty, off the north-western coast of New Guinea, he reached the Pacific Ocean, whence, sailing around the eastern and northern shores of the Philippine Islands, he finally reached Macao on 3 April 1759. This pioneering voyage was immediately recognised as marking the beginning of a new era in the history of the China trade, and in recognition of his feat the East India Company's grateful Court of Directors bestowed upon the commodore its gold medal. The discovery of this new route benefited the Company's maritime service in two ways; in the first place it meant that East Indiamen could henceforth sail to and from China at any season of the year instead of their voyages having to synchronise with the prevailing monsoon in the South China Sea, and second, in time of war, this new Eastern Passage would enable these ships to reach Macao and Canton even when an enemy controlled both the Straits of Malacca and Sunda, hitherto the principal means of access to China for ships approaching from the west.[2]

The use of this new route, however, did threaten to entail political tension with both Spain and Holland. In the first place, its discovery coincided with Alexander Dalrymple's attempt to open a new trading post for the East India Company in the Sulu Archipelago. He was trying to find a base outside the sphere of effective Spanish or Dutch occupation or control, and not too far from China, a port which both East Indiamen and Chinese junks would find it convenient to reach and which would enable them to trade with each other free from the vexatious and expensive interference of Chinese officialdom.[3] But as Captain (later Admiral) Richard Kempenfelt observed, even though the prospects were promising, 'I apprehend it will require a nice Judgment and Dexterous Management to Effect this, in such a manner as not too much to alarm and raise the jealousy of other European states.' The perspicacity of this remark was underlined by Dalrymple's assuring him that 'we may if we please have a share in the Spice Trade without interfering with those Islands the Dutch have settlements at, as in the S.E. part of those Seas are many islands probably not known to the Dutch abounding with Spices, some of them producing Cinnamon equal to that of Ceylone [*sic*] besides several other Commodities for Commerce'.[4]

This was precisely what the Dutch feared. Their monopoly of the Spice Trade was based upon treaties concluded with the Sultans of Ternate and Tidore, whereby the production of cloves and nutmeg was confined to the islands of Amboina and Banda. Outside this area, all spice trees were ordered to be exterminated. To enforce this system, annual expeditions were organised consisting of fleets of armed proas, manned by Amboinese and Bandanese islanders and commanded by Dutch officers. It was the task of these fleets to visit the coasts of other islands in the region and to cut down all unlicensed spice trees found growing there. By this means, the production of spices in the Moluccas was reduced to a quarter of what it had been before the Dutch East India Company gained control of the region. This was obviously beneficial from the Dutch Company's point of view, but it was disastrous for the welfare of the islanders at large in the archipelago, who thus lost their principal means of livelihood. Hence, the Dutch were very apprehensive at the opening up of this new route to China, which would bring the powerful ships of the English East India Company into close proximity of the Moluccas and of the numerous islands to the eastward. The Dutch saw this as a threat to the continuance of their monopoly of the Spice Trade, a threat that would be reinforced if Dalrymple's Sulu scheme was allowed to go ahead. Furthermore, while the British might argue that the Sulu Archipelago lay outside the sphere of effective Spanish control, the Spaniards would certainly not admit this to be the case, nor allow the establishment of a British trading post there to go unchallenged.

Given this background, the Dutch had reacted to Commodore Wilson's new discovery with predictable hostility. Because the *Pitt* was a large new East Indiaman of 600 tons displacement, and carried fifty guns, it had been impossible for the Dutch on the spot to do more than shadow this ship's progress, but when another East Indiaman followed this same new route to China in 1760, it was stopped and its captain was informed that no English ship was in future to navigate in those seas since 'all the countrys [*sic*] round belong'd to the Dutch Company'. In addition, fearing that the English were planning to establish a settlement on the island of Salawatty, off the north-west coast of New Guinea, in 1762 the Dutch authorities despatched an expedition with orders (so the Directors of the English East India Company reported) 'to extirpate all the English which might be found there, to make an effective cruise all along the coast of Pa-pos [i.e Papua], to set on fire all the vessels they might meet with on that coast, to take no prisoners, to be as auxiliaries to the Kings of Tidore and Ternate in doing this, and effectually to root out and destroy all interlopers'.[5]

While this Dutch fear for the preservation of their spice monopoly posed one difficult problem for the English East India Company, relations with Spain were even more strained. Spain's belated entry into the Seven Years' War had promptly led to the British capture of Manila. Had it been practicable, at the war's end, for Britain to retain this prize with its superb harbour, this would have revolutionised the East India Company's trade with China and would have greatly added to the security of its sea-lanes to Macao and Canton, but if such a move was ever in the Company's mind, any such thoughts soon had to be discarded. For, as Parkinson pointed out, the Spanish settlement in the Philippines incurred a heavy annual financial loss to Spain, the deficit in the revenues having to be met by an annual subsidy from Mexico of at least one million dollars, this sum being brought in by the famous Manila galleons sailing from Acapulco. Manila, in turn, supplied the whole of the East with its currency, including the British settlements, and with the British capture of Manila this source of specie had suddenly dried up.[6] So Manila was returned to Spain at the peace, and to avoid causing further friction with either Spain or Holland, the English East India Company thereafter avoided making further use of the Eastern Passage so long as the peace endured. For the ending of the Seven Years' War had seen France deprived of her powerful position and influence in India and the East, and this was a loss that her statesmen were determined, if possible, to avenge. The British therefore had to beware of creating a situation where the Dutch and the Spaniards would be tempted to form a triple alliance with France against Britain in any future war in the East.

Furthermore, Anglo-Spanish rivalry also extended to Latin America. Britain, in the early stages of her industrial revolution, was anxious to open up new markets for her manufactures in Latin America, and when the Spanish Government sought to exclude British goods from entering these colonies, Britain responded by opening free ports in the Caribbean. Traders from central and south America soon found their way to these ports, and thus British goods were enabled to reach these markets, to the irritation of the Spanish authorities.

In the case of the Pacific, too, Anglo-Spanish tension was soon to arise again. In the two decades that preceded the Seven

Years' War, English and French writers had been calling for the exploration of the Pacific, arguing that such an enormous expanse of ocean, covering approximately one-third of the earth's surface, could be expected to contain a great landmass, the fabled *Terra Australis Incognita*.[7] As soon as the Seven Years' War was over, both the French and English were anxious to put these theories to the test. The French were very eager to replace the empire that had been lost in this war, and it was no coincidence that the man chosen to lead the first French expedition to the Pacific, Louis-Antoine de Bougainville, had played a distinguished role in the war in Canada as ADC to General Louis-Joseph de Montcalm. The British, however, had one crucial advantage in their exploration of the Pacific. Unlike the French, they knew precisely where to look for any great landmass, since Alexander Dalrymple, as a preliminary step to any such exploration, had made a careful and prolonged study of all the known discoveries that had hitherto been made in that ocean, thus demonstrating precisely within what limits any such continent must exist. This vital contribution to the success of the great subsequent searches and discoveries of Captain Cook has never yet received the recognition that it should be accorded.[8]

In ignorance, as yet, of the prevailing winds that blew in the Pacific Ocean, both the French and the British, unbeknown to one another, yet contemporaneously and in the persons of Bougainville and Byron, established rival settlements in the East and West Falklands respectively in 1764–65, in preparation for exploratory voyages to the Pacific Ocean. It was believed that these settlements would provide an essential base for such work, but when Byron accidentally came across Bougainville in the Strait of Magellan he abandoned the search that he had been ordered to undertake for a possible passage linking California ('New Albion') with Hudson's Bay, and instead, after sending back charts and an announcement of his change of plans, raced back to England by the most direct trans-Pacific route. It seems highly probable that he was anxious to get back home as quickly as possible in order to report in person on this unexpected French presence in Patagonia, and what it might mean, before playing a leading role in the preparations for the follow-up voyage of Wallis and Carteret. France and Spain were both Bourbon monarchies, allied in the Family Compact. It is not impossible to imagine Byron haunted by a fear that Bougainville's presence in the Strait of Magellan might presage a Franco-Spanish design to hinder a British approach to the Pacific via this strait or Cape Horn.

The Spanish government reacted sharply to the presence of these settlements in the Falkland Islands, and the Spanish ambassador at Paris was instructed to demand that the French base should be surrendered to Spain. In view of the importance of the Family Compact for France's plans for the future, the French felt compelled to comply with this demand, and in April 1766 Bougainville himself was sent to Madrid to negotiate for the surrender of the islands to Spain. But the British case proved more difficult. A follow-up voyage by Captain Macbride had been organised in 1766, with instructions to establish a fortified settlement at Port Egmont and to continue the survey of the islands begun by Byron. Egmont himself, the First Lord of the Admiralty, not only described the Falklands as 'the key to the whole of the Pacific Ocean,' but considered that the British settlement 'must command the Ports and trade of Chile, Peru, Panama, Acapulco, and ... all the Spanish territory upon that sea'.[9] In 1768, the Madrid Government sent instructions to the Captain-General at Buenos Aires that no English settlements were to be permitted in the islands, and that any existing ones, after due warning, were to be expelled by force. In pursuit of these orders, a Spanish squadron appeared off Port Egmont in February 1770, and though the squadron returned to Buenos Aires without further incident, a second expedition large enough to expel the British settlement was in due course landed, opened fire on the fort and obliged the defenders to surrender.

What made the crisis all the more dangerous was the fact that the Family Compact implied that Spain would be backed by France, and the latter was now in the process of becoming a formidable naval power. Aware that the loss of France's overseas possessions in the late war had largely been due to her lack of adequate sea power, steps had now been taken to put this right. Under the able and energetic leadership of the Duc de Choiseul, a large number of new ships, many of them of improved design, had been constructed, French arsenals and dockyards had been brought up to scratch, and great attention was being paid to the professional training of naval officers. Within a few years of the ending of the late war, the French navy had thus been built up into a formidable force, and this had been achieved at the very time that the British navy was being run down in the interests of economy after that financially stressful war.

What made the Falkland Islands crisis of 1770–71 seem particularly dangerous was the fact that Choiseul had nominated the year 1770 as that in which France and her navy would be ready for war. Thus it came about that with Great Britain and Spain on the brink of war, in the autumn of

1770, the English East India Company decided that the time had come to make use of the Eastern Passage for its China-bound East Indiamen once more. However, the need to do so soon passed in the wake of a series of developments aimed at defusing the crisis. First, King Louis XV, despite having given orders in 1763 for the preparation of a comprehensive plan for a future war with England, dismissed the Duc de Choiseul on 24 December 1770 and wrote to King Charles III of Spain asking him, if possible, 'to preserve peace without injury to your honour,' while Lord North had also concluded that the islands were not worth fighting for. War had thus been narrowly averted,[10] and with peace once more assured, the East India Company's ships promptly discontinued their use of the Eastern Passage and reverted to their customary routes leading to the South China Sea.

While this Latin American crisis had now been safely resolved, however, that between Britain and her North American colonies was becoming ever more dangerous, and the French were closely following developments in order to gauge the most opportune moment to intervene, and this was judged to have arrived when news was received of Burgoyne's surrender of his army and the signing of the Convention of Saratoga on 17 October 1777. This induced the French Government to recognise the newly proclaimed United States of America and to conclude treaties of alliance and commerce with the new country, the alliance being formally concluded in February 1778. Thus, Britain and France were once more at war, and French pressure was immediately brought to bear upon Spain to join in as well. This left the Spanish authorities in a quandary. A successful war might allow them to recover Gibraltar and Minorca, but they realised that a war waged on behalf of Britain's rebellious North American colonists would send a most dangerous signal to Spain's own increasingly restive Central and South American colonies. Her response was accordingly unenthusiastic, nevertheless by June 1779 she had entered the war against Britain. In the case of the Dutch, the Republic did not choose to go to war, but became involved through its readiness to risk all in the pursuit of trade. First, from their West Indian island of St Eustatius the Dutch were carrying on a very large-scale and lucrative arms trade with the rebellious colonists, and at the same time were supplying naval stores to both France and Spain. Then, when Empress Catherine II of Russia persuaded Sweden and Denmark to join Russia in forming the Armed Neutrality in August 1780, the Dutch, exasperated by British seizures of their shipping, appeared ready to join. They apparently calculated that Great Britain would not dare to involve herself in war with yet another European Power, and that Russia and her partners would be ready to give them direct support. Since the Dutch were totally unprepared for war, this was a rash gamble, and they were soon to pay a very high price for their miscalculation when the British declared war on them on 29 November 1780.

It was now no longer possible for the British to look upon the recovery of the North American colonies as being likely to prove practicable, and as early as 22 March 1778 Lord Howe had been advised that 'the object of the war being now changed' and 'the contest in America being a secondary consideration, the principal object must now be the distressing France and securing his Majesty's own possessions against any hostile attempts'.[11] In this new situation, the subcontinent of India and the surrounding seas, including the sea-lanes leading to China, became a main focus of attention, and once more

East Indiamen began using the Eastern Passage to and from China.[12] And on 3 February 1779, in anticipation of France being joined in the war by Spain, and possibly by the Dutch as well, the East India Company, greatly concerned over the security of its sea-lanes to China, appointed Alexander Dalrymple as its official hydrographer. The most immediate problem related to the Malay Archipelago, especially if the Dutch joined in the war, when the usual routes by way of the Straits of Malacca and Sunda would no longer be available. Dalrymple therefore set to work studying alternative routes at the eastern end of that archipelago, which were beyond the limits of Dutch control, including the Eastern Passage, as well as Pacific routes to the east of Australia and New Zealand. The result was his Memoir concerning the Passages to and from China wherein he listed five distinct Passages.[13]

The winding up of the virtually bankrupt French East India Company in 1769 had left many footloose adventurers searching for employment, and it had become French policy to encourage these men to serve in the armies of the various independent Indian princes, while simultaneously maintaining French diplomatic influence in these same princely courts, thus seeking to undermine the political and economic power of their British rivals.[14]

Fierce naval engagements in the Bay of Bengal between the fleets of Admirals de Suffren and Hughes had proved indecisive, while British attempts to capture the Cape of Good Hope and Trincomali had proved unsuccessful. But it was the Nawab of Arcot's attempt to repay his debts by seizing some rich lands in neighbouring Mysore that created a serious crisis for the East India Company when the ruler of Mysore, Haidar Ali, retaliated so fiercely that his troops came within sight of the Company's base at Fort St George, Madras, before a force under Sir Eyre Coote was able to relieve that station. A French expeditionary force under de Bussy, in alliance with Haidar Ali, tried to exploit that opportunity, but it arrived too late, after Haidar Ali's death, and the chance was lost, and when peace negotiations began in Europe, the Company's position in India remained intact.

Great Britain had come out of the war in rather better shape than might have been anticipated, but the Dutch had suffered severely. Their woes in Europe will be discussed in the next chapter, but in Asia, too, their East India Co. was in dire straits. A characteristic feature of the Dutch empire in the East was the way in which its trade with the rest of Asia had been concentrated in the port of Batavia. In the recent war this had increased the vulnerability of the Dutch Co., which had been unable to prevent an effective British blockade of its ports in the Malay Archipelago. As a result, all direct communication between the Dutch East Indies and the Netherlands had been severed and great quantities of unsold tropical products had accumulated in the storehouses of Batavia. Not only were the usual supplies of silver and copper coins from Holland no longer forthcoming, but the Company's directors, in their blind commitment to the maintenance of their monopoly of the spice trade at all costs, would not allow Batavia to sell these goods, worth many millions, on the open market, which would have procured for the Company the cash it so urgently needed. Hence, as Vlekke observed, 'they dealt a death blow to their own Company'.[15]

At the same time, the Dutch negotiators were trying their hardest to prevent the English from obtaining, as they were demanding in the peace talks, 'liberty to navigate and trade in the Eastern Seas without Molestation'. Faced with fierce opposition from the Dutch negotiators, the English were prepared to concede that 'it was by no means the intention of the East India Company to pretend to any Trade with the Dutch settlements there ...' But it certainly did want the Country Traders to be active in that area. The financing of the China trade had now become heavily dependent upon the Country Trade with the Malay Archipelago, and this is what the East India Company surely had in mind when it presented its original demand for liberty to navigate and trade in those seas without molestation. Furthermore, the English Company's refusal to give up its claim to a free navigation in the Eastern Seas was obviously necessitated by its determination to preserve its right to use the various forms of the Eastern Passage to China in times both of peace and of war. The security of the China trade was dependent upon that right. But from a Dutch perspective, the passage of heavily armed English East Indiamen through waters in close proximity to their Spice Islands posed a dangerous threat to the continuance of their spice monopoly, where the Dutch commerce was based, for the most part, not upon territorial possession, but upon treaties and contracts concluded with the local rulers. It was not difficult to foresee that any fresh occurrence of Anglo-Dutch friction might tempt these same rulers to forswear their existing allegiance, thus putting these treaties and contracts, and the whole Dutch monopoly of the Spice Trade, at risk.

Chapter Two

THE ANGLO-FRENCH STRUGGLE TO WIN OVER THE ALLEGIANCE OF THE DUTCH REPUBLIC

The peace that followed the American War was a very fragile affair, since France, Spain and the United Provinces were all dissatisfied with the peace terms that they had been obliged to accept. The French were unhappy at having failed to recover their former influence in India, Spain was disappointed at having failed to regain Gibraltar, while the Dutch had been compelled to grant the English East India Company free navigation for its ships in eastern waters, a capitulation which they feared might endanger the future of their monopoly of the spice trade. In addition to these causes of instability, an acute rivalry was also developing between Austria and the Dutch Republic, and any dispute involving the latter and a European Power was always likely to be of concern to Britain on two counts.

In Europe itself, the Dutch controlled British access to some very valuable markets on the continent, while, from a military viewpoint, the Dutch Netherlands had always been seen as providing a potential base for any enemy planning an invasion of the British Isles. Hence, it had long been a maxim of British policy to prevent any major European Power from gaining control of that strategic coastline. Overseas the Dutch East Indies controlled vital sea-lanes on the route to China, which was why British ministers were particularly apprehensive over the likelihood of a new Franco-Dutch alliance being formed.

The new Austro-Dutch rivalry was a direct consequence of the American War. For, as the Annual Register noted at the time, the war years had seen the transfer from Holland to the Austrian Netherlands 'of that vast commerce, which ... England carried on with that and other Eastern and Northern continental countries'. At the same time, attacked, at once, in every part of the world, and nearly overwhelmed by the multitude of her enemies, Great Britain was forced in large measure to abandon the protection of her own commerce, so that her fleets in foreign parts might be sufficiently powerful to defend her very numerous foreign possessions. This was a situation which English merchants had never experienced in any other war, and which had compelled them to seek 'the protection of foreign flags for the first time'. These factors had combined to make Ostend 'a general mart to all the neutral, as well as the belligerent states; and such an influx of trade was carried into that city and port, that it arrived, even early in the war, at a degree of opulence and commercial importance, which it never before enjoyed, or was expected to attain'.

Furthermore, this writer noted, the imperial flag, which had hitherto been considered of negligible importance by the maritime powers, 'was now conspicuous in every part of the world, and the seas covered with ships under its protection'. All these circumstances had combined to encourage a spirit of commercial adventure in every part of the Austrian Netherlands and had stimulated the citizens of Antwerp to visualise a revival of their city's historic fortunes, For Antwerp had once been the world's greatest port, but had seen its prosperity decline in the sixteenth and seventeenth centuries after the Dutch had closed the river Scheldt to navigation. In March 1781, the Emperor Joseph II had begun a five months' visit to take personal possession of the Austrian Netherlands, in the course of which he had visited Antwerp where he had been presented with a memorial requesting that he would take measures for the opening and reestablishment of that port. This, therefore, became the primary aim of his foreign policy in 1784, as soon as peace had been re-established.[1]

By way of contrast, the Dutch republic had suffered severely as a result of the war and had revealed a radical weakness that 'had never before been suspected, even by its nearest neighbours,'[2] and it was this weakness in a country that was 'convulsed and torn to pieces by intestine dissensions' which encouraged the Emperor to act. In the first place, he forced the Dutch to withdraw their garrisons from the Barrier Fortresses, whose continued existence he considered to be an anomaly. Then, in early April 1784, the Austrians made their first test of the firmness of Dutch resolve by attempting to send a ship down the river from Antwerp towards the sea, an attempt which resulted in the vessel being fired upon as it passed the Dutch fort at Lillo.[3]

With the Emperor thus bent upon opening the river Scheldt to navigation in the interests of the citizens of Antwerp, and the Dutch committed to an obdurate defence of its closure in the interests of their own prosperity, the prospects for the immediate future did not look promising, and Sir Robert Keith, British ambassador in Vienna, agreed that 'the opinion of the Foreign Ministers in London that a Storm on the Continent is to be expected, seems to be confirmed by a variety of circumstances'.[4] The danger of war appeared still greater when, on 23 August 1784, Count Belgiojoso, the Governor of the Austrian Netherlands, made a final demand for the opening of the Scheldt. Thereupon everything, reported *The Annual Register*, 'seemed tending rapidly to the most decisive and alarming crisis,' when, in addition to 'the entire and free navigation of the Schelde from Antwerp to the sea,' Joseph II not only demanded that the Dutch should dismantle and demolish the forts which had been erected to enforce their monopoly of the navigation of that river, but had added what the reporter described as a new, extraordinary demand, namely for 'a free navigation to and in both the East and West Indies ... A requisition which,' the writer commented 'taken to its full extent, would have reached to their monopoly of the Spice Islands, and even to their trade in Japan'. This was followed by the grave development of 8 October 1784, when an imperial brig, having passed Lillo and some other forts without examination, was sighted by a Dutch naval cutter near the mouth of the river. When all other methods of persuasion had failed, the Dutch cutter fired a broadside and threatened to sink the imperial vessel if she did not immediately bring to, whereupon her captain, whose orders expressly forbade him to submit to any detention, left his ship, and a Dutch boarding party took over.

This incident resulted in the imperial ambassador at The Hague being recalled, and the Brussels negotiations between the Austrians and the Dutch breaking up. With an Austrian army of some sixty thousand men already reportedly preparing to march north to the Netherlands, war was generally thought to be imminent.

It was at this stage that the British authorities began to pay particular attention to the naval implications of recent developments In the first place, the situation in the Baltic, which was such an important source of naval supplies, was causing increasing concern. There the conduct of Sweden was coming under close scrutiny, and early in 1784 Carmarthen, the new Foreign Secretary, had informed Sir Robert Keith, the British ambassador in Vienna, that he had lately received intelligence 'of a most extraordinary plan, adopted by the court of Sweden, and no doubt at the instigation of France, ... of an invasion of Norway ... during the ensuing Spring'. Since Norway was then a part of the Kingdom of Denmark, he believed this to be part of 'one great system ... calculated to involve the Court of Petersburgh [*sic*] in a Northern war, in order to prevent any exertions of that power in the East'.[5] Kaunitz, the Austrian Chancellor, had told Keith that the fear of such an invasion had 'very lately engaged the Court of Copenhagen to prepare a fleet, and to embark some regiments, in order to put Norway in a complete state of defence'.[6]

This was followed, during the summer, by the King of Sweden's visit to Paris, during which Dorset, the British ambassador, reported that 'whispers ... have been circulated concerning the cession of Gottenburg, or some Port of Sweden, to France'. He himself doubted that an actual cession had been agreed to, but did believe that 'the liberty of building and fitting out ships of war in that or some other Port has really been offered'. Then, when he approached de Vergennes on the subject, the French Foreign minister had told him that in return for the Caribbean island of St Bartholomew the King of Sweden had 'consented to allow Gottenburg, instead of Wismar, to be an entrepot for the French trade in the Baltic'. This was an obvious threat to Britain's naval supplies, though Pitt thought that it might be turned to political advantage by becoming 'a ground work of some further connexion with Denmark and Russia,' who had both reacted angrily to the Swedish move. Then Hailes, the Secretary of the Embassy, told Carmarthen that while he had at first thought that any French advantage from gaining free use of the port of Gottenburg was 'extremely problematical, not to say visionary, from the very little protection [France] would be able to give to its Fleets arriving from that port, without one in the Channel,' further reflection had persuaded him that this was the explanation for the work then in progress to develop the port of Cherbourg. 'Everything concurs to induce me to believe,' he wrote, 'that the construction of this Port is the grand object of the Cabinet at this moment, and the very peculiar advantages it will possess from its spaciousness and situation must render it very formidable to England ... The Harbour will be able to contain a hundred Ships of the Line.'[7]

With regard to India, Lord Torrington, the British minister at Brussels, had supplied information which, the chairman of the East India Co. told Carmarthen, was 'so perfectly consonant to those instructions which Mons. De Bussy set out with, when he sail'd to India, that I tremble for the consequences'. He described the measures contemplated by the French as being 'so well plan'd, and ... calculated to so effectually assist the Natives in their wars against us, without awakening jealousy or distrust in their minds, of any latent views on the part of France afterwards to enslave them, that I much fear it may have too successful an effect for our interest'.[8]

It had long been anticipated that the French and the Dutch would conclude an alliance, and one of the first acts of Lord Carmarthen, on becoming Foreign Secretary, had been to instruct Lord Dorset, the British Ambassador in Paris, to investigate whether there was any evidence of this. In reply, on 26 February 1784, Dorset had stated that such a proposal was indeed 'in agitation' and that he had reason to believe 'that transactions of an alarming nature and materially affecting the interests of Great Britain are carrying on between France and the States General'.[9] Now, a month after the Austrian ultimatum, this information appeared to take more concrete shape when Torrington forwarded what were claimed to be a copy of the treaty and its secret articles. His dispatches of 14 and 16 September 1784 made worrying reading, for in addition to the anticipated mutual guarantee of the two countries' possessions both in Europe and overseas, the enclosed articles not only included provisions to ensure the closest cooperation between the naval and military forces of the two powers, but specific stipulations that were certain to create unease in Great Britain. The fifteenth article, for instance, laid it down that the French were to be responsible for the defence of Trincomali, which followed upon an article arranging for

French Commissioners to be stationed at both the Cape of Good Hope and at Batavia, to ensure that the arsenals at both places were kept fully equipped to meet the needs of both the French and Dutch naval and military forces in the region in all foreseeable eventualities. The dominating role of France in the alliance was underlined by the provision that in all cases where French and Dutch troops were serving alongside one another, the overall command was always to lie with the French. But most worrying of all was the eighteenth article stated that the French and Dutch would maintain in East Indian waters, either continuously or in a condition to arrive quickly in case of need, a naval force of some fourteen ships of the line and seven frigates, of which force France would supply eight and four vessels respectively, and the Dutch six and three.[10]

Soon, however, doubts began to creep in as to the authenticity of these documents, which Torrington failed to dispel. Nevertheless, this purported information continued to trouble Carmarthen's peace of mind. These secret articles might yet prove genuine, and this made him doubly anxious to learn of the size of the French and Dutch fleets in the Eastern seas and of French plans for Trincomali. For previously, on 19 August, Torrington had reported that the French were paying unprecedented attention to their Marine; 'everything,' he had written, 'is neglected for that object, which will be carried to a pitch to surprise all Europe,' and he had added that there were persistent reports in both Holland and France that the Dutch were to yield up Trincomali to the French.[11]

The day after Carmarthen had written to Torrington requesting information as to his sources, an event occurred in the Netherlands which appeared to bring Europe to the very brink of war. In the negotiations which were being carried on in Brussels between Austrian and Dutch delegates, the Austrians had insisted that pending a final settlement the Emperor's subjects 'should occasionally exercise their undoubted right' of navigating the river Scheldt, and they had served notice that two ships were then being prepared for that very purpose. The plan was for one of these vessels to proceed down the Scheldt from Antwerp to the sea, while the other was to sail up-river from Ostend to Antwerp. Belgiojoso added the warning that 'the first shot fired upon the Schelde would be considered by his master as a declaration of war'. In the brig sailing down river from Antwerp passed Lillo and some other forts without being stopped, but when it approached the mouth of the river on 8 October it was sighted by a Dutch naval cutter. The brig's captain had been expressly forbidden 'to submit to any detention, or to any examination whatever, from any of the ships belonging to the republic'. Nevertheless, the Dutch cutter, after all other methods of persuasion had failed, fired a broadside and threatened '*to send the imperial brig* to the bottom if she did not immediately bring to'.

Refusing to comply with the Dutch demands, yet wishing to save his ship, the captain of the brig thereupon quitted his vessel and a Dutch boarding party took control.

In view of Belgiojoso's warning, this appeared to signal the outbreak of war. The imperial ambassador at The Hague was recalled, the negotiations at Brussels were broken off, and an imperial army of sixty thousand men was placed under orders to make preparations for marching north from Austria to the Netherlands.

By November 1784, the outlook appeared particularly bleak. This was a time when Keith was describing Austria's war preparations as being 'very serious and extensive,' and the Dutch had reportedly begun to have resort to that ultimate defensive tactic of flooding parts of their country. Carmarthen took the opportunity, therefore, to have a long conference with the French Ambassador, the Comte d'Adhemar, regarding the Austro-Dutch dispute, and he had been informed that a note had been sent from Versailles to Vienna wherein it was acknowledged that fresh engagements had been entered into between France and the Dutch Republic. It was therefore decided that the time had come for Sir James Harris to take up his appointment at The Hague. He had in fact been appointed to this post more than a year earlier when Fox was the minister responsible, but his move to The Hague had been delayed, initially through ill health. Yet when he had recovered, he was still held back by Carmarthen. Hailes, secretary at the Paris embassy, fretted that British interests in Holland were being jeopardised by 'the want of some able and active Person to counteract the assiduity of French intrigue,' while Pitt himself, in June had referred to 'the Necessity of Dispatching our Minister to The Hague as soon as possible; and indeed in that I think there should not be a minute lost'. Yet Carmarthen had still hesitated, prompting Harris, in some impatience, to remark, 'I presume it is still your opinion that till we can see which way to steer it will be injudicious for me to set out.'[12]

Now, however, the time was judged to have finally arrived, and it was the implications of the crisis for Britain's position in the East which had proved the spur to action. Back in the spring Torrington, it will be recalled, had provided information which the chairman of the East India Company had likened to the earlier plans of de Bussy and which, he had said, made him 'tremble for the consequences'. And Hailes had told Carmarthen that it was a M. Launay, who had once served with Haidar Ali, who had convinced the French authorities of the possibility of persuading the princes in the Indian subcontinent to revolt. These warnings did not go unheeded, and Dundas was in no doubt as to their import: 'India is the quarter to be first attacked,' he warned Sydney.[13] So when Harris finally departed for The Hague, a few days after privately dining with Pitt, he was armed with instructions from Carmarthen to concentrate his attention primarily upon developments relating to the East, rather than on affairs within Europe itself. It was more necessary than ever, he was told, to be informed of the extent of the new Franco-Dutch engagements referred to by the Comte d'Adhemar, 'and particularly so in respect to the East Indies ... [and] to be apprised as accurately as possible of the Naval and Military forces the Dutch either have, or purpose to have, in that part of the world.' He was also to travel by way of Brussels, which, it may be surmised, would give him the opportunity of weighing up the evidence underlying Torrington's reported 'secret articles,' as well as the chance to meet senior Austrian officials in that city. Harris had been sceptical on this score from the first, and his visit to Brussels did nothing to persuade him that these supposed secret articles really existed, nevertheless, he did believe that something very closely corresponding to them was in contemplation.

Harris had been at his post at The Hague barely a month when news leaked out of the Emperor's proposed exchange of the Austrian Netherlands for Bavaria, and he was dumbfounded. He believed that it would entail the overthrow of the balance of power in Europe, and it seemed to him that the situation on the continent had 'never ... been so critical, at any epoch since the breaking out of the Thirty Years War'. What he particularly feared was that France would then be in a position to dominate the former Austrian Netherlands which, taken in conjunction with her increasing influence over the Dutch Republic, might end up with 'France having the command of that whole extent of coast from Ostend to the Texel'.[14]

This followed closely on the news that a French General, de Meillebois, had been appointed to take command of the Dutch army, and that de Calonne, the French Comptroller General, had laid before the King in Council a plan to form a new French East India Company that was to be under the control of the Government, while the merchants who had given their names as subscribers were 'not to have any management or concern whatever in the territorial possessions of France in that part of the world'.[15] At this very time, Dorset was warning, 'I don't see how a war is to be averted,' and Harris concurred, saying that 'a war on the Continent is now become an almost certain event'.[16] And though these pessimistic assessments proved wide of the mark, and by the end of March there appeared to be hope that the Austro-Dutch crisis might be on the eve of resolution, this in no way abated the sense of crisis in Britain. For the only thing that was holding up the signing of a Franco-Dutch alliance was the danger felt by France that, as an ally of the Dutch, she might be dragged into an Austro-Dutch war. If the Austrians and the Dutch were able to negotiate an end to their dispute, and the pro-French Patriot party remained in power in the Dutch Republic, the immediate conclusion of a Franco-Dutch alliance could then be anticipated. Should the Bavarian Exchange follow, then France could indeed find the entire coastline from Ostend to the Texel under governments devoted to her interest, in which case the Low Countries would no longer act as a barrier to France, and Britain would be vulnerable both militarily and economically.

By the summer of 1785, it was clear that the Emperor's foreign policy initiatives had come to grief. In Hailes' view, his drive against the Dutch had been predicated upon the assumption that France was unable to go to war, but this assumption, if it existed, was dispelled when, on 17 November 1784, a French note was sent to Vienna warning the Emperor that if he staged an attack on the Dutch Republic, France was prepared, if necessary, to support the Dutch by force.[17] Then his plans for the Bavarian Exchange were brought to grief when Frederick the Great, in July 1785, succeeded in forming the League of the German Princes which was opposed to the whole idea. It was at that stage that Lord Cornwallis was sent to Prussia to see whether there was any possibility of Britain being able to conclude an alliance with that state. Cornwallis, however, found Frederick the Great in a pessimistic frame of mind and convinced, like[18] Harris, that the balance of power in Europe had been destroyed. He argued that France, Spain, Austria and Russia were all united, with the Dutch Republic also in the power of France. Against this combination, Britain and Prussia were isolated and without allies, and on their own they were not a match for such an allied force. In any war,

England would have to contend with the fleets of France, Spain, Holland, and possibly Russia, while he himself would be left to face the armies of France, Austria and Russia. The close connection between France and Austria was enabling France to concentrate all her attention on her marine, which would be used against England, and while there were circumstances in which such an unequal contest could be maintained, 'it was not a game to be played often'.[19]

In these circumstances the Emperor decided to make his peace with the Dutch, with whom a treaty was signed, at Paris, on 8 November 1785 and, as anticipated, this was followed the very next day by the conclusion of the long-awaited Franco-Dutch Alliance. The British reaction was to try to prevent ratification of the Alliance if at all possible, but should this measure 'so alarming to the interests of this country' be formally concluded, 'it must then become our care to endeavour to excite such an opposition to the ruling party ... as at least to render the effects of it as little pernicious as possible to our prosperity and safety'.[20]

In the summer of 1784 Dorset had reported that in their search for a way out of their economic woes the French were invariably directing their attention 'to an increase in power in the East, to which quarter they look forward, as if it was to be the scene of future hostilities,'[21] and both Dundas and Harris had likewise warned, in Harris's words, that the French Government believed that 'our possessions in the East are our vulnerable part, and in any future war will begin its operations there'. The steps which Britain took to strengthen her lines of communication with the East, now that the danger of a future war seemed to have greatly increased, will be dealt with in the next chapter, but it is now necessary to focus on the political rivalry that ensued.

As Frederick the Great had implied in his conversations with Cornwallis, French foreign policy concentrated upon isolating Great Britain in Europe. In this way, France sought to ensure that she would be freed from any threat of war on the continent, and would therefore be free to concentrate her whole attention upon building up her sea power for future use in the East. As part of this policy of isolating Great Britain in Europe, France sought to widen the Franco-Dutch Alliance. The first initiative in this respect came from the King of Sweden, though in a roundabout manner. In what was meant to be a highly secret approach to the Dutch government, he proposed an alliance with that republic. 'No secret, however, is kept here,' Harris noted at The Hague, who reported that though the proposal did not, as it stood, represent a bid to accede to the Franco-Dutch Alliance, he had every reason to believe that it was made with the full approval of the French government and would, if it took place at all, 'end in a formal accession'. But Harris immediately alerted the Danish and Russian envoys as to what was afoot, and a month later was able to report that the Dutch, under French pressure, had turned down the proposal, 'knowing that it has spread a kind of alarm both at Vienna and Petersburg'.[22] It was an essential element of French policy to maintain good relations with both those countries while the ground was being prepared for challenging Great Britain's position in the East.

The country which the French really wished to see become a member of that alliance, however, was Spain. If France could establish a strong hold over the Dutch East Indies and at the same time develop even stronger ties with the Spanish Philippines than her influence at Madrid through the Family Compact already assured her, then Britain's domination over the rapidly growing China trade would become extremely precarious.

Under the vigorous lead of King Charles III, and spurred on by the implicit threat to Spanish sovereignty in the Philippine Islands posed by the opening up of the Eastern Passage to China, the Spaniards had been strengthening their position in that archipelago for several years.[23] This had culminated in the formation of Spain's own East India Company, the Royal Philippine Company, contemporaneously with the formation of the new French East India Company in early 1785. At the same time, the *Annual Register* reported how Spanish exertions for the improvement and increase of her naval power had been unremittingly continued and, since the conclusion of the late war, 'carried on with fresh vigour, and in a more extensive degree'. And it was anticipated that this would continue 'so long as the French influence predominates at the Court of Madrid.'[24]

In trying to persuade the Court of Madrid to join the Franco-Dutch Alliance, the French government was tempted to support the claims of the Royal Philippine Company to use the route to the Philippines by way of the Cape of Good Hope, but this threatened to endanger their influence in the Dutch republic.[25] Baulked by this Dutch intransigence, de Vergennes had hit upon another tactic. Hailes, in Paris, informed Carmarthen that for several years France and Spain had been trying to fix their frontier 'at the foot of that part of Pyrenees called the Pays de Basques'. For this purpose, commissioners had been appointed by both countries, 'but it was not until very recently that the line could be agreed upon and settled definitely by the commissioners ... A district held by France for upwards of four centuries, near twelve leagues in length, and tho' naturally unproductive rendered by the industry of the inhabitants uncommonly fertile, is ceded to the Spanish Monarchy by the demarcation.' What made this cession still more remarkable was the fact that 'there is now in this territory a quantity of wood capable of supplying the whole navy of France, and the inhabitants of it have at all times shown themselves uncommonly attached to the French government'. Everybody had been puzzled by this cession, and there had been dark hints of bribery at work, but Hailes believed that it was probably owing to the French desire 'to forward as much as possible the access of Spain' to the Franco-Dutch Alliance.[26]

It was not only the threat posed by the build-up of French and Spanish naval power that was causing consternation in Britain, however, but attention was also being paid to the potential danger posed by Dutch sea power as well. In an attempt to lessen the maritime threat to Britain's predominant position in the East, it had been agreed in London that the most desirable outcome would be for both Britain and France to agree 'to withdrawing the whole [naval] Force on both sides,' and Howe informed Carmarthen that at one stage orders had, in fact, been sent out for the recall of the British squadron from India. But as Harris sensed, and as de Castries, the French Minister of the Marine, was later to confirm, this settled nothing. For when Harris pressed the Dutch for information as to what size of naval force they planned to keep up in the East Indies, they replied that it was impossible to give a precise answer 'on account of their not knowing what protection their Company may want against the different princes there, with whom they are at variance'. Harris rightly believed that the Dutch had been pressed by the French not to reveal such information to the British, for as de Castries was to tell Vergennes, whereas France and Britain had a verbal agreement on the subject, the Dutch had given no such undertaking and could retain what naval force in the East they wished. This would face the British with a dilemma; they could either themselves maintain a similar force to the Dutch, thus breaking their agreement with France and justifying the latter to do the same, or they could honour their agreement with France. In either case, the Franco-Dutch forces would end up as superior in size.[27] Furthermore, apart from the Dutch navy, the ships of the Dutch East India Company had to be taken into account. A memorandum in the Carmarthen/Leeds papers described how the greater part of the larger number of ships which the Dutch employed in their trade with Asia were 'of a large construction, much larger than the ships presently used by the English East India Company. These Dutch ships are so constructed, too, that they are easily convertible into ships of war, ... [being] formed for carrying two tiers of guns; they actually carry twenty to thirty, and are qualified to carry forty or fifty guns'. The writer feared that a large fleet of such ships would not only be dangerous in time of war, when acting in conjunction with a French force, but would have it 'in their power to injure [British commerce and interests in the East] by surprise, and to strike such a severe blow either before any declaration of war, or in the commencement of hostilities, as would not be easily retrieved on the part of Great Britain'.[28]

The French government was determined to gain control of the Dutch East India Company through its political allies the Patriots (or the Faction, as Harris styled them), who had gained control of the government of the Dutch Republic. In this, however, they had to contend with the fierce opposition of the maritime Province of Zeeland. The first approach of the French was made immediately after the signing of the Franco-Dutch Alliance and took the form of a demand that the Dutch must improve the defences of the Dutch East Indies by increasing the number of troops in the service of the Dutch East India Company. Those Directors of the Company who came from Zeeland, however, argued that the impoverished state of the Company's finances made this quite impossible at the present time, and their arguments were so well founded that even the Directors who came from Amsterdam, the home of the Patriots, were convinced. This, Harris reported, meant putting off for at least a year 'the intended enormous increase of Dutch European troops in the East Indies, [and also] prevents the Company from becoming entirely dependent on Government'.[29]

To get around this opposition, the Patriots now planned to take over the government of the Dutch East India Company from its traditional directing body, the Assembly of Seventeen, and to invest it in a committee of six deputies who would have their permanent base in Amsterdam, the committee itself being chosen from the pro-French party. Then as soon as this change had been put into effect, the Patriots intended to increase both their naval and land forces in the East. Such a wholesale change in the way of governing the Company, however, inevitably aroused intense opposition and now 'the whole body of the Directors absolutely refused ... to submit to any alterations whatsoever in their mode of proceeding'. However, reported Harris, 'this was an object of too great magnitude to be neglected by the French,' who, by bribes and every other kind of persuasion, prevailed upon the directors from Amsterdam to agree to a compromise, but even then only after one Patriot director declared that 'he could assure them, from authority, that the present Government ... were resolved to suffer the Company to become a Bankrupt rather than let the Direction remain totally independent of their inspection and authority'. Harris declared this threat to be 'a mere bugbear ... [since] the whole Republic would be, more or less, involved in the ruin'. Nevertheless, the threat was sufficient to enable the Patriots to gain a majority of one in the Assembly of Seventeen, and Harris warned that 'the Patriots are in the plenitude of their power' and that 'if the direction of the East India Company falls into their hands (and I very much fear it will) you may be assured that all its force, wealth and resources ... will be employed against us in India the moment France chuses [*sic*] to give the signal'.[30]

The French government, however, became increasingly exasperated at its inability to get the Directors of the Dutch East India Company to take the action it desired swiftly, and it intimated to those leaders of the Patriot party in which it placed the greatest confidence that 'a rupture with England in Asia, is not at a very distant period' and that it was therefore of the utmost consequence that no time should be lost in augmenting the Republic's naval and land forces in the East. To circumvent the delays entailed in trying to get the Company's Directors to take the necessary action, as well as to avoid the unwelcome publicity that that would entail, which would defeat the great object of such a reinforcement, it urged the States General to take upon themselves the ordering and financing of this measure. And the French representative, M. Cotleuri, was reported to have 'whispered ... that France is preparing new troubles for us in India' and would not be behind-hand in reinforcing her own fleet and army in the East. As a result of this pressure, it was stated that the Patriots had resolved among themselves to send as soon as they could be got ready four ships of the line and four frigates, with as many troops as they could hold, to the Cape, where they were to await further orders.[31]

Through the spring and early summer of 1786, Harris felt that the Dutch Republic was 'hastening to its fate' and was much closer to dissolution than recovery, and in his view it was of almost equal value to France to be able to reduce the Dutch Republic to a state of anarchy and confusion so that that Republic would necessarily be made, in consequence, dependent upon France.[32]

The compromise solution which the Patriots had forced upon the Dutch East India Company was that six new directors were to be added to the number of its traditional Direction, and these new directors would be invested with new and greater authority than the others and would, of course, be selected 'from among the creatures of the faction'. This move, however, elicited a violent reaction from the Chamber of Zeeland, which declared it to be an act of arbitrary power to which they would not submit. They even went so far as to declare 'an intention of separating themselves from the union and flinging themselves on the protection of some foreign Power'. Three weeks later the Pensionary of Zeeland had two secret conferences with Harris to outline his thinking, and to try to persuade Great

Britain to undertake the protection sought. He intimated that he was ready to see Zeeland's share of the Dutch East India Company annexed to England, provided that his Province's whole trade could be carried on under the English flag, and that its ships would be afforded the same protection in India as England's own ships. He argued that this threat of secession, backed by Britain, would not mean war, but would 'spread a terror among the Patriots' and give encouragement to those anxious to restore the Company's old system of administration. Even if war did result, Zeeland, despite its small population, was 'by far the most important Province of the Union 'because of its strategic location, and because in Flushing it had the only port in the Republic capable of admitting large ships of war. Because of its natural defences, he said, six frigates would suffice to protect it from invasion, while its position gave it 'command of the German Ocean, secures the Baltic trade, and an English fleet stationed at Flushing would ... prevent any vessel from coming out of the Texel unobserved ... No junction between the French and Dutch fleets could take place; the French would never venture among the shoals and currents of the North Sea, without having one port where they could take shelter, and the Dutch must either go north about or through the Channel'.[33] The British response to this dramatic approach was naturally a cautious one, but it served to underline the exceptional stresses that were developing in the Dutch Republic.

By the summer of 1786, it was clear that opposition to the Patriots was beginning to increase as a result of their efforts to gain control on the Dutch East India Company, and when the Pensionary of Dordt suddenly left on a short visit to Paris without any authority or order from his superiors, Harris surmised that he was seeking French support for 'all his levelling measures by offering her the absolute disposal of the Dutch East India Company'. He himself had 'a promise of a majority in the Assembly of Seventeen (who meet in the autumn) to refuse the admittance of the six new Directors,' and it was clear that violent measures were now being contemplated, and it was evident, he said, 'that matters are hastening, very fast, to a crisis'.[34] He was to add, a month later, that the Patriots were straining every nerve to crush in its infancy the party which was forming against them, knowing that if it continued to gain strength their own fall was certain. They were prepared to resort to 'the last extremities' to retain power, and the French Ambassador had apparently promised to subsidise their militia, the Free Corps.

From this point onwards there was an all-out struggle for control of the Dutch Republic, and thus of the Dutch East Indies, and as the position of the *Patriots became ever less* secure, so did their resort to violence increase. In the very week that the Botany Bay decision was announced, Harris was reporting from The Hague that conditions 'beggar all description,'and that the leaders of the ruling faction, in collaboration with the French, were using as their chief instrument the militia known as the Free Corps, 'which they term The majesty of the People'. With this armed mob they were driving 'from the civil government of the towns such Regents as are inimical to their views'. They appeared determined, he wrote, 'To prosecute their designs to the full extent of party rage.'[35]

Meanwhile, the French were intent upon exploiting the

predominant position which they had already established in the Dutch Republic so as to get as many of their own troops to the East Indies as they could. At the same time they were encouraging the Dutch to concentrate on their marine, and to build docks and to form magazines at the Cape of Good Hope, Trincomali, Malacca and Batavia, all key bases on the sea-lanes to India and China, while French agents were also busily recruiting, especially at Amsterdam, any men they could find who had personal experience of India. In forwarding a copy of a Memorial which the French Ambassador had just submitted, Harris noted that it proved 'how greatly the attention of France is turned towards India and how earnest that Court is to spread its emissaries over every part of it'.[36]

By the early summer of 1787, however, the position of the Patriots was becoming desperate. In the previous autumn Harris had expressed his fear that if the unrest in the Dutch republic continued, France would take advantage of the situation and, without waiting for any Dutch request to do so, would send her own troops into the Dutch East Indies, on the pretext of defending them, and would then 'appropriate them to herself.' Now he revealed that the French Ambassador had warned his government that the position of the Patriots was so critical, and the probability of their party being overthrown was so very likely, that nothing remained for the French to do but to advise and support the violent measures. As a result of this new crisis, the Rhinegrave de Salm had suddenly returned from Paris, and permission had been granted for 'money to almost any amount' to be forwarded from France. The fact that the French authorities had agreed to such an enormous expenditure at a time when their own finances were in so ruinous a state revealed, said Harris, 'The immense importance [France] sets on the success of her operations here.' Harris clearly felt that France's deepening financial crisis provided the ideal opportunity for Britain to take a decisive stand over the course of events in the Netherlands. In three separate despatches in as many days, he urged that the critical moment had arrived when the British Cabinet must decide whether to support their partisans in the republic on a commensurate scale to that provided by France to the Patriots, or whether to continue with a non-committal stance. If Britain did commit herself to such support, he was confident that 'the Republic will act under our direction, and connect our interests with theirs,' whereas failure to provide such support would mean that 'nothing short of a miracle can save this Republic from immediately becoming an appendage to the French monarchy'.[37]

As he himself had suggested, Harris was thereupon summoned to return to London for consultation, and on 23 May 1787, just ten days after the First Fleet under Captain Arthur Phillip set sail for Botany Bay, he attended a Cabinet meeting where the whole situation was discussed. At this gathering, Harris argued that France was not ready for war and that nothing would provoke her to go to war with Britain until she was ready. Her purpose was not to fight for possession of the Dutch Republic, but, when ready, to fight against the British in the East in collaboration with the Dutch. A more favourable moment would not present itself for 'England to hold a high and becoming language to France'. Pitt, on the other hand, while admitting 'the immense consequence' of the Dutch Republic's being preserved as an independent state, argued that war was only possible, not probable, at the present time. This was therefore a moment for careful reflection. Was this the right occasion for taking action against France? Could anything repay 'disturbing that state of growing affluence and prosperity in which [Britain] now was' an affluence that was increasing so fast that it promised 'to make her equal to resist any force France could collect some years hence?'[38]

Meanwhile there had been riots in Amsterdam, and there was a very real danger of civil war. The French government was in a quandary as to how to respond and it was left to the bold Princess Wilhelmina of Orange, wife of the irresolute Stadtholder William V, to make the decisive move which finally brought matters to a head. On 28 June, she set out for The Hague with proposals for a moderate settlement, in a deliberate attempt to force the Patriots' hand. In the event, some republican troops made the grave error of arresting her on the way. Since she was the sister of the new King of Prussia this was a serious misjudgement. For a while, Frederick William contented himself with demanding an apology and satisfaction to the Princess, and the massing of some twenty thousand troops, but the Patriots were no longer willing to be guided by the French, who were anxious to avoid any further friction with Prussia, and who therefore urged the Patriots to give the required apology. French influence, however, had taken a nose-dive after the French Ambassador's visit to Amsterdam in the third week of June. His intention had been to rally the hard-pressed Patriots, but when he was asked, as Harris put it, 'whether, if they proceeded to extremities, and were in ... distress and danger, France would come with troops to their support, he replied (after endeavouring to avoid the question) that he had no authority to say that they would,' an answer that had provoked 'bickerings and altercations'.[39]

Hitherto the Prussians had been cautious about committing themselves, but with Russia and Turkey now at war Frederick William felt free to act, and on 9 September, he issued a four-day's ultimatum to the province of Holland. On the 14th, no answer having been received, the Prussians crossed the Dutch frontier. There was little effective opposition and though the French Foreign Minister, de Montmorin, made some 'warlike noises,' he had no desire to become involved in the war, which was effectively over by 7 October. By 10 October, the Dutch had accepted the Anglo-Prussian terms for a settlement and finally, on 27 October, the French officially disclaimed any intention of having desired to intervene.[40]

However, this British diplomatic triumph of 1787 proved to be only an illusory and short-lived success and it did no more than buy time. For over the next five years it proved impossible to negotiate an Anglo-Dutch treaty of alliance, the problem of the free navigation in the Eastern Seas creating an impasse which it proved impossible to resolve. In Dundas' words, 'The jealousies and apprehensions of the Dutch relative to the Navigation of the Eastern Seas ... rest on the ground they dare not avow. I mean their consciousness of the radical and internal weakness of the sovereignty they claim in the Eastern Isles, and they are afraid that the communication we may have with the Natives would lay the dependence in which they are held by the Dutch ... '[41]

The result of this failure was a resurgence of the political fortunes of the Patriots. Once war had broken out and the

French revolutionary government had gone over to a policy of military expansion, its armies were able to invade the Dutch Republic, and after May 1795, the Patriots were able to set up their Batavian Republic, allied, once more, to France.

Chapter Three

SAFEGUARDING THE SEA-LANES TO INDIA AND CHINA

*Part 1. The Routes to the Bay of Bengal
and India, 1784–93*

While Sir James Harris, at The Hague, was seeking to prevent the signing of a Franco-Dutch alliance or, if that proved impossible, to help in the creation of an anti-Patriot (and thereby an anti-French) opposition party in the Dutch Republic, steps were simultaneously being taken to strengthen the security of Britain's lines of communication with the East. To enable this to be achieved with the greatest effect the Younger Pitt, immediately after winning the general election in 1784, hurried through Parliament the enactment of his India Bill and the Commutation Bill, the former giving the Government political control over the East India Company by making the office of Governor-General in India a Royal rather than a Company appointment, while leaving the Company in control of purely commercial affairs. This transfer of political control to the Government was further enhanced by the creation of the Board of Control, whose chairman, for many years, was Henry Dundas, Pitt's right-hand man.

There were three separate lines of approach to the Orient that had to be considered, namely, the direct approach by way of the Mediterranean, the Indian Ocean, the Bay of Bengal, the Strait of Malacca and the South China Sea, and the two routes that passed by way of South Africa, the one to the west of 'New Holland' and through the Eastern Passage into the Pacific, the other – after the decision to establish the Botany Bay settlement had been taken – to the south of 'New Holland' and so again by way of the Pacific Ocean to China. And added urgency was given to this task by the fear that in any future war a triple alliance of France, Spain and the Dutch Republic was likely to prove a far more effective and formidable combination than had been the case in the recent past, for during the American War, not only had Spanish attention been focused upon the Mediterranean rather than upon the East Indies, but Spain had been a reluctant participant in a war that had been setting a most dangerous precedent for her own restive colonists in Central and South America. As for the Dutch, in the recent war they had still been under the authority of the Prince of Orange, whose dynasty had traditional ties with England, whereas now the pro-French Patriots were in the ascendant and were aiming to conclude a treaty of alliance with France. This was particularly worrying at a time when Sir James Harris was reporting from The Hague that the Dutch had 'already a larger naval force in that part of the globe [i.e. the East Indies] than any other European Power,' and that the French had substantial garrisons, outnumbering the Dutch, both at the Cape and at Trincomali.[1] Furthermore, the French navy had been continuing to develop in both size and efficiency, and, as a result of Vergennes' policy of isolating Britain in

Europe, it would now be possible for it to concentrate its full force in the East Indies in a way that had not been possible during the American War.

In seeking to make the sea-lanes to the Orient more secure, the British also had to accept the fact that the two most important strongholds on these seaways, namely the Cape of Good Hope and Trincomali, were Dutch possessions and it was impossible to take any action against them in time of peace. It was nevertheless evident that in the event of another war both would again become targets for early attack.

In the case of the direct route, Warren Hastings, during his period as Governor-General, had already appreciated that use of the route through Egypt would significantly reduce the time taken for communications to pass between India and Great Britain. Now, in the spring of 1785, attention was again focused on this region in the wake of a report from Sir Robert Ainslie at Constantinople.

Despite the fact that an imperial edict of 1779 had specified that vessels carrying the flags of Christian nations were not to be allowed to proceed beyond the port of Jeddah, he stated, rumours were rife that an exception was now to be made in the case of French vessels, which would obviously be to the disadvantage of the English East India and Levant Companies. Furthermore, he suspected that the French were planning to evade such restrictions in the Red Sea and in Egypt by trading in conjunction with Tipu Sultan of Mysore, who was known to be in touch with the Porte, or with other Muslim allies. A similar warning came from Dorset, the British ambassador at Paris, who told of a rumour that the French had submitted a proposal to the Porte that the latter should cede to France *'une petite partie de l'Egypte,'* including the ports of Jeddah and Suez, with permission for the French to fortify them, in return for which French troops would assist the Porte to re-establish its authority in Egypt. He further warned that he had 'much reason to believe that the French cabinet have serious designs of making an establishment in Egypt whenever a favourable conjunction shall offer itself'.[2]

In the light of these warnings, Dundas asked George Baldwin, a merchant with long experience of the region, to prepare a memorandum on Egypt, and the latter's report described it as 'the resort of all the traders of the world and the entrepôt to all the interior parts of Africa'. For England, its principal significance was that it provided the most direct route to India, but for France it could mean much more. She would have no great difficulty in seizing it from the degenerate Turkish Empire, and once in possession of Egypt she could develop it into 'the emporium of the world,' and at the same time be able to transport her troops thee in any number and at any time, thus ensuring that England would thereafter 'hold her possessions in India at the mercy of France'.[3]

Another who was consulted on French interest in Egypt was John Bruce, formerly a professor at Edinburgh University whom Dundas had persuaded to leave his university post and to join the India Board in order that he, Henry Dundas, as the effective head of the Board of Control, might make constant use of his expertise. And Bruce reinforced Baldwin's argument by demonstrating that French interest in Egypt was one of long standing.

The prospect of the most direct line of communication between England and India being at the mercy of a French presence in Egypt was one which the British Government was determined to do everything in its power to avoid.

When Carmarthen told Ainslie of the Government's alarm at the possibility that France might be able to induce the Porte to allow her the use of the ports of Gedda and Suez, Ainslie implied that the rumour was not without substance, though noting that the Porte was suspicious in equal measure of France, Russia and Austria, all of whom, in their efforts to undermine the Turkish Empire, had employed agents who had endeavoured 'to stimulate the Beys [of Egypt] to absolute independence'.[4]

Meanwhile, worried by his inability to get reliable intelligence quickly enough regarding developments in Egypt, Ainslie had appointed a retired merchant well known to him, named Brandi, as his own personal agent. Brandi had known Egypt for a quarter-of-a-century, and within a week of his arrival at Alexandria he was reporting that the French had negotiated a commercial treaty with the government at Cairo for the introduction of goods from India into Egypt by way of Suez, a treaty which had been negotiated, said Ainslie, without the knowledge of, or authority from, the Porte. A report on the same treaty from Sir James Harris contained further worrying details, stating that under its terms the new French East India Company was to be allowed to transport its imports from India through Suez, that French merchants were to be allowed free access to all the ports belonging to the Government of Cairo, that particular respect was to be accorded to the French King's ships, and that the French consul and French subjects were to enjoy privileges superior to those of any other nation.[5] Carmarthen was further worried by the spreading of reports that Russia, in her determination to undermine the Turkish Empire, was planning to win French backing for her plans in exchange for an agreement that Egypt should be ceded to France.

With the knowledge that French, Russian and Austrian agents were all seeking, for their different reasons, to undermine the authority of the Turkish government, and that the Beys of Egypt, who had, said Ainslie, 'aimed at absolute independence ever since the time of Ally Bey [1772],' were their potential allies, the British Government now decided that the time had come to appoint Baldwin British Consul in Egypt with a brief 'to discover the motions of the French' and to conclude a treaty with the Government of Egypt that would enable the English East India Company to trade through Egypt and to open up a new official line of communication between Great Britain and India.

Farther east, in the Indian Ocean, the French were already established in the Ile de France (Mauritius), the Ile de Bourbon (Réunion), Rodriguez and the Seychelles, and they had been the first to establish a small settlement on the island of Diego Garcia. On 8 July 1785, the Court of Directors of the English East India Company similarly ordered the Bombay Presidency to take possession of that island. However, both the French and the British soon withdrew their settlements, having found the island 'nothing better than a convenient station for surveying and exploring the numerous islands and shoals about, and to the southward of the Line'. This initial attempt, however, did result in Archibald Blair of the Bombay Marine sailing on 8 May 1786 to undertake an important survey of the whole Chagos Archipelago, the neighbouring Laccadive islands having already been surveyed by Wedgborough in 1785.[6]

In the Bay of Bengal itself the need for increasing the security of the British settlements on the coast of the subcontinent was particularly pressing, their vulnerability having been dramatically exposed by the operations of de Suffren in the recent war. As the year 1784 drew to a close and the outbreak of a European war appeared to be imminent, with Dundas predicting that India would be the first quarter to be attacked, acute anxiety had been aroused by a report regarding supposed Franco-Dutch plans in that Bay, and Carmarthen ordered both Hailes in Paris and Sir James Harris at The Hague to investigate the matter, though only with 'the utmost secrecy and caution.' The report concerned 'a plan which M.de Suffren expressed an eager desire of carrying into execution (even before he left India) of establishing a French settlement in Acheen.[7] This place ... must from its situation be of the utmost importance to British interests should it fall into the hands of France, or Holland. Trincomalé on the Western and Acheen on the eastern side of the Bay of Bengal, would indeed render the safety of the British interests in that part of the world to the most alarming degree precarious'.[8]

In the event, both Hailes and Harris reported that the rumour appeared to be without foundation, nevertheless in the search for means whereby the English settlements could be made less vulnerable, in addition to Acheen other possible locations being considered were the Nicobar and Andaman Islands, Penang and the Mergui Archipelago. The latter had, in fact, been recently surveyed, if somewhat by chance, by Thomas Forrest, who had sailed from Calcutta in the Esther brig with the intention of surveying the Andaman Islands, but who, having failed to stand sufficiently far to the westward after leaving the Ganges, had failed to reach those islands and had, instead, been blown down the Tennasserim coast as far as Kedah. This had allowed him to have a close look at the Mergui Archipelago, that long string of islands lying off the coast of Tennasserim.

Forrest's arrival in this vicinity came shortly after its naval value had been dramatically demonstrated following a naval engagement between the French ship *Arrogant* and the British ship *Victorious*. In the aftermath of this battle both ships had been forced to make for a port in order to carry out repairs, but whereas the *Arrogant* was able to put in to Mergui, the British ship had been compelled to go all the way back to Bombay, reminiscent of the situation that had occurred after the final naval engagement between Hughes and de Suffren in 1782. The case put forward for the Mergui Archipelago as a site for a trading settlement and naval base was that it could provide shelter from both monsoons, while a free port there would be able to attract trade not only from Burma and Siam, but from the northern Malay states as well. Nor were the British alone in displaying a growing interest in this area. For in 1785 Bruni D'Entrecasteaux, on taking up the command of France's East Indies squadron, had been instructed to undertake an examination of the Andaman Islands, the Mergui Archipelago and the Strait of Malacca.[9]

Suffren's recent demonstration of the vulnerability of the Company's possessions on the Coromandel coast, as well as of its trade by way of the river Ganges, prompted the Court of Directors, in April 1785, to make another attempt to find out more about the Nicobar Islands and, if possible, to establish a small settlement at Nancowry Island. Its harbour had been surveyed back in 1762 by Alexander Dalrymple, now the Company's hydrographer, and the arrival of Lord Cornwallis to take over as the new Governor-General carried this project forward. Fully convinced of the overriding importance of finding a good harbour for ships of war in the Bay of Bengal, Cornwallis was to spend the next two years in accumulating an exact knowledge of Bengal's adjacent islands and coasts before despatching Lieutenant Archibald Blair of the Bombay Marine on an expedition to explore and survey the Andaman Islands in December 1788.

Five months later Blair returned to Calcutta with a detailed description, accompanied by maps and charts. After discussing this matter with his brother, Commodore (later Admiral) Sir William Cornwallis, the Governor-General felt most encouraged, and decided to send Blair back to take formal possession of the Islands and to establish a pilot settlement at what he had named port Cornwallis on Great Andaman (later Chatham) Island.

Meanwhile Francis Light, after a decade of trading in this region, had come to believe, by 1785, that the time was ripe for Britain to begin establishing control over the Malay peninsula, thereby not only opening a vast new market for the products of India, but also opening a potential new source of supply for the China trade. Furthermore, he was beginning to fear that Siam, having recovered from her 1767 defeat by Burma, was now showing signs of pursuing an expansionist policy herself by envisaging taking the whole of the Malay Peninsula under Siamese jurisdiction. Kedah, located on the northern fringes of the Malay world, already recognised Siam, her immediate powerful neighbour to the north, as her tributary overlord. Light therefore suggested that the Sultan of Kedah should now seek the support of the East India Company for granting it access to the strategically located island of Penang. In the event, however, the Company exploited the Sultan's vulnerability to force him to give it actual possession of that island in return for a pension as compensation for his lost territories.[10]

Part 2. The Approaches to China

The crucial problem still awaiting solution was how to reach China in the event of a war in which the French, the Dutch, and possibly the Spaniards too, were all in alliance against Britain, thus making the usual routes by way of the Straits of Malacca or Sunda and then the South China Sea unavailable to East Indiamen. The Eastern Passage did offer one alternative, but it was potentially vulnerable both in the vicinity of Pitt's Passage off western New Guinea, and in its passage past the Philippine Islands.

During the American War, when that precise hostile triple alliance had sided with the rebel colonists against Britain, the East India Company had experimented with using the alternative route to China by way of Cape Horn and the Pacific Ocean, and Captain Henry Wilson in the *Antelope* had been sent to examine this route's practicability for China-bound East Indiamen. Dalrymple, who, as the Company's new hydrographer, played a leading role in planning the expedition, intended this voyage of reconnaissance to include an examination of the north coast of New Guinea, so after reaching the atoll of Eurpik in the Caroline Islands, to the east of the Palaus, Wilson altered course and took a southerly heading until he reached the north coast of New Guinea. He then sailed west as far as Dorey Harbour in Geelvink Bay. Nine years earlier, during Herbert's ill-fated settlement on the island of Balambangan, in the Sulu Archipelago, that enterprising seaman, Thomas Forrest, had been sent from that settlement to undertake a voyage of reconnaissance in the *Tartar* galley, which had carried him as far as this same Dorey harbour. He had visited London in 1779 when his account of that expedition was published, and on 2 March 1780, he was Dalrymple's guest at a dinner at the Royal Society club.

When the *Antelope* reached Dorey Harbour, Captain Wilson declared that 'we have no further business upon this coast as he [i.e. Forrest] saw all the coast to the westward and much better than we can venture to do in a ship. Therefore we shall haul to the northward ... and get to some place of refreshment [off] this inhospitable coast'. Thereafter, sailing to the south of Mindanao, they put in at the island of Basilan for supplies, and thence sailed on to the island of Balambangan before heading up the South China Sea to Macao.[11] On her return voyage, the *Antelope* was wrecked off the Palau Islands on the night of 9 August 1783, but the local ruler, Abba Thule, proved a kind and generous man, and Wilson and his crew were able to build a new vessel, the *Oroolong*, in which they sailed back to England, accompanied, at Abba Thule's request, by his second son, Lee Boo, in the hope that when he returned, he would bring back things which he had learned for the benefit of his own people.

Four months before the *Antelope* was wrecked, the *Northumberland* East Indiaman, in attempting to use the Eastern Passage, had reached the south-west coast of New Guinea too far to the eastward, and was struggling with light winds and 'the uncertainty of our situation, and no charts'. After a month on this coast, and suffering the loss of some of her crew in an affray with the local inhabitants, the *Northumberland* did finally manage to reach China and was back in England in 1784, and her story only underlined the urgency of learning more about the western coasts of New Guinea, though that had to wait for a few more years.

Meanwhile, the Commutation Act, by reducing the duties payable upon imported tea from a variable rate of between 79 per cent and 127 per cent to 12.5 per cent, brought about an immediate threefold increase in the amount of tea imported by the East India Company, and therefore a large increase, first in the number of, and then in the size of, the East Indiamen sailing to and from China. This gave the vulnerability of the Eastern Passage in the vicinity of Pitt's Strait a still greater significance. The Company intended to respond to this new situation by establishing a fortified base in or close to Pitt's Strait, Such a base, the Company argued, would not only serve as a place of refreshment for the China-bound East Indiamen, but would also help in 'awing the Dutch to prevent a rupture with them,' while at the same time, should such a rupture nevertheless occur, enable the Company 'to break effectively their spice monopoly'.

It was now that the value of Pitt's India Act was manifested. The Government, more sensitive to political considerations than was the Company, saw the dangers in establishing a fortified base in Pitt's Strait. In the first place it was known that the French felt a particular affinity to the islands surrounding Pitt's Strait as a result of the spice-gathering expeditions of Pierre Poivre in the 1740s and later. Second, it could be anticipated that the Spaniards in the Philippines would be suspicious of the establishment of any such British base.

Dundas therefore sought to persuade the Dutch that there was no essential conflict of interest between the Dutch and the British in the East, and that Britain had no desire or interest in wresting from the Dutch their monopoly of the spice trade.[12] Hence Cornwallis, who had had long talks with Pitt and Dundas before leaving England for India, and so knew their thinking, felt free to ignore the Company's orders on the plausible grounds that a base near Pitt's Strait would be too far away for the Bengal authorities to defend it in case of emergency.

In the meantime, various enterprising individuals were dreaming up projects whereby they hoped to be able to exploit the discoveries made in the Pacific Ocean by Captain Cook, and thereby reap a reward, should the charter of the East India Company, shortly due for renewal, be terminated by an administration some of whose leaders, including Pitt himself, were known to sympathise with the free trade doctrines of Adam Smith. Among the first in the field of such projectors was James Matra who, on 28 July 1783, wrote to Sir Joseph Banks seeking information about plans that he had heard of, some relating to New South Wales. in which Banks himself, and Lords Mulgrave and Sandwich, were said to be interested, while another scheme was said to be the brainchild of Sir George Young and 'Mr Jackson, formerly of the Admiralty.'[13] On the strength of what he had then been able to find out, Matra produced his own scheme which he forwarded to Lord North at the Home Office on 23 August 1783 for his consideration. Among other arguments, Matra suggested that a settlement at Botany Bay might help in the development of the China trade and, in the event of another war involving the Dutch and/or the Spaniards, might allow for the despatch of expeditions against the Dutch East Indies, on the one hand, and the Acapulco-Manila galleon trade and the coasts of Latin America on the other. He also suggested the possibility of opening new markets in Japan and Korea.[14]

The Government, meanwhile, having forestalled the East India Company over the matter of a fortified base, was thereby obligated to have an alternative route available, should use of the Eastern Passage prove too hazardous to use in the event of war, and the obvious choice was the route passing to the south of Tasmania before heading north past the eastern coast of New South Wales, past New Guinea and then past the eastern and northern coasts of the Philippine Islands, and so to Macao. That Ministers were thinking along these lines at an early stage is suggested by the fact that when, during the acute international crisis in the autumn of 1784, Sir George Young, in cooperation with Matra, presented his own plan for a settlement at Botany Bay, Nepean, the Under-Secretary at the Home Department, aware that these were dangerous and largely uncharted waters, sought confirmation that this was a practical alternative route to China, Matra was able to assure him that the captains of East India men familiar with those seas, who had been consulted by Young, had confirmed that this was so.

Furthermore, when Sydney had interviewed Matra regarding his own original plan for such a settlement on 6 May 1784, he had hinted that Matra should incorporate the use of convicts in his scheme. For as William Eden, a member of the Committee on Transportation, had observed, 'criminals have always been judged a fair subject of hazardous experiments to which it would be unjust to expose the more valuable members of a State,'[15] words which make it very clear that those convicts were a means to an end and not the prime object of the Botany Bay settlement.

In the early months of 1785, the political situation in Europe was beginning to look very dangerous in the wake of Emperor Joseph II's proposal that he should exchange the Austrian Netherlands for Bavaria, a proposal that threatened to upset the balance of power not only in Germany but in Europe as a whole. 'I don't see how war is to be averted,' Dorset warned Carmarthen from Paris, and Harris at The Hague shared his sense of foreboding, expressing the view that the situation in Europe had 'never been so critical at any epoch since the breaking out of The Thirty Years War'. It was against this deteriorating political background that the House of Commons decided to reconvene the Committee on Transportation under the chairmanship of Lord Beauchamp on 20 April 1785.

The convict problem had a twofold aspect: there was the immediate need to relieve the pressure of the prisoner population in the hulks on the Thames and in the prisons, and there was the long-term need to find a way of using convict labour for the lasting benefit of the nation. Hence in the first session of the Committee's meetings, which lasted from 26 April to 3 May, it was the immediate need to relieve the pressure of the growing convict population that held centre stage, when Lord Sydney's proposal for establishing a penal settlement on the island of Lemane far up the Gambia River in West Africa was considered and heavily criticised. This first session was brought to an end with the issue of the committee's interim report on 9 May. Having failed to find a solution to the immediate short-term problem, the committee now entered upon the second stage of the hearings which began on 6 May and focused upon finding a long-term productive use for convict labour. The arguments for Botany Bay were now the centre of attention, and it was at this time that the East India Company, now under Government control, published Dalrymple's hitherto secret 1782 *Memoir concerning the Passages to and from China*, as its own contribution to the debate.

The first witness to be examined, when the Committee met on 6 May 1785 to begin the second stage of its hearings, was James Matra, but at the very moment when he began to give his evidence a dramatic report was received from Lord Dorset at Paris who, on 5 May, told Carmarthen that La Pérouse was about to sail from Brest on a voyage of Pacific exploration, and that he was reported 'with some degree of authority, [to have] orders to visit New Zealand, with a view to examine into the quality of the timber of that country. This plan is recommended by Mons. de Suffren, who says that ships may with little difficulty go from the Mauritius to that country. It is believed that the French have a design of establishing some kind of settlement there ... as it will be necessary to tap the trees at least six months before they fell them, in order to lighten the wood'. This report was followed by one from Lord Dalrymple on 8 June who, also writing from Paris, told Carmarthen of information that had come his way 'by a mere accident', stating that sixty persons had been taken from the prison of Bicêtre and put on board La Pérouse's ships at Brest for transportation to New Zealand, 'there being a design to make a settlement in that country'. This information was repeated by Dorset the next day, who added that the transfer of prisoners had been carried out with great secrecy and that it was 'imagined that they are to be left to take possession of this lately discovered country'. One can easily imagine the concern with which these reports must have been received.[16] It was indeed ironic that when La Pérouse finally sailed from Brest on 1 August, the French were likewise convinced that the British were planning to establish a settlement at Queen Charlotte Sound in New Zealand!

When the time came for Lord Beauchamp to frame his final report, after the Committee had finished its detailed study of the evidence relating to Botany Bay, the chairman was placed in a quandary. As he himself remarked, as chairman he should have stated some place, but, in an obvious reference to Dorset's original report of 5 May, 'a particular circumstance occurred during the sitting of the committee, that rendered it improper for me to mention it at the time'.[17] It is not difficult to visualise some of the reasons that may have prompted this decision to remain silent. One probable consideration would have been the likelihood that if the British announced an intention to colonise Botany Bay, with the presumption that that of New South Wales would follow, the French might very well respond, once La Pérouse arrived, with a similar claim to all of New Zealand. Another major consideration would almost certainly have been the likely reaction of the Dutch and the Spaniards. The various advocates for the establishment of a settlement in New South Wales had laid emphasis upon the likely value of such a colony, in time of war, for attacks upon the Dutch and Spanish possessions, while in peacetime it had been argued that a trade was likely to develop between such a settlement and the Spanish colonies in South America. Vergennes, the French Foreign

Minister, was trying hard at this time to persuade the Spaniards to be ready to join a future Franco-Dutch Alliance, and there was every reason to fear that any announcement at this time of a decision to establish a settlement at Botany Bay, taken in conjunction with the anticipated early arrival of the French in New Zealand, would be sufficient to persuade the Spanish Government to join a Triple Alliance with France and Holland, a move that would pose a very dangerous challenge to British interests in the Far East.

The fact that the Committee, after concluding its hearings on Botany Bay, gave details only of its findings on Africa, and then recommended Das Voltas Bay, has sometimes been presented as though these were alternative solutions to the convict problem. It is much more logical to see them as complementary proposed solutions. Both were desirable and, together, could be seen as providing a permanent solution to the problem of the overcrowding of prisons and hulks, while simultaneously helping to secure the sea-lanes to the Orient, and it made sense to give priority to Das Voltas Bay, if that was found to be practicable, since the African station would have been of value to all East Indiamen, whether they were trading with India or China, whereas Botany Bay would be of use only for those engaged in the China trade. In the event, of course, when the *Nautilus* returned from her voyage of reconnaissance on 28 July 1786, her commander had to report that he had found 'no Bay, River, or Inlet' in the reported latitude, but only a barren and rocky coastline which extended at least as far south as 16°.

So this was now clearly the time for an immediate concentration on Botany Bay. Furthermore, reports from Sir James Harris at The Hague showed that there was now a need for haste. For on 1 August Harris reported that he had reason to believe that the French Ambassador had recently received 'some very important Instructions, relative to the future plans of the French in the Dutch East Indies,' the main drift of which was 'to place French garrisons in the Dutch settlements in Asia,' a step which implied 'an actual making them over to France'. Three days later he added that the French plan appeared to consist of representing 'Ministerially' to the Dutch authorities that if they were relying on France to 'fulfil the article of the late Treaty by which she guarantees to them their possessions in that part of the globe,' then they themselves must put their military establishment in the East Indies 'upon a more respectable footing'. This was represented as meaning the presence of some fourteen thousand European troops, of whom five thousand would be 'lent' by France, and would be transported to the East by the Rhinegrave de Salm, who was to take up the supreme command of all the Dutch forces in Asia.[18] Two years earlier, when Dorset had referred to the uneasiness created in England by reports of additional forces being sent by France to the East Indies, Vergennes had disingenuously replied that 'the Settlements of the Dutch were much too far to the Eastward to be of any real advantage to the French'. This was not an answer calculated to allay British fears.

Dundas was already at work reorganising the military defence of the British settlements on the Indian subcontinent, having told Sydney that, in the event of war, he took it for granted that India was the quarter to be first attacked. For its part, the Cabinet in London moved swiftly to put the Botany Bay plan into execution, and on 16 August 1786 Lord Hawkesbury, though not officially a member of the Cabinet, was also asked to come up to London. As head of the newly formed Board of Trade, and the minister responsible for the quickly expanding Southern Whale Fishery, he was obviously closely concerned with the decision to go ahead with the establishment of a convict settlement at Botany Bay, the formal decision for which was announced on 21 August. The fact that the key appointment of Captain Arthur Phillip to take command of this enterprise was announced within a week of this decision strongly suggests that the intention to go ahead with this project when the moment was adjudged opportune had been known to the key officials concerned for a while.

As Lord Beauchamp had sensed in 1785, however, it was necessary to proceed with this project with considerable delicacy if this move was not to result in catapulting into existence the very triple alliance of France, Spain and the Dutch Republic whose formation British diplomats had been trying so hard to prevent. For on the one hand opposition to the pro-French Patriots was growing apace, while on the other the Pitt administration was working hard to conclude a commercial treaty with Spain. Pitt and Dundas also favoured a proposal which had been put forward by Spain's new Royal Philippine Company whereby a freer market in India would be allowed for the sale of Spanish goods in return for the sale of Indian products in Spain and the Spanish Empire. Apart from encouraging the growth of British trade in the Philippines, this plan would facilitate the entry of British trade to Spanish American markets.[19] Anglo-Spanish relations had already been put under strain at this very time over the 'Mosquito Shore' question in Honduras Bay, and with so much at stake it was obviously desirable that as far as possible these relations should not be put under still more severe stress by the Botany Bay decision. Similarly, it was essential not to undermine the opposition to the Patriots in Holland by allowing the Botany Bay decision to be portrayed as an aggressively anti-Dutch move.

Therefore, in giving reasons for the new settlement, all the anti-Spanish and anti-Dutch motives assigned by Young and Matra, as well as any mention of this as an alternative route to China, were carefully omitted, and the focus of attention was confined to the question of naval stores, an argument given increased plausibility by contemporary developments in the Baltic. Even the prediction that 'Most of the Asiatic productions may ... without doubt be cultivated in the new settlement, and in a few years render recourse to our European neighbours for those productions unnecessary' would not have been wholly unwelcome to the Dutch, for though, if it proved true, it could mean their loss of an important market, at the same time it might remove any temptation for the British to seize control of the Spice Islands for themselves, and would therefore tend to strengthen the Dutch position in the East Indies. It was for this same reason that when the Botany Bay settlement was duly established, the western boundary of Britain's territorial claims for New South Wales was fixed at 135°E, the reciprocal of the 'Pope's Line' established at the Treaties of Tordesillas (1494) and Saragossa (1529), which had divided the Portuguese and Spanish imperial claims of that era. Since the Dutch were the successors to the Portuguese in this part of the world, their claims in New Holland did not extend beyond this old dividing line, hence the British claims in New South Wales did not imply any conflict of interest or of territorial claims with the Dutch in New Holland.[20]

Having thus established a safe alternative route to China, should the Eastern Passage become too hazardous to use in time of war, attention was next directed towards attempting to reorganise the way in which Britain's trade with China was carried out. The inspiration for such a change came principally from David Scott, a merchant who had returned to London in the summer of 1786 after twenty-three years' residence in Bombay, where he had run his own very successful business. The situation with regard to the Eastern trade was indeed most unsatisfactory, with the annual cost of the Company's purchases of tea, silks and china-ware amounting to not less than £1,300,000, whereas its annual sales of goods at Canton amounted to a paltry £150,000 or less, the balance having to be paid in specie. Yet British exports, in this early stage of the Industrial Revolution, were booming, increasing in value from over £12 million in 1782 to over £20 million by 1790. Even apart from other considerations, this was a potentially precarious situation, since in the not unlikely event of a renewal of war in Europe, Britain's European markets would rapidly be closed. Scott argued that there needed to be a large increase in British exports to China (as well as to India). But this would require Britain's acquisition of a settlement on the coast of China for a magazine, where goods could be unloaded and stored in warehouses 'until a convenient season'. For under existing conditions at Canton, ships had to dispose of their cargoes on arrival 'at whatever price a company of monopolists at Canton please to give,' or else to bring them back. Scott's initial memo. was submitted to the Court of Directors in April 1787, a few weeks before the First Fleet's departure for Australia.

It was no mere coincidence that, at the very time that the First Fleet was approaching Botany Bay, a China-bound

expedition led by the Hon. Charles Cathgart MP sailed from
Spithead in an attempt to persuade the Chinese Emperor to
allow Anglo-Chinese trade to be transacted on a new basis,
but this initial approach failed when Cathgart died on the
outward voyage. Five years later a second mission on a much
larger scale, led by Lord Macartney, tried again, but to no
avail, with the unhappy result that, thereafter, opium became
the means of financing the China trade. As for Britain's
French rivals, when La Pérouse finally sailed from Breston
1 August 1785 on what was intended to be an epic voyage of
discovery, a French response to the voyages of Captain Cook,
his expedition had been planned to involve two phases. In
the first he was to concentrate on the South Pacific Ocean,
and this phase was to culminate with a counter-clockwise
navigation of the Australian coastline from the Gulf of
Carpentaria to the south coast, followed by a crossing to
New Zealand, where the crews could rest and restore their
energies, while the ships could undergo repairs and have a
refit. The second phase was to begin with an examination
of the north-west coast of America and its (temporarily)
thriving fur trade, followed by an exploration of the Asiatic
coastline opposite and of the islands in between.

Although this was not spelt out in the instructions, it is
reasonable to assume that a major purpose of the circuit of
the coast of Western Australia was to throw light on whether
there did, in fact, exist a channel linking the northern and
southern coasts of the continent. That was certainly in
English minds at that time, as Eden demonstrated when
he observed that 'for any thing we can positively affirm to
the contrary, New Holland and New South Wales may be
actually two different islands'.[21] If that proved true at a time

when the French were busily sending reinforcements to other colonial possessions of their Dutch allies, this could prove of major consequence in the case of New Holland, for if a safe harbour, or harbours, were discovered on its western or southern coasts, or both, French warships would be able to use such a base or bases in time of war from which to intercept English East Indiamen using the Eastern or Outer Eastern Passages. In the event, however, La Pérouse made use of the power of discretion that had been given to him to switch the sequence of his Instructions, and to explore the North Pacific Ocean first, but his expedition was tragically cut short when, after interrupting his North Pacific exploration in order to check up on the arrival of the First Fleet at Botany Bay, his ship was wrecked shortly after that brief visit, so that the proposed circuit of the Australian coastline from the Gulf of Carpentaria to the south coast, still remained to be undertaken.

The Search for La Pérouse

It was some time before a search for the missing navigator was undertaken, but on 9 February 1791 the National Assembly petitioned King Louis XVI to arrange for the organisation of an expedition to the south-west Pacific to try to discover what had happened and at the same time to carry out the work that La Pérouse had not lived to undertake. For this task the choice fell on D'Entrecasteaux, a man peculiarly well fitted for the job. Not only had he recently been in command of France's East Indies squadron, but he had also been Governor of the Ile de France, and was thus very familiar with the whole region and its possibilities and problems. Even more to the point, he himself had been the

first Frenchman to make use of the Eastern Passage when in
1786, on a secret mission to China, he had sailed that way
without charts, a voyage that he later described as having
been 'very tricky,' his ship having been 'surrounded by reefs
in all directions and fenced in by fog'.[22]

Sailing from Brest on 28 September 1791, D'Entrecasteaux
reached Van Diemen's Land, as Tasmania was then called,
on 21 April 1792, and some valuable exploratory work on
the southern coast followed, this region being of particular
interest to the French as a potential port-of-call for ships
sailing from the Ile de France for New Zealand and the
Pacific. The expedition then continued on its way and called
in at New Caledonia where D'Entrecasteaux, at considerable
risk, sailed along the dangerous western coast, which Cook
had not visited. From there he passed on to the Solomons,
and then the Admiralty Islands, where a rumour picked up at
the Cape of Good Hope had suggested evidence of a possible
clue to La Pérouse's disappearance. Finding no trace of the
missing expedition, D'Entrecasteaux went on to Amboina
for refreshments, whence he had intended to follow the
western coast of New Holland to its southernmost point, but
adverse winds making this impracticable, he sailed straight
to Cape Leeuwin. Here his orders told him that, in following
the coast from Cape Leeuwin to the islands of St Francis
and St Peter, discovered by Peter Nuyts in 1627, he was to
examine it as closely as 'if he was making its first discovery'.
This strongly suggests that the French were on the look-out
for a possible channel joining the Gulf of Carpentaria to
the south coast. That, as we have seen, was certainly a
concept which, in the wake of Dampier's observations in an
earlier age, was exercising English minds at this time, for, as

William Eden put it, 'from the eastern extremity of Nuyt's Land to the most westerly of Van Diemen's, being a range of about three hundred and fifty leagues, we know not so much as the coast'.[23]

It was very frustrating for D'Entrecasteaux, however, that when he had reached the vicinity of St Francis Island the persistence of strong easterly winds and the very low state of his expedition's water supply necessitated a return to the south coast of Van Diemen's Land. This was all the more disappointing in that the strong westerly flow of the current made D'Entrecasteaux strongly suspect that Van Diemen's Land was, in reality, an island, the proof of which conjecture he was compelled to leave to another. Once the expedition was back in Recherche Bay, more important surveying was carried out, leading D'Entrecasteaux to observe that 'I do not believe that elsewhere in the globe there is such a great area of excellent anchorages assembled in so small an area'.[24]

After leaving Van Diemen's Land for the last time, the expedition left for a short visit to northern New Zealand, before heading north, by way of the New Hebrides, to north-eastern New Caledonia, after which the Solomons and the Louisiade Archipelago were visited. Here much important exploratory work was done and new discoveries made in the Louisiades, with the addition of the D'Entrecasteaux Islands being made to the map of the world. But on the way back to Java, sailing westwards along the northern coast of New Guinea, D'Entrecasteaux himself died on 30 July 1793. Kermadec, the expedition's second-in-command also died a few weeks earlier.

When the expedition finally put in at the port of Surabaya in the Dutch East Indies at the end of 1793, it was only to discover that France and the Dutch Republic were now at war, and the members of the expedition were all made captive. Thereafter, the expedition disintegrated, with the officers and scientists divided in their political loyalties.[25] Furthermore, the charts and specimens of the expedition were captured by the British as they passed through the English Channel, but French interest in Australia was far from over.

The Final Discoveries before the Outbreak of War

While the proposed settlement near Pitt's Strait had been dropped, the English East India Company nevertheless still went ahead with work to improve the safety of ships making use of the Eastern Passage. For this to be achieved, it was essential to gain more knowledge of the coastline of New Guinea – and of its nearby islands – for instance, there was controversy over the true location of the Solomon Islands, discovered by the Spaniards in the sixteenth century Alexander Dalrymple had already shown a theoretical interest in this region, as controversy developed over the true location of the Solomon Islands, discovered by the Spaniards in the sixteenth century. Some, like Carteret, disbelieved in their very existence, while both Dalrymple and Captain Cook, believed that their true location lay in the island of New Britain off the north coast of New Guinea, whereas Philippe Buache, rightly as it turned out, surmised that they must lie between Santa Cruz Island and New Guinea.

If East Indiamen were to use the proposed Outer Eastern Passage, it was essential that this matter should be resolved. Furthermore, if other ships should ever find themselves in a position similar to that of the Northumberland, it would be invaluable if the first explorers of this region were found to be correct, for Dalrymple recalled how 'the early Portuguese writers say that Papua, or New Guinea as it is since called, is not a continued Land, but an assemblage of Islands'.[26] Dampier, too, thought that he had detected evidence of a possible strait. Dalrymple also knew that Forrest, while at Dorey Harbour, had been told of a deep inlet to the south. Clearly, a careful survey of this whole area was called for, and for this work Dalrymple wanted to secure the services either of Archibald Blair or of John McCluer, the two most experienced surveyors of the Bombay Marine. Both these men, however, were currently engaged in other surveys, Blair in the Andaman Islands and McCluer off the west coast of India.

When McCluer at last became available, orders for the voyage were despatched to Bombay on 23 March 1790, wherein it was stated that the principal object was to examine 'what appears to us as the most eligible Passage [on account] of the frequent occasions which Our China ships lately have had to go by unfrequented Passages and the probability that it will be expedient in future to proceed in like manner'. McCluer was provided with a map taken from the English translation of Leinschoten (1598)[27] that indicated 'that there is a channel thro' Papua or New Guinea to the N.E.ward of the Aroe Islands, which if practicable for an Indiaman, would be the most eligible Passage for our ships to China at a late Season'.[28]

It was intended to combine this survey with a humanitarian voyage to the Palau islands to advise Abba Thule of his son's death in London on 27 December 1784 from smallpox. In addition to this genuine humanitarian concern, there was every reason for the East India Company to be taking a new interest in this island group so close to the track being followed by East Indiamen using the Eastern Passage. Thus, McCluer left Bombay on 24 August 1790, and after sailing by way of Macau he reached the Palau Islands on 21 January 1791. Here he broke the news of Lee Boo's death and handed over presents, in return for which Abba Thule granted the British the island of Corrorah, upon which McCluer thereupon laid the foundation-stone of a fort.

It was not until 24 June 1791 that McCluer was ready to sail for New Guinea, and fresh delays because of unfavourable conditions forced him to travel by way of the islands of Bouro and Amboina. It was on 26 October 1791 that he and his men finally entered the Inlet that was soon to bear his name and they carried on in an easterly direction until, on 28 October, they decried 'a huge chain of Mountains [that] extended from the N. to the S.E. and our water began to decrease fast'. Eventually, after going 'as far as I could possibly go,' with the river 'not above twice the vessel's length in breadth,' McCluer decided that it was time to return to the open sea.

Sailing by way of Bencoolen and Sulu, McCluer was back in the Palau Islands on 20 January 1793, and feeling that he had now completed the task that he had been given, he took the unprecedented step of handing over his command to Wedgeborough, and then staying on at the islands for the next fifteen months. Apart from liking the lifestyle of these islands, it may well be that McCluer thought that the Company would forgive this step if he was able to acquire influence and much vital information of an island group so strategically situated for ships using the Eastern Passage.

Be that as it may, after making an adventurous journey in an open boat, McCluer was back in Macau after fifteen months, and there he met John Hayes, who had planted a colony at Dorey Harbour in New Guinea which was in dire need of provisions. McCluer agreed to take these provisions with him as he began to make his way back to India in a vessel which he had purchased in Macao. He reached Dorey Harbour safely and delivered the supplies he was carrying, but after setting sail for India was never heard of again.

Meanwhile, on 1 February 1793, just as McCluer was beginning his sojourn in the Palaus, Revolutionary France had declared war on Great Britain, Holland and Spain, and the very crisis which had underlain all the above moves to strengthen the various sea-lanes to the East was now at hand. In the years that followed, however, East Indiamen still found themselves able to use the Eastern Passage, which became the regular route to and from China, since France's revolutionary leaders, in their radical frenzy, undermined all the work that had been accomplished since the ending of the Seven Years' War in rebuilding the French navy. It took a further two decades for French sea power to recover from this mad work of destruction which so handicapped Napoleon, and which paved the way for a century of British worldwide naval supremacy and all that that entailed.

Chapter Four

THE DEFENCE OF THE EASTERN TRADE DURING THE REVOLUTIONARY WARS

The French declaration of war against Great Britain, Holland and Spain on 1 February 1793 came at a moment when the newly established French Republic had set out on an expansionist course and had announced its intention of establishing the Rhine and the Alps as France's 'natural frontiers'. This would inevitably involve French absorption of the Austrian Netherlands and the Dutch Republic, and once again seriously impinge upon the economic and military security of Great Britain.

The outbreak of war, though a great blow against Pitt's programme of economic reform and recovery, did have some compensating features. In the first place, it coincided with the undoing of much of the work of the Duc de Choiseul and his successors over the last three decades in creating a really powerful and formidable French navy. The fine new ships, of course, were still there, but a navy is only as good as its technical prowess, discipline, training and morale can make it, and in all these respects, the outbreak of the French Revolution had had the most deleterious effects. For as John Dunmore has observed, not only did disturbances occur in all the French seaports in late 1789, but in the fleets themselves 'insubordination soon developed into anarchy,' and while the aristocratic officers were either in prison, or had been relieved of their commands, or else had fled into exile abroad, those captains who remained were compelled to negotiate with committees set up by the sailors.[1] And though some semblance of order had been restored after a couple of years, it has been estimated that it was not until about 1810 that the French navy had once more become the effective fighting force that it had been before the outbreak of the Revolution. Second, the fact that the revolutionary wars began with both the Dutch and the Spaniards ranged against, rather than with, Revolutionary France meant that the formation of a triple alliance against the British in the East was, for the time being, off the political agenda. Hence, the war, to begin with, was confined to Europe and, for Britain, the immediate objective was to prevent the French from dominating the Low Countries and thus gaining control of the mouths of the Scheldt and the Rhine.

The French decision to go to war had, it is clear, been a recognition of the fact that no British Government could have allowed such a policy of expansion to go unchallenged, but it did entail a problem for both belligerents. The French now had to discover how a land power like France could come to grips with British sea power, and vice versa. One possible answer to this conundrum was that proposed by Vice-Admiral Armand Comte de Kersaint, a French hero of the American War and one of the few senior French naval officers who had hitherto survived the Revolution and was still living in France. He had even been elected to the National Convention, and in a belligerent speech to that body on 1 January 1793, just a month before the declaration of war, he had argued that the apparent economic strength of the British Empire was in reality illusory, and that an invasion of England would meet with massive popular enthusiasm among the British people. Then on 13 January 1793, when presenting the official report of the Committee of Defence, he went on to say, 'The credit of England rests upon fictitious wealth; the real riches of that people are scattered everywhere ... Asia, Portugal and Spain are the most advantageous markets for the productions of English industry; we should shut those markets to the English by opening them to the world. We must attack Lisbon and the Brazils, and carry an auxiliary army to Tippoo Sultan. The Republics of Italy offer you maritime prizes, the losses of which will fall on English commerce.' These ideas were to continue to influence French policy for the next two decades.[2]

In practice, the defence of the Dutch Republic was to prove beyond Britain's power, and in the winter of 1794–95, with the Belgian provinces already under French control, Pichegru's army overran Holland, captured the Dutch fleet while it was ice-bound in the Texel, and set up the Batavian Republic which, under the control of the pro-French Patriots, was to remain in existence until 1806. As the French army swept over the country, however, the Stadtholder, William V, fled to England and settled down in exile at Kew. The British Government, fully alive to the danger posed to the security both of the China trade and of the British position in India, should the French ever gain control of the Dutch East Indies, was determined to take full advantage of this development and on 7 February 1795 the Stadtholder, after consultations with the British ministers, was persuaded to issue the following orders addressed to the various Dutch colonial governments overseas from his residence at Kew: 'We have thought it necessary ... to write that his Britannic Majesty's troops shall be admitted and take possession of the troops in our colonies, and that they are to be considered as the troops of a Kingdom in friendship and alliance with their High Mightinessess in case the colonies should by summoned by the French.'

This was accompanied by a letter addressed to the government of Batavia in Java, describing how the frost had 'enabled the enemy to pass over the rivers in nearly every place,' so that the resort to the usual defensive tactic of flooding the country 'affording us no means of defence, they have penetrated into Holland, the states of which province as well as those of Utrecht thought fit to capitulate ... Their High Mightinesses remaining in The Hague could no longer act as Freemen and are in the situation of a King made a prisoner of war.' He himself, in his place of exile, had found the British determined to succour the Republic 'and to free it from the yoke of the French, and his Britannic Majesty has caused me to receive the strongest assurances that all the colonies or ships of which he should take possession should be restored at the Peace to their High Mightinessess'. His own purpose was 'to prevent the French from making themselves masters thereof,' and he was anxious to effect this end without compelling the British to obtain possession by force, which would allow them to consider themselves 'freed from their promises'.[3]

Although surrenders under this letter of Kew only took place in the cases of Surat, Padang and Amboyna, this document was undoubtedly influential in lowering Dutch morale and reducing resistance to a minimum. Hence, within weeks of the setting up of the Batavian Republic the colonies of the Dutch in the East began to fall. From the viewpoint of the English East India Company, priority needed to be given to those posts commanding the lines of communication with the East. The first to fall was Malacca, on 17 August 1795, followed by the two key strongholds of Trincomali (26 August) and the Cape of Good Hope (16 September).[4] With these key strongholds in their hands, the British next turned their attention to the Spice Islands, where Amboyna surrendered on 16 February 1796, to be followed by Banda on 9 March. The control of these islands not only deprived the Dutch and their French allies of an important economic resource, which was now at the service of their British foes, but was even more significant for the security that it bestowed upon English East Indiamen sailing to and from China by way of the Eastern Passage; for their use of this Passage in time of war became very hazardous whenever enemy cruisers were based in these nearby islands.

While the situation in the Malay Archipelago had thus turned to Britain's advantage, the situation farther east was far otherwise. In what is now Vietnam, civil war had been raging since 1772. In the south of that land, then known as Cochin China, where the Nguyen family had formerly ruled, that whole clan had been massacred with the sole exception of a young prince named Nguyen Anh, and he now made it his life mission to restore his family's fortunes and put an end to the Tayson rebellion. In 1774, shortly after the rebellion had started, a French missionary bishop named Pigneau de Behaine had arrived in the country as Apostolic Vicar to Cochin China, and had quickly become a close adviser to Nguyen Anh.

He hoped that he could help this prince to reunite the country, and as his own missionary work prospered he visualised that this might yet become an Asian Christian kingdom.

In 1785, the French had re-established their East India Company, and within two years their activity in this region was beginning to cause some concern to the British. For in February 1787 D'Entrecasteaux, the new French naval commander in the East, sailed to Canton from Pondichéry by way of the Eastern Passage on a secret mission aimed partly at improving Franco-Chinese relations and, it was believed, at establishing a new French commercial base in Cochin China. Furthermore, in that very same month Pigneau de Behaine was in Paris, at the head of a mission from Cochin China (which included Nguyen Anh's eight-year-old son), and having interviews with King Louis XVI and some of his senior ministers. He was arguing that French military intervention in Cochin China would help France establish a commercial base there, which in turn would benefit French trade with China itself. All this was well publicised in the French press, and so was well known in London, too, and on 28 November 1787, the French Government signed a treaty with Cochin China, whereby Nguyen Anh would cede to the French Crown 'absolute ownership and sovereignty' over Tourane[5] and Pulo Condore, and would grant the French 'entire liberty of commerce in all states of the Kingdom of Cochin China, to the exclusion of all other Europeans,' in return for French military aid against the Tay Son rebels.

Under the terms of this treaty France promised to despatch to Cochin China four ships carrying 'twelve hundred infantry, two hundred artillery, and two hundred and fifty Kaffirs,' complete with arms and ammunition.

On paper, Pigneau appeared to have won a great victory, and had this treaty been put into effect the English East India Company would have had every reason to be deeply worried. Unknown to Pigneau, however, was the fact that Vergennes, the French Foreign Minister, had made the execution of this treaty subject to the approval of Governor Conway of Pondichéry, and such approval was not forthcoming. However, Pigneau was not prepared to return empty-handed, and on 19 June 1789, after a stay of thirteen months, he left Pondichéry for Saigon with two merchantmen and a private army of several hundred volunteers whom he had been able to recruit, and this force was to be of material assistance in helping Nguyen Anh to improve his position.

In China itself, on the other hand, the situation was steadily deteriorating. The long reign of the Emperor Ch'ien Lung (1736–95) was drawing to a close. He had extended the Chinese Empire to its greatest extent, but in the process had strained the empire's resources, and in 1774, the first Chinese rebellion in nearly a century had broken out in Shantung under the leadership of the White Lotus Society. Muslim revolts in Kansu had followed in 1781 and 1784, and then a revolt in Formosa was suppressed in 1786–87, as were revolts in Hunan and Kweichow in 1795–97. But once the old emperor abdicated and his prestige was removed from the scene, the reign of his successor who ruled from 1796 to 1820 was filled with revolts, beginning with that of the White Lotus Society in the provinces of Hupei, Szechuan and Shensi which it took the government more than seven years to suppress (1796–1804).

Thus while conditions in Vietnam were slowly beginning to stabilise, the situation in China was getting steadily worse.

This led J. W. Drummond, the East India Company's President of the Select Committee of Supercargoes at Canton, to suggest that it might be wise to establish a new settlement in that neighbouring territory while waiting for the situation in China to improve. 'There is,' he wrote, 'a vast field opened for the formation of a settlement, or for a commercial intercourse, with the King of Cochin China, whose successes against the usurpers of his Throne and Kingdom have lately given him possession of nearly the whole of his dominions; and, from the best authority, I have heard that he is inclined to solicit support from us or listen to any proposals made him on the part of the English. The Extent of Territory he can now call his own is immense, and rich in all the produce of the East; and although no immediate advantages might be reaped ... in consequence of the 27 Years Civil War which has existed ... still it might prove ultimately beneficial, by offering a place of security to resort to, so close to the Empire of China, and from whence all its produce could be procured by means of Junks, in the event of disturbance of this Government.'[6] Drummond was, in fact, well informed, for on 13 January 1798 Nguyen Anh had written to the British Governor at Malacca to suggest that the British should establish friendly relations with his court, pointing out that he had heard 'that the Governor has under his charge a large supply of Arms and Military stores' of which he himself was 'in great want'.[7] But there were cautionary voices as well. John Barrow, who visited Vietnam as a member of the 1792–93 Macartney mission to China, warned that the 1787 Franco-Cochin Chinese treaty had been 'evidently directed at the building ... of a naval force that should one day overcome our territorial possessions in the East'.[8]

Meanwhile, after the capture of the Spice Islands, an attack on Batavia would have been the logical next step, thus saving the Dutch East Indies as a whole from French control, but in December 1796 news was received of the signing of the new Franco-Spanish alliance, thus creating uncertainty as to whether Batavia or Manila would be the best choice for the next expedition. Manila was not far from Canton and could prove a perfect base for an enemy naval force intent upon attacking the English East India Company's East Indiamen, whether they were sailing by way of the South China Sea or the Eastern Passage, and it was for this reason that Manila was chosen. In the course of preparing the expedition, however, plans went awry when some transports failed to arrive on time, and then, on 3 September 1797, Rear Admiral Rainier wrote to the Admiralty to explain why the expedition had had to be abandoned at the very last moment, stating that:

...almost on the instant of my quitting [Madras Road] with His Majesty's ships and the last Division of Transports, an express was received from His Majesty's minister at Constantinople by this Government ... announcing the important intelligence of the Emperor of Germany having concluded a Peace with the French Nation, [a development that would leave the latter free to execute] their long projected plan of attack on the British Possessions in this country in concert with Tippoo Sultan with whom they have had much friendly intercourse of late. [It had therefore been decided] to relinquish in toto the expedition to Manila, which would have entailed exposing the Possessions and acquisitions we now have [to great risk] if attacked by two such formidable Powers [at a time when] so large a part of the troops and most of the King's ships were detached on a service so distant.[9]

Nevertheless, the significance of Manila continued to exercise the minds of the authorities in India, and in October 1800, Arthur Wellesley urged upon Dundas the need for naval and military reinforcements for the conquest of the Philippine Islands. 'France,' he said, 'is reported to have opened a negotiation with Spain a few years past for the exchange of the Philippine Islands, and it may be reasonably supposed that she has not relinquished her views upon these valuable possessions, which, in the hands of the French, would prove the destruction of our trade with China'.[10] And in his letter, quoted above, recommending a possible move from Canton to Vietnam, J. W. Drummond had, in 1801, stated that he had considered that the acquisition of Luzon, the major northern island of the Philippines, 'might be of very great national consequence'.

While the British, having failed to keep the French out of the Low Countries, had in these ways been concentrating upon seizing control of the Spice Islands and thus safeguarding the use of the Eastern Passage by East Indiamen sailing to and from China, the French had been gaining control of the Mediterranean, Britain's direct route to India. To begin with, Bonaparte's first Italian campaign had brought to an end the Venetian Empire, which had allowed France to seize control of the Ionian Islands, formerly a part of that empire, This had given her mastery of the Adriatic Sea, tempting Bonaparte to declare boastfully that 'soon we shall feel the necessity of seizing Egypt in order to destroy England'.

Then, on the other side of the Italian peninsula, the brief British occupation of Corsica came to an end as a result of the French capture of Leghorn, which was the port from which the British drew their supplies for their military forces on that island. The consequent British withdrawal took place in October 1796, leading to the reversion of the island to French control.

Finally, French supremacy had also been established in Spain, whose government had fallen into the inexperienced and incompetent hands of Godoy. Initially, Spain had been allied to Great Britain, but after a series of Spanish defeats at the hands of the French, Godoy, fearful of the spread of revolutionary propaganda in the wake of these advancing French armies, and aware that Spain did not have the military strength to hold them back, decided that he had no option but to withdraw from the coalition, and by the Treaty of San Ildefonso in 1796 the traditional alliance with France was renewed, despite that country's revolutionary republican government. It was in this context that the British, after the loss of Leghorn to the French, decided to withdraw their naval forces from the Mediterranean altogether.

In order to establish complete French mastery over the Mediterranean, Bonaparte now planned to seize control of the islands of Malta and Sicily, islands which he was later to describe as constituting 'an impassable barrier'. In the case of the former he recommended the seizure of Malta from the Knights of St John in May 1797, and the Directory signified their approval on 27 September. This allowed Bonaparte to send a French commissioner on a spying mission to the island, under the guise, so often resorted to, of being on 'a commercial mission'.[11] The time for action with regard to Sicily, however, had not yet come.

As part of this plan to establish complete French mastery over the Mediterranean, Bonaparte was fully alive to the need to build up France's sea power in the region. Indeed, in his student days he had even contemplated a naval in preference to a military career, and had actually applied to the British Admiralty for admission to the English naval college at Portsmouth. How the course of world history had hung upon the Admiralty's reaction to that application![12] Now, in the wake of his Italian triumphs, a French fleet was stationed in the Adriatic under the command of Admiral de Brueys, capable, it was believed, of meeting on equal terms any British fleet that might appear in the Mediterranean.

Meanwhile, preparations had also been going ahead for a possible invasion of England under Bonaparte's command. But he himself had had grave doubts as to the practicality of such a venture. He knew that France would not have command of the English Channel if she attempted such an invasion, since the fleets of both her Spanish and Dutch allies had suffered serious defeats at the hands of the British during the course of 1797. He further knew that Hoche had recently been unable to land a much smaller force than his own in Ireland.

Furthermore, a large number of the officers and men in his new army were inexperienced or even raw recruits. All in all, the conditions did not look propitious, and as he confided to Bourrienne, if, after a careful tour of inspection, he concluded that the success of such an attempted invasion was doubtful, then 'the Army of England shall become the Army of the East'.[13]

His careful tour of inspection confirmed his doubts, and when he advised the Directory accordingly on 23 February 1798, and pointed out that an eastern expedition would menace Britain's trade with the East, his advice was not only echoing the thinking of Kersaint, but was also very much in the French tradition. There had been earlier proposals for the seizure of Egypt, and in 1738 d'Argenson, a former foreign minister, had even advocated the construction of a Suez Canal. Bonaparte's own interest in the Orient had been inspired by his reading of Raynal's *Philosophical and Political History of the Two Indies*, which had impressed upon his mind the vast potentialities of that region.

While Bonaparte was thus preparing the way for the launch of his Egyptian expedition, Tipu Sultan of Mysore, whom Admiral Rainier had rightly described as having lately had close contacts with the French, had himself been busy in sending agents as far afield as Arabia, Afghanistan, and Constantinople, in addition to France, in his search for allies against the British. For he was determined to recover the half of his dominions which had been taken away from him after his defeat by Cornwallis in 1792. Nor was he Bonaparte's only potential ally in India, for French officers and soldiers were serving in the armies of the Marathas, Hyderabad and Mysore, and General Perron, who had succeeded to the command of the army of Scindhia, perhaps the most powerful of the Maratha princes, was believed to sympathise with the revolutionary government in Paris.

In the case of the Nizam of Hyderabad, there had been a deliberate increase in the number of such recruits since 1795, and these French officers, described by Wellesley as 'men of the most violent principles of Jacobinism,' were known to be in correspondence with their French colleagues in Scindhia's service. All in all, it was clear that Bonaparte had much useful material at hand wherewith to stir up unrest against British authority in India and that a revival of de Bussy's plan of the 1780s was to be expected in some form or other; and Bonaparte's correspondence with Tipu showed that he was fully alive to this possibility.

Tipu had, in fact, already taken the initiative as the result of a visit by a disabled French privateer, in 1797, to his port of Mangalore for repairs. The captain of this vessel, a certain Ripaud, wrongly represented himself as an official French agent from the Ile de France seeking Tipu's cooperation against the British, and Tipu had followed this up by sending envoys to that island with proposals for a Franco-Mysorean alliance against the British in India.

The preparations for Bonaparte's expedition had been on an immense scale, and he set forth with some forty thousand troops carried on four hundred transport vessels, escorted by fifteen ships of the line as well as frigates, corvettes and other vessels, and his instructions stated that the purpose was to capture Egypt and expel the British from 'all their possessions in the East to which the general can come'. Bonaparte was further instructed 'to have the isthmus of Suez cut through' and to gain for France 'the exclusive possession of the Red Sea'.[14]

With this great force, Bonaparte sailed from Toulon on 19 May 1798, and his departure from France closely corresponded in time with the arrival in Calcutta of Richard Wellesley, the Earl of Mornington (soon to become Marquess Wellesley), to take over as the new Governor-General of India. Thus two strong-willed commanders were about to take control of the Anglo-French struggle for dominance in the Orient, the one committed to driving the British out of the Mediterranean and seizing control of Egypt, the other to excluding the French from the subcontinent of India and the surrounding seas.

As the French expedition worked its way eastward through the Mediterranean, it was able to effect the bloodless surrender of the island of Malta on 12 June, and after spending a short while setting up a new French administration for the island Bonaparte continued on his way to Egypt, where he disembarked the expedition on 1 July. Soon afterwards, his army was in possession of the port of Alexandria, and then of Cairo, whereupon the rule of the Mamelukes was at an end and a French administration was in control of the government of Egypt. And it was not long before Bonaparte was in communication with Tipu Sultan of Mysore, telling him of his desire to deliver the sultan 'from the yoke of England'.

Tipu's own proposal for a Franco-Mysorean alliance against the British in India had been forwarded to France for consideration. In the meantime, Governor Malartic explained to Tipu's envoys that not only was Ripaud no envoy of his, but that he himself was in no position to offer Mysore any effective assistance in the immediate future since most of his troops were at present at Batavia, where they were helping France's Dutch allies. All he could do, he explained, was to invite volunteers to serve under Tipu in Mysore. For this purpose he thereupon issued a proclamation stating that in serving Tipu the volunteers would be helping a ruler who 'only awaits the moment when the French shall come to his assistance to declare war against the English, whom he ardently desires to expel from India'.[15]

This proclamation reached Calcutta only a few weeks after Wellesley's arrival there, and in issuing this document, the

French governor had displayed a marked lack of imagination and foresight. He apparently had not realised that the change of Governor-General in India portended a far more aggressive British regime in India. Wellesley was a forceful and hard-working man who was already conversant with Indian affairs as a result of his former service on the Board of Control, and though at first he suspected that the proclamation might prove to be a forgery, he decided to work on the assumption that it was genuine and to prepare for an early move against Tipu Sultan before the latter sensed the danger that he was in.

Meanwhile, Bonaparte had suffered a very severe setback in Egypt where Nelson, after finally discovering the location of the French fleet in Aboukir Bay, had virtually destroyed it in a daring manoeuvre which Admiral Brueys had thought impossible. As a consequence of this Battle of the Nile (1 August 1798) Bonaparte's army was now isolated and could expect neither reinforcements from, nor regular communication with France.

Characteristically, Bonaparte sought to reap some positive advantage from this devastating blow by concentrating all his resources and the minds of his men upon establishing an enlightened French administration in the country, which would offer a favourable contrast to that of the Mameluke period. For as he had confided to his brother Joseph before leaving Toulon, even if the war in Europe went well for France, and 'a political general like me appears and centres the hopes of the people on himself ... then still in the Orient I shall perhaps do greater service to the world than he'.[16] Some 3,800 years earlier, the great Pharaohs of the Feudal Age in Egypt had dug a canal from the north end of the

Red Sea westward to the nearest branch of the Nile in the eastern Delta, thus making it possible for the Pharaoh's Mediterranean ships to sail up the easternmost mouth of the Nile, then to enter the new canal and, passing eastward through it, to reach the Red Sea.[17] Now, in pursuit of his instructions, Bonaparte was planning to renew that concept, and when, in addition to his administrative reforms, he instituted a programme of scientific discovery in Egypt, he reserved for himself, assisted by General Max Caffarelli of the Engineers, the all-important task of studying this ancient canal. At the same time, another engineer, La Pere, was entrusted with making a survey of the whole isthmus.[18]

The fear that the construction of such a canal might be attempted by the French had been worrying the British, too, and Henry Dundas had conferred with Alexander Dalrymple on the subject, the latter having crossed the isthmus in 1776. Dalrymple had replied that while such a project would be possible, it would be an exceedingly costly undertaking. Bonaparte likewise concluded that its construction would be too costly to be practicable at the present time.[19] However, since the whole concept was directly related to the expedition's purpose of threatening the security of the English East India Company's position in India and the Far East, and knowing that Bonaparte habitually refused to acknowledge the validity of the word 'impossible,' it is far from certain that he would not have attempted the construction of this canal later, had he remained in Egypt. As it was, and despite everything that had happened, he still assured the Directory on 8 September 1798 that 'France, mistress of Egypt, will in the long run be mistress of the Indies'.[20]

The French occupation of Egypt, however, involved strained relations with the Ottoman Empire, for although it had become virtually an independent state under the Mamelukes, nevertheless it still owed nominal allegiance to the Sultan. In his anxiety to avoid a war with the Turks over this issue, Bonaparte had arranged that after he had occupied Egypt Talleyrand, as the Directory's Foreign Minister, should travel to Constantinople to open negotiations with the Turks. The idea was that Talleyrand, who was an experienced and skilled (not to say devious!) politician, would then be able to negotiate from a position of strength, and it was hoped that the signing of a new Franco-Turkish treaty would be the result. Talleyrand, however, did not honour his promise to travel to Constantinople to open negotiations, and the very development that Bonaparte had feared now eventuated: Turkey declared war on France. Bonaparte thereupon decided that his best policy was to make a preemptive strike against Syria, which at that time included the Holy Land, and in February 1799 he marched his army into Syria. By a strange coincidence, this was the very time that Wellesley ordered the invasion of Mysore to begin. On 4 May, Seringapatam, the capital of Mysore, was carried by assault and Tipu was slain, while on 20 May Napoleon was forced to abandon his siege of Acre and begin his retreat back to Egypt. He did manage to get the bulk of his army back, and when the Turks landed their own force near Alexandria, he was able to attack and defeat them in the Battle of Aboukir on 25 July.[21] It was soon after that battle that a packet of newspapers reached Bonaparte, including the *Gazette française de Francfurt* of 10 June 1799, which depicted a very serious deterioration of affairs in France itself. The Second Coalition had now been formed, so that France faced five enemies[22] instead of Britain alone, and hostile armies were now active in Holland,

Switzerland and North Italy, while a Turco-Russian fleet had captured Corfu, the most important of the Ionian Islands. Furthermore, France was in a state of economic collapse, and it was believed that it was only a matter of time before Louis XVIII sat on the French throne.

Before leaving Toulon, Bonaparte had told his brother Joseph, 'If France needs me; if the number of those who think like Talleyrand, Siéyès, and Roederer increases; if war breaks out, and is unlucky for France, then I shall return.'[23] He now sensed that such a moment had come, and though he knew that he would be accused of deserting his army, he nevertheless decided that the situation called for his return to France, and on 23 August 1799, he handed over control of the army to Kléber and, accompanied by a handful of officers and civilians, returned to France, managing to evade the British blockade in the process. On the way, his ship had put in at the harbour of Ajaccio in Corsica, and there he had learned of further French reverses and the dissolution of the republics which France had set up in Italy. On 8 October, Bonaparte landed on the French coast at Fréjus, and was welcomed back by the people at large as a conquering hero.

Chapter Five

NAPOLEON'S CHALLENGE TO BRITAIN AND AUSTRALIA: THE FIRST PHASE

Bonaparte, as the new First Consul, needed a period of peace in which to establish and consolidate his new regime, and on 25 December 1799, Talleyrand, his foreign minister, forwarded a letter from Bonaparte addressed to King George III proposing peace between the two countries. Two years earlier Pitt had made the same proposal to no avail, and now it was Britain's turn to be uncooperative. Lord Grenville, the foreign secretary, argued that while the proposed negotiations would relieve France from 'numerous and alarming difficulties,' they would not relieve England from any. 'The ports of France,' while her army in Egypt, now deprived of all intercourse with the republic, could then be brought back. And whereas the commerce and manufactures of France would greatly benefit from the lifting of the blockade, this country would be left merely in its present position. Above all, the First Consul was untrustworthy, Grenville said. He enumerated many instances in which Bonaparte had violated the treaties which he himself had made. As a particularly revealing example of such devious behaviour, he instanced the case of the Egyptian expedition where, he stated, Bonaparte had solemnly declared to the Porte that he had no intention of taking possession of Egypt, while at the same time stating the very opposite to his own generals, and then assuring the people of Egypt that he had taken possession of the country with the consent of the Porte. Britain should not enter into any negotiation, Grenville said, until she could anticipate getting some advantage from it.[1]

This made it very evident to Bonaparte that he must first seek to break up the Second Coalition and then, if still necessary, bring economic pressure to bear upon Britain to negotiate. As a result, within five months of this unsuccessful approach to Britain, Bonaparte was launched upon his Second Italian Campaign, and on 14 June 1800, after crossing the St Bernard Pass with 40,000 men, had defeated the Austrians at the Battle of Marengo, though only by an extremely narrow margin. This was followed by Moreau's victory at the Battle of Hohenlinden on 3 December, and on 9 February 1801, the Austrians were forced to conclude the Treaty of Lunéville. Once more the French position in Italy, and therefore in the Mediterranean, was a very strong one, with the Austrians being forced to recognise the Cisalpine and Ligurian Republics in Italy, as well as the Helvetian Republic in Switzerland and the Batavian Republic in the Netherlands. Furthermore, Tuscany now became the Kingdom of Etruria.

A fortnight before the coup d'état in Paris, the Tsar had withdrawn in disgust from the very Second Coalition that he had played a leading role in creating, which had left Austria to face the French on her own. Now these French successes persuaded him to link his fortune with Bonaparte's rising star. He had been deeply dissatisfied with the conduct of both the Austrians and the British in the operations of the Second Coalition, while the British actions over Malta had incensed him even more, and Bonaparte skilfully exploited his feelings of resentment. It was hard work to begin with for, as he told O'Meara in later years, at first the Tsar 'was strongly prejudiced against the revolution, and every person concerned in it, but afterwards I ... rendered him reasonable and ... changed his opinions altogether'. The Tsar, who had wished to gain Malta for Russia, had re-established in Russia the Order of the Knights of St John – the Order that had ruled Malta until the island had been captured by Bonaparte –, and had thereupon been elected Grand Master of the Order on 27 October 1798. With the French garrison on the island being blockaded by the Royal Navy, Bonaparte made a virtue out of necessity by promising the Tsar that if the French garrison was compelled by famine to withdraw, he would be prepared to hand over the Island to the Tsar as its Grand Master. This was a promise that cost him nothing to make, though in point of fact the garrison was forced to surrender to the British on 5 September 1800.

Nine days earlier the Tsar, doubtless resigned to the fact that he was not going to get possession of Malta, had invited Prussia, Denmark and Sweden to join Russia in re-establishing the Armed Neutrality of the North which his mother, Catherine the Great, had originally organised in 1780. To gain still further merit in Paul's eyes, Bonaparte promptly expressed his support, and declared that he would not negotiate a peace with the British 'until England shall have acknowledged that the sea belongs to all nations'.[2] The ploy worked, and to Bonaparte's delight the Tsar sent an envoy to Paris on 15 January 1801 to negotiate a peace treaty.

Bonaparte already controlled the European coastline from the Batavian Republic right round to Naples with the important exception of Portugal, Britain's closest European ally and trading partner. It was Bonaparte's intention to close the European continent to British trade, and the formation of the Second Armed Neutrality, which became a reality by 18 December 1800, added a very promising new ingredient to the economic pressure that was being brought to bear upon the authorities in London. For as part of this renewed Armed Neutrality, Danish forces entered Hamburg on 19 March 1801, occupied Hanover and Bremen and similarly declared the Weser and Ems closed to British trade. Bonaparte could see the consequential tightening of the economic noose, and in order to complete France's control of the coastline of Western Europe he now brought pressure to bear upon Spain to invade her smaller neighbour, and on 3 March 1801, a reluctant Spanish government complied.

The invasion of Portugal had important implications for Britain's trade with the East. Portugal's overseas empire still included eastern Timor, Goa, and the port of Macao. Goa was of particular immediate concern, since it was surrounded by the territories of the Maratha Confederacy in whose armies so many French adventurers were serving. If the port of Goa were to come under French control, it would create great opportunities for the French to undermine British influence and authority in the Indian subcontinent. This consideration persuaded Governor-General Wellesley to conclude a treaty with the Portuguese Viceroy of Goa whereby 1,100 British royal infantry were added to his garrison. The Bengal Government would have liked to have taken similar action with regard to Macao, whose roadstead was much frequented by East Indiamen on their way to Canton, and which was the settlement where the East India Company's supercargoes were required to reside, by Chinese regulations, at the close of each trading season at Canton. A proposal was therefore made for the despatch of British troops to help the Portuguese to defend that settlement from possible French attack. The Company's supercargoes, however, strongly opposed this idea. Appreciating the fact that Macao belonged to China, and not to Portugal, they were fully alive to the alarm that had already been aroused in China by the British conquests in India. Any such expedition to Macao, they warned, would only 'tend to confirm the unfavourable sentiments they already entertain relative to the restless and intriguing temper of the English nation'. They went on to reassure their superiors in India and London that even if the French captured Macao, they could not endanger the China trade so long as Britain continued to possess 'a Superior and Commanding navy in those seas'.[3]

Meanwhile, shortly after concluding his peace treaty with France, the Tsar approached Bonaparte with a proposal for a joint Franco-Russian invasion of India. 'He sent to me for a plan,' Bonaparte recalled years later at St Helena. 'I sent him one, with instructions in detail.' There are some apparent discrepancies in the accounts given of this plan. According to one version, a Russian army was to march from Orenburg through Bokhara and Khiva, while a French army was to pass down the Danube and proceed to Taganrog, and thence by the Don and the Volga to Astrakhan. The two forces would then combine and proceed by way of Herat and Kandahar. In his account at St Helena, on the other hand, Napoleon had stated, 'My troops were to have gone to

Warsaw, to be joined by the Russians and Cossacks, and to have marched from thence to the Caspian Sea,' saying which, he had shown O'Meara on a map the routes which had been planned. Perhaps there were two French detachments involved. Napoleon had gone on to say, 'I was to subscribe 10 millions in order to purchase camels and other requisites ... I had ... made a demand to the King of Persia [*sic*] for a passage through his country ... Though the negotiations were not entirely concluded, [they] would have succeeded as the Persians were desirous of profiting by it themselves.'⁴ Some of this had been picked up by the British press, which was soon reporting that the Emperor of Russia was collecting together an army that rumour stated was intended to march overland to attack the British possessions in India.

At this point, however, events ceased to go Bonaparte's way. In the first place, his efforts to maintain the French army in Egypt, whose possession by France was so crucial to his plans to attack British trade and possessions in the East, had gone awry. In January 1801, Rear Admiral Ganteaume left Brest with seven ships of the line carrying 5,000 troops, but after successfully passing the Straits of Gibraltar the Admiral, instead of continuing on his way and landing the troops in Egypt, had made for Toulon, believing that he was being pursued by powerful British naval forces, and that Keith's ships were in front of him. The chance had been missed, and it was the British who landed a fresh army in Egypt in March, an army that was slowly to gain control of the whole country and to force the French army there to surrender.

His next setback was in the Baltic. Faced with the escalation of the blockade following upon the formation of the Second Armed Neutrality of the North, and aware that the Northern

Powers between them possessed some forty-one sail of the line, with the Tsar himself being poised to form an alliance with France, the British Government decided to strike back. A fleet under Parker and Nelson was fitted out for the Baltic, and after forcing the passage of the Sound it fought the Battle of Copenhagen on 2 April, whereat Nelson took possession of the Danish fleet. Meanwhile, an even greater blow had befallen Bonaparte with the murder of Tsar Paul on 24 March 1801, and in a moment of time, the entire prospect of the war had been transformed. The projected joint invasion of India was dead, while the Second Armed Neutrality of the North was doomed to an almost immediate extinction. And since the new Tsar wanted better relations with Great Britain, the blockade of her trade was greatly weakened. Then, after the capitulation of the French army in Egypt in September, the way was open for immediate peace negotiations with Britain. These began in October 1801, and on 25 March 1802, the Peace of Amiens was finally signed.

The Peace of Amiens

Both France and Britain had become anxious for peace in 1802. Bonaparte needed a period of calm in which to establish his new regime, while the Addington Ministry was anxious to see an end to the prolonged hostilities which had resulted in high unemployment and high prices for food, a combination that inevitably led to much popular discontent. Thus, the coming of peace was warmly applauded in both countries. When the terms upon which the peace had been concluded became known, however, it became clear that this was a peace dictated upon Bonaparte's terms, and as this became more generally understood it was realised that only the French had genuine grounds for celebration. For under the terms of the treaty, Britain had agreed to surrender all the conquests she had made during the war to France and France's allies, with the exception of Trinidad, which was ceded by Spain, and Ceylon, which was ceded by the Dutch. Thus the Cape, but not Trincomali, was returned to the Dutch, while Minorca once more became a Spanish possession. It was also laid down that Britain was to return the island of Malta to the Knights of Malta.

These terms were disillusioning in themselves, but worse was to follow. British merchants had expected to find the Continent open to Britain's trade now that the war was over, but this was not the case. For Bonaparte shared the protectionist economic concepts of his Revolutionary predecessors, whereby British merchants had seen the importation and sale of their goods forbidden throughout the territory of the French Republic. He had refused to allow discussion of any new commercial agreement between the two countries during the negotiations for a new peace, and when the treaty was eventually signed, these merchants were aghast to find that the wartime bans were in no way to be abated now that peace had returned. In fact, their position now was even worse than during the years of war, when bans could be circumvented in ways that were hardly available in time of peace, and when they had been able to benefit from prizes captured at sea. Now very high protective tariffs virtually excluded British goods from an enlarged France that included Belgium, and which stretched as far as the Rhine. Thus, whereas the value of Britain's foreign trade had almost doubled during the eight years of war between 1792 and 1800, now that peace had returned it had begun to decline, as did the total tonnage of ships leaving the United Kingdom.[5]

Bonaparte's intervention in Switzerland only served to increase British suspicion. Before and during the peace negotiations he had been providing new institutions for the countries bordering France so as to strengthen French control therein. At the same time, the map of Germany had been redrawn under Bonaparte's guidance in a way that was designed to weaken Austria's influence. The British had found it hard enough to accept Bonaparte's high-handed imposition of a new constitution upon the Dutch at the very beginning of the peace negotiations, but his latest intervention in Switzerland, on the ground that France must have a strong and friendly government on the borders of Franche Comté, tested British patience to the limit.

In addition to these worries, there was also much cause for concern regarding the interest that Bonaparte was showing in developing an imperial policy, both in the West and in the East. Talleyrand had advocated such a policy as an antidote to revolutionary fervour and restlessness in a paper that he had delivered to the Institut National in July 1797. Drawing upon his experience in the United States of America, where he had lived for a short while and had seen how, after their own Revolutionary War, the people had concentrated all their energies upon taming 'forest, flood and prairie' and in developing their expanding frontier, he had argued that France needed a similar outlet for the 'restlessness of mind and need of movement' left behind by the unsettling effects of the Revolution. This could best be met, he had suggested, by a policy of colonial expansion, and he had pointed to Egypt and Louisiana as offering the most promising possibilities.[6] This was a concept that appealed to Bonaparte, and in studying Abbé Raynal's volumes he would have noted the considerable space devoted to the original French discovery of this region and to its potentialities. In *1763*, France had ceded Louisiana to Spain in compensation for her losses during the Seven Years War, and in subsequent years, she had made repeated efforts recover possession of this great territory, culminating in Bonaparte's repossession of it in *1801* in exchange for the Italian states of Tuscany and Parma.

With the conclusion of the treaty of Amiens the way was now clear for Bonaparte to proceed with his colonial plans. In the West, the great expanse of Louisiana bordered on Spanish Florida, and the two together comprised the whole northern shores of the Gulf of Mexico. Farther south, the territory of French Guiana stretched as far as the Amazon river. Thus, France now controlled the mouths of the two greatest rivers on the American continent. In addition to this, a French settlement had existed for more than a century on the western part of the island of San Domingo, where modern Haiti is located, in the middle of the Caribbean Sea. On this island Bonaparte was visualising the establishment of French naval and military bases, in the centre of his nascent French Empire of the West. For the British, however, this whole plan was alarming. In Europe Bonaparte had already demonstrated that he shared with his Revolutionary predecessors belief in an economic policy of strict protectionism, and it could be safely be assumed that he intended to extend that policy to this planned new French empire in the Americas. Spain, of course, had long pursued a policy of economic exclusion in her Latin American colonies, but her weak hold on these possessions had enabled British merchants to evade the Spanish restrictions with some success. With Bonaparte's increasing domination of the Spanish monarchy, however,

POSTSCRIPT

Books by mail since 1987

Secure online shopping at psbooks.co.uk where you can browse our entire range
Advanced search tool ● **Easy Order Form** for quick ordering
Bestsellers ● New Arrivals ● Back by Popular Demand

Follow us on Twitter   Like us on Facebook

Subscribe to our email newsletter online or join us on Facebook and Twitter
to be the first to hear about our special offers.

To speak to one of our helpful and friendly operators, call:
Customer services – 01626 897123
Order line – 01626 897100
available Monday to Friday 8.30am to 5.30pm

Up to 75% off publishers' prices

www.psbooks.co.uk

POSTSCRIPT
Books by mail since 1987

Thank you

Thank you for ordering from Postscript and we hope that you enjoy your books.

For over 30 years Postscript has been buying overstocks and out of print books from major publishers, as well as specialist presses, and passing on exceptionally high discounts to our customers.

A range of over 10,000 discounted titles to choose from
Subjects include history, biography, art, literature, military history, science, philosophy, politics, fiction and children's books as well as sale titles
Also gift ideas such as notecards, calendars, journals, puzzles and games

- Free monthly catalogue with over 600 titles, 200 of which are new in stock •
- Original descriptions written by our team of expert writers •
- Special offers including free books and free P&P •

Up to 75% off publishers' prices

www.psbooks.co.uk

there was every reason for British merchants to fear that the policy of economic protectionism would now become far more effective and widespread in this whole region in the future.

On the other side of the world, Bonaparte was involved with another enterprise that might well lead to some form of colonial expansion in the future.

For on 25 March 1800, he had had an interview with Nicolas Baudin[7] who, with support from the Institut National, was proposing to undertake a new voyage of discovery. In first proposing this expedition, Baudin had had in mind the completion of the work that La Pérouse had not lived to complete in his famous but ultimately tragic voyage. That expedition had sailed from Brest in 1785, the year when the French East India Company had been re-established and when the fur trade between the North-West coast of America and China had been burgeoning in spectacular fashion, and the main thrust of La Pérouse's instructions had been a call for a close examination of the potentialities of that trade. Nevertheless, the expedition had also been expected to carry out further exploration in the South Pacific, as well as to circumnavigate the Australian continent in an anti-clockwise direction from the Gulf of Carpentaria to the southernmost part of the southern Van Diemen's Land.[8]

Baudin's original far-ranging proposal had been honed down by the Institut National to a detailed exploration of the Australian coastline, apart from the well-known eastern seaboard and its British settlement. And the man who played a leading part in planning the expedition and drawing up its instructions was Charles-Pierre de Claret, Count of Fleurieu, who had played a similar leading role in the planning of La

Pérouse's voyage. In Baudin's case, the overall plan was for the exploration of the Australian coastline to be carried out in two stages, in the first of which Baudin was to explore the eastern seaboard of Van Diemen's Land (Tasmania) and to find out whether the British had established any settlements there. This was to be followed by an examination of the south, west and north-west coasts of New Holland before going on to Timor for supplies and refreshments. In the second stage, he was to sail from Timor past the island of Ceram and to make for the straits separating the island of Waigeo from New Guinea, these straits being, of course, in the immediate vicinity of Pitt's Passage and Pitt's Strait, the most vulnerable stretch of water for ships using the Eastern Passage. He was then to examine the south-western and southern coasts of New Guinea until getting as far as Cape Deliverance,[9] and was then to pass over to the Gulf of Carpentaria, after exploring which he was to head back westwards, examining the northern coasts of the continent until reaching Cape North-West. A very strict timetable was laid down in these instructions so as to enable the expedition to complete this vital final phase in harmony with the onset, first of the north-west and then of the south-east monsoons. Then, once the expedition had fetched up at Cape North-West, it was to return to the Ile de France. The plan was for the expedition to return to France by the spring of 1803.

Bonaparte could see great possibilities in this plan. Van Diemen's Land was of prime significance for French interests, since it was hoped to establish a port of call there for ships sailing from the Ile de France to New Zealand. Admiral de Suffren had affirmed that New Zealand could supply the dockyards of the Ile de France with the timber that they lacked, and a settlement in New Zealand would enable the French to command their share of the whale fisheries and trade of the great Pacific Ocean. The examination of the south coast of Australia that was to follow would prove or disprove the widespread theory that New South Wales was separated from New Holland by a strait linking the Gulf of Carpentaria with some point on the south coast, probably in the vicinity of the isles of St Peter and St Francis in the Nuyts Archipelago. If true, this would give France and her subservient Dutch ally very strong claims to New Holland on the grounds of prior discovery, particularly in view of the fact that the British, when proclaiming their annexation of New South Wales, had specifically delineated the longitude of 135° E as marking the western border of that colony. If France could set up settlements on Van Diemen's Land and on the south coast of a possibly insular New Holland, and establish her sovereignty over both, she would be in a position to intercept English shipping bound for New South Wales and China in time of war. But above all, the close examination that Baudin was called upon to make of the south-western coasts of New Guinea and the north-western coasts of New Holland would reveal to the French the best ways in which to intercept China-bound English shipping making wartime use of the Eastern Passage.

With all these factors in its favour, and in view of the backing given to the voyage by such influential figures as Fleurieu, Bougainville, and the scientist Lacépède, it is no wonder that when Baudin met Bonaparte on 25 March 1800, the latter gave his enthusiastic backing to the whole undertaking. Since the expedition was to be launched in the midst of a worldwide war, however, it was necessary for a passport to be obtained from the British Admiralty guaranteeing it a safe passage, and for this to be obtained it was essential for the whole mission to be depicted as a purely scientific undertaking. This did not prevent the British from having strong suspicions that this was not the real purpose of the voyage, however, and later comments by both Baudin himself, and by Péron, one of the most active of the scientists on board, and the man who was to be appointed the official historian of the expedition, showed that those suspicions were wholly justified.

At about the time that the French were applying to London for their guarantee of a safe passage, Matthew Flinders was preparing to leave Australia for England. Before setting out he wrote to Sir Joseph Banks, on 6 September 1800, expressing his belief in the likelihood that 'an extensive strait separates New South Wales from New Holland,' and his desire to have the opportunity to establish once and for all the true nature of the whole continent. His offer to lead such an expedition was taken up as soon as he arrived back in England. He, in his turn, also had to be armed with a passport from the French authorities, but by the time that Flinders was ready to leave, Baudin already had a big lead, having sailed from Le Havre on 19 October 1800, whereas Flinders was not able to leave England until 18 July 1801.

Had Baudin been able to keep to the original timetable laid down in this instructions, he would have completed his survey before Flinders arrived on the scene, and the two expeditions would not have met. Baudin's two ships would not have been forced to repair to Port Jackson, and the British would have remained in the dark as to what, precisely, Baudin had been doing, and what discoveries he might have made. Without knowing the extent of Baudin's work in Tasmanian waters, Governor King might not have felt the urgent need to establish a settlement there as a preemptive move at that time. Baudin himself would have been able to complete his all-important surveys in the north in harmony with the prevailing monsoons, and on his return to France Bonaparte would have been presented with some promising options for the future. On the other hand, Bonaparte would not have gained the information that was to come his way with regard to the progress that the British had made in developing Port Jackson, nor of the Pacific ambitions that they were suspected of nurturing.

In fact, however, a mixture of faulty judgment and ill luck put the expedition seriously behind schedule from the very start. In his instructions, Baudin had been told that after taking in supplies at Santa Cruz in Tenerife he was to endeavour to sail non-stop to the Ile de France, but if a call *en route* proved necessary, this should be at the island of Santa Catarina off the Brazilian coast. This implied that he was expected to follow the standard practice adopted by English East Indiamen bound for the East, which first headed for the Brazilian coast, and then headed south to latitudes where the prevailing westerlies gave them a rapid passage eastwards so as to double the Cape of Good Hope.[10] Baudin, however, decided to risk taking the shorter route down the African coast, where fickle winds and adverse currents had to be contended with, and it was a gamble that did not pay off, for instead of arriving at the Ile de France in late January and then being in a position to leave again by 15 February, as planned, he did not reach the island until 15 March, docking the next day.

Once arrived, he was to lose a further month through circumstances not entirely of his own making. He was to blame for the fact that his long voyage out meant that he now required a far larger quantity of stores than the authorities at the island had been led to believe. But it was his ill fortune that he arrived at a time when an English attack was expected, making it far harder to obtain the necessary cooperation from the islanders and the local authorities. It was presumably in an attempt to pressurise the latter into giving him the supplies that he needed without further delay that he confirmed, in a letter to the administrators, that behind the stated scientific objectives there was a substantial political end in view.[11]

Even at this early stage, there was no longer any realistic hope of catching up with the original timetable, and Baudin's decision, upon leaving the Ile de France on 26 April, to make for Timor rather than Van Diemen's Land after he had reached Cape Leeuwin, made it impossible beyond recall. This decision was based upon his belief that conditions off the coast of Van Diemen's Land at that season would make it impossible to carry out useful hydrological and natural history research, a belief that seems to have been vindicated by his experience off that coast a year later.

It is not necessary to detail, here, the story of Baudin's voyage, but only to remark upon some specific aspects that are of relevance to our main topic. After leaving Timor and carrying out some extensive research around the south-east coast of Tasmania, the two ships became separated, and Baudin started coasting the mainland in a westerly direction. On 8 April 1802, the two expeditions of Flinders and Baudin met at Encounter Bay, the meeting coming as a great surprise for Baudin, who knew nothing about Flinder's voyage, whereas the latter was better prepared for such an encounter. Port Jackson had already been informed about this French expedition, so it was no surprise when first the *Naturaliste* and then the *Géographe*, entered Port Jackson in May and June 1802, respectively. By this time Baudin had completed his belated but very thorough survey of D'Entrecasteaux Channel and the east coast of Van Diemen's Land, and a preliminary survey of the south coast as far as the Nuyt's Archipelago, though much remained to be done. But now, at Port Jackson, while the French received every help for their worn-out crews, scientists and ships that the English settlers were able to provide, and readily acknowledged as much, nevertheless suspicions were inevitably aroused. Indeed, misgivings had been expressed at the very outset. Thus, when Flinders had set sail C. F. Grenville, a director of the East India Company, had written to Brown, the botanist on board, to say, 'I hope the French ships of discovery will not station themselves on the north-west coast of Australia,' rightly sensing that the French were seeking to discover how best to threaten East Indiamen using the Eastern Passage.

Now, after the expedition's extended stay at Port Jackson, Governor King wrote to Lord Hobart, the Minister for War and the Colonies, to send this warning about Baudin: 'Notwithstanding the very great collection he has made in every branch of Natural History,' he wrote, 'yet I am inclined to think from his Geographical pursuits that collecting alone is not the principal object of his Mission, as it has very forcibly struck me that they have an intention of looking for a place proper to make a similar Establishment to this, on the north or north-west coast. It has also occurred to me that they may have some intention of laying a claim to Van Diemen's Land, now it is known to be insulated from New Holland: my only reason for this supposition is the length of time and the very accurate and extensive survey he has taken of what is called by us 'Storm Bay Passage' and by the French 'Le Canal D'Entrecasteaux'. If Baudin had not met Flinders at Encounter Bay, and if the ships had not been compelled to make that long stay at Port Jackson, the facts that had made Governor King so suspicious would not have been known to the British. King's belief that the great scientific collections were 'not the principal object of his Mission' had not only been hinted at by Baudin himself at the Ile de France, but was categorically confirmed by Péron in his admission that 'all our natural history researches, extolled with so much ostentation by the Government, were merely a pretext for its enterprise and were intended to assure for it the most general and complete success.'.[12] Even allowing for his bitter enmity towards Baudin, this would have been a difficult admission to make for one who had played such a prominent role in the pursuit of those very researches, but it afforded striking confirmation of King's suspicions which were surely correct on both counts.

As things now stood, however, the failure to keep up with the timetable set, and the impossibility of keeping the British at Port Jackson unaware of what had been done, allowed Governor King to take the necessary countermeasures, and to send Lieutenant John Bowen to establish a settlement at Risdon Cove on the Derwent River, where he and his companions arrived on 8 September 1803. This was followed by the Colonial Office's despatch of Colonel William Paterson to found a second settlement at Port Dalrymple in

November 1804. Thus, the French had lost an opportunity of stealing a march on the British in this southern island.

As for the hoped-for settlement in the north, Baudin, now a dying man, had been unable to leave Timor until 3 June 1803, whereas his instructions had nominated early December (1801) as the target date, a time of year which would have enabled the expedition to catch the north-west monsoon for the first half of its northern reconnaissance. This belated departure meant that he was having to battle against rather than sail with the monsoon, and so was unable to complete the all-important final phase of his mission. As he had originally been warned, 'the monsoons are in command,' and his inability to observe that truth in practice now finally forced him to give up the struggle and return to the Ile de France, where he died a few weeks later with his mission unfinished. Thus, he had been unable to search for and locate a suitable site for a French settlement on the north or north-west coast of New Holland from which to intercept English East Indiamen using the Eastern Passage.

The English East India Company had every reason to be relieved at the inconclusive outcome of the Baudin mission. If that relief was to be more than temporary, however, those servants of the East India Company who were most directly involved in trading in and through the East Indies were anxious to see further precautions taken for the future. On 7 October 1802, a copy of the definitive treaty of Amiens had reached the Governor-General, and under its terms, all the French and Dutch settlements and possessions in the East which had been captured during the war, with the exception of Ceylon, were to be returned to French and Dutch control. R. T. Farquhar, the British Resident at Amboyna, thereupon decided to try to get control of other islands lying in close proximity to the Eastern Passage, and chose Obi, to the south of Celebes (Halmahera) and Geby, to the west of the island of Waigeo, and to this end he negotiated treaties with the Sultans of Batjan and Tidore. The Company's directors in London were sympathetic with this policy, But Governor-General Wellesley and Governor Lord Clive of Madras were not. Clive's opposition was grounded upon legal considerations, but Wellesley's was based upon considerations of policy. In his view, the most immediate danger facing the East India Company was the challenge to its authority emanating from the Maratha Confederacy, and the last thing that he wanted was to have resentful Dutch foes in his rear. Hitherto the Dutch in the East Indies had been reluctant allies of the French, but Wellesley sensed that if the English planted themselves in the heart of the Dutch Moluccas, this passive attitude would be transformed into fierce hostility. Therefore, Farquhar, now forgiven for using his initiative too boldly by being appointed Commissioner for the restoration of the Moluccas to the Dutch, was instructed to proceed with caution. Obi was dropped from consideration, perhaps because of its close proximity to the Dutch settlements, while in the case of Geby he was instructed to 'refrain from the assertion of any right of occupancy' and to confine himself to stating 'that the British Government is anxious to possess a port in the Eastern seas, to which British vessels may occasionally resort for shelter or for supplies of provisions, or for the purpose of repairing any occasional damages, without interfering in the trade of the Spice Islands'.

While refusing to go further than consenting to this tactful request to the Dutch authorities for permission to establish a settlement at Geby, Wellesley did determine to authorise Farquhar to revive British claims to the island of Balambangan off the north-west coast of Borneo, where Alexander Dalrymple had obtained permission from the Sultan of Sulu to establish a settlement in 1762. So, with the Moluccas handed back to Dutch control by Col. Oliver on 1 March 1803, Farquhar left Malacca for Balambangan in August with the necessary military personnel to form a new settlement there. This island did not offer the immediate advantages to ships using the Eastern Passage that Obi and Geby would have done, but it did have other advantages. It was positioned, in the first place, in a location where piracy had always been endemic, and so could be expected to add to the maritime security of the region. In addition, it was described as 'possessing a safe and commodious harbour' located where it would 'afford shelter and supplies of provisions to British ships navigating the Eastern seas. Furthermore, it 'would enable us to obtain information with regard to the proceedings of any European power possessing establishments in that quarter of the Globe' as well as facilitating 'military and naval operations against the possessions or the maritime force of any power in these extensive islands with which we may eventually be engaged in war'.[13]

The European powers referred to in the above statement were clearly, in the first instance, the Dutch in the East Indies and the Spaniards in the Philippine Islands, both subservient allies of the French under the rule of Bonaparte. Another source of potential danger was French influence in Vietnam, which shared a common border with the Empire of China, and whose shores faced the island of Balambangan far away on the opposite side of the China Sea. There the ruling prince,

Nguyen Anh, who had now adopted the title of the Emperor Gia Long, had just emerged victorious from a prolonged civil war with the help of French arms.

In view of the breakdown of law and order in the Chinese Empire following upon the abdication of the long-reigning Emperor Ch'ien Lung[14] Vietnam was becoming a focal point of increased international interest. Back in 1787, when the Vietnamese civil war was at its height, two notable French missions were undertaken. One was led by Admiral D'Entrecasteaux, the newly appointed naval commander in the East, the other by Bishop Pigneau, the French Apostolic Vicar of Cochin China.[15] In an effort to put the newly re-established French East India Company on a firmer footing, D'Entrecasteaux had sailed from Pondichéry to Macao by way of the Eastern Passage, seemingly the first Frenchman to make use of that route, on a secret mission to improve Franco-Chinese relations as well as to seek to establish a French commercial base in Cochin China. The other mission, headed by Pigneau, with the eight-year-old son of Nguyen Anh in its ranks, headed for Paris. There the bishop's meetings with senior ministers and with King Louis XVI had been widely publicised in the French press, and were therefore well known in Britain too, and they had resulted in the signing of a French treaty with Cochin China, whereby Nguyen Anh undertook to cede to the French crown 'absolute ownership and sovereignty' over the important port and harbour of Tourane[16] and over the island of Condore, and to grant the French 'entire liberty of commerce in all the states of the kingdom of Cochin China to the exclusion of all other Europeans' in return for French military aid against the Tayson revolutionary forces.[17]

On paper, Pigneau appeared to have won a great victory. Unknown to him, however, Vergennes, the French foreign minister, had made the execution of this treaty dependent on the approval of Governor Conway at Pondichéry, and this was not forthcoming. Nothing daunted, Pigneau had thereupon raised, on his own initiative, a private army of several hundred volunteers, and had left Pondichéry with this force in two ships on 19 June 1789. These soldiers had been of great assistance to Nguyen Anh. The outbreak of the French Revolution, however, had prevented France from exploiting the advantage that she had thus won.

By the turn of the century, the British President of the Supercargoes at Canton, T. W. Drummond, was also paying close attention to Vietnam, which was seen as a territory both of great promise and of potential danger. With China now subject to serious civil unrest, whereas the civil war in Vietnam was coming to an end, Drummond was considering moving the East India Company's base of operations from Canton to Vietnam, where he visualised 'a vast field opened for the formation of a settlement, or for a commercial intercourse with the King of Cochin China' who, he understood, was willing to hold discussions with the English, and whose Kingdom was 'immense and rich in all the produce of the East'. Even though, in the aftermath of twenty-seven years of civil war, no immediate commercial advantage was to be anticipated, yet 'it might prove ultimately beneficial, by offering a place of security to resort to, so close to the Empire of China, and from whence all its produce could be procured by means of junks, in the event of disturbance of the Government. And it is with this idea,' he continued, 'That I have considered the acquisition of Luconia might be of very great national consequence.'[18] The French, because of their domination over Godoy's Spain, were already assured of the use of Manila, and could concentrate on Vietnam. For the English East India Company, on the other hand, it was worrying to have French influence predominant on either side of the approach to the Chinese Empire by way of the South China Sea, and to have France's subservient Spanish ally in control of the Philippine Islands alongside the routes to China followed by East Indiamen using either the Eastern Passage or the various alternative approaches by way of the Pacific Ocean.

With regard to the potential danger of Cochin China, one traveller, after visiting Saigon in April 1799, recorded having seen an armament of 80,000 men and of more than 1,000 vessels being fitted out, while Nguyen Anh had approached the Governor of Madras with requests for arms and ammunition, and although he had granted free ingress to English ships into all the ports of Cochin China, nevertheless French advisers, hostile to the English, were known still to have considerable influence at his court. The growth of British power in India, and the belief that the British were hoping to acquire Tourane or some other port in the country were not helpful to the British cause. This led John Barrow, who had visited the country in 1792–93 as a member of the Macartney embassy to China, to remind his countrymen of the Franco-Cochin Chinese treaty negotiated by Pigneau in.1787 which, though it never came into force, was indicative of French thinking. That treaty, he argued, had 'evidently been directed to the building of a naval force that would one day overcome our territorial possessions in the Far East,' an attempt that he believed, when writing in 1806, that France might well renew.

Meanwhile, Wellesley was concentrating upon making the Indian subcontinent safe from an attack. What he particularly feared was the influence among the Marathas of a French mercenary, General Perron, who, in 1796, had succeeded Count de Boigne as commander of Sindhia's army. Perron had a reputation of being far more friendly towards the revolutionary regime in France than his predecessor. According to Compton, whose book closely reflected the outlook of Wellesley himself, Perron had sent an embassy to France in 1801 and had pressed his views on the attention of Bonaparte. 'An arrangement was actually settled,' he wrote, 'for the assignment to the Court of France of all the districts that Perron held, the transfer of which was to be confirmed by the Emperor Shah Allam' who was under Sindhia's control. 'Perron,' he continued, 'only waited a full complement of officers from France to cooperate in any attack which the First Consul might order'.[19]

In the summer of 1802, Bonaparte appointed General Decaen Captain-General with the task of receiving back, under the terms agreed by the treaty of Amiens, the French settlements in India. When his expedition sailed, Bonaparte was not anticipating a resumption of war in the immediate future. British suspicions, however, were aroused by the unduly large number of senior officers on board in relation to the relatively small number of troops being carried out, and the natural deduction drawn was that the French were planning to raise new sepoy regiments which would then come under the command of these officers. The secret instructions issued to Decaen by Bonaparte on 15 January 1803 showed that there was substance for these suspicions. In these instructions, Decaen was told that, to begin with, his mission was to be one of observation regarding the political and military situation in the Indian subcontinent. Every six months he was to report back to Paris, outlining the attitudes of the different peoples of India and reporting on the strength of the various English establishments, as well as on what hopes he himself might have of finding the support that would enable him to maintain himself in India in the event of war. To prepare for the latter eventuality, he was to fix upon some place that could serve as a *point d'appui*, since the French would 'would not be masters of the sea and could look for little succour,' and in such circumstances he was given full powers of discretion as to whether to fall back on the Ile de France and the Cape, or whether to remain in India. What Wellesley feared was that Decaen and Perron would join forces.

Decaen arrived off Pondichéry on 10 July at the very time when relations between the British and the Marathas were extremely tense, and Wellesley was demanding to know whether the Maratha leader Sindhia intended peace or war. Receiving an equivocal answer, the Governor-General issued what amounted to an ultimatum, and in early August, war between the British and the Marathas began. Meanwhile, Decaen received news from Europe that a resumption of war between France and Britain appeared to be imminent. Realising that the British were likely to learn of its outbreak before he did, and that his expedition would then be liable to immediate capture, he was forced to make an immediate and dramatic escape from Pondichéry and arrived at the Ile de France on 16 August, just a few weeks after the return of the Baudin expedition at the termination of its mission.

While Wellesley's precautionary moves to counter the French threat in India thus led to the Maratha wars, so

Bonaparte's own actions, which had been intended to lay the foundations for his planned empire in the West, were similarly leading to war in Europe. As we have seen, it was on the island of San Domingo that Bonaparte had envisaged establishing the naval and military bases for his proposed empire in the Caribbean and the Americas. Since the seventeenth century the western part of San Domingo, namely Haiti, had been a French possession, while the rest of the island was a Spanish colony, but by the treaty of San Ildefonso in 1795 it had been stipulated that once a general peace had been concluded, the Spanish portion of the island was to be handed over to France. In Haiti itself, however, a Negro leader, Toussaint L'Ouverture, had exploited the opportunity provided by the outbreak of the French Revolution to gain power and establish Haiti as a black-governed French protectorate. When he heard of Bonaparte's seizure of power, he decided to forestall any new move on the part of the First Consul by himself leading his own army into the Spanish colony and capturing the capital, the town of San Domingo, on 26 January 1801. Bonaparte responded by sending an expedition under his brother-in-law, General Leclerc, to restore the old regime. This French army, however, was decimated by yellow fever, Leclerc himself being one of the victims, and the only result of this expedition for the French was the loss of more than twenty generals and some 30,000 troops. As the French Emperor was to acknowledge during his final exile at St Helena, the despatch of this expedition was 'one of the greatest follies I was ever guilty of ... I committed a great oversight and fault in not having declared St Domingo free, acknowledged the black government, and before the Peace of Amiens sent some

French officers to assist them. Having once acknowledged them, I could not have sent an army out there during the peace. But after the peace,' he continued, 'I was continually beset with applications from proprietors of estates in the colony, merchants and others. Indeed, the nation had *la rage* to regain St Domingo, and I was obliged to comply with it. But had I, previous to the peace, acknowledged the blacks, I could under that plea have refused to make any attempt to retake it.'[20]

Before he knew of this disaster, Bonaparte had dispatched Colonel Sebastiani on a reconnoitring mission to the eastern Mediterranean which, in the light of subsequent events, was clearly intended to lay the foundations for a future challenge to Britain's domination of Europe's trade with India and the Far East. In his secret instructions, dated 5 September 1802, Sebastiani was told, among other things, to visit Alexandria and to 'take note of what is in the harbour, the ships, the forces which the British as well as the Turks have there, [and] the state of the fortifications,' after which he was to check up on 'all that has passed since our departure both at Alexandria and in the whole of Egypt'. Finally, he was to pass on to Acre where he was to make a similar study of the fortifications.[21] When he reached Cairo, Sebastiani emphasised that his task was merely a fact-finding mission as a first step towards the reestablishment of French commercial activity in the region. That was indeed the official line. Brigadier-General Stuart, who was in command of the British troops still in Egypt, did not believe this, however, and in his report to London expressed his belief that Sebastiani's real purpose was 'totally foreign' to what he had stated, which was nothing less than preparing the ground for the reestablishment of French 'preponderance and authority in Egypt'.[22] This suspicion was well founded, for when he got back to France and gave the First Consul a full report, Sebastiani concluded by stating his conviction that in view of the general unrest in Egypt, and the poor state of its defences, a force of 6,000 French troops would be sufficient to reconquer the country. Bonaparte thereupon had the report published in the official *Moniteur* on 30 January 1803, a decision which J. Holland Rose plausibly suggested may well have been intended to divert public attention from the disastrous French setback in San Domingo, news of which first reached Bonaparte in early January and was bound to become public knowledge before long. Whatever the reason, the publication of the report, which caused a sensation both in Paris and in England, proved to be a major blunder, for it helped to precipitate a war for which Bonaparte was not ready, a process that began with the decision of the British Government to retaliate by refusing to evacuate Malta, and ended with the British declaration of war on 16 May 1803.

Chapter Six

GREAT BRITAIN'S STRUGGLE WITH NAPOLEON: THE SECOND PHASE

War had come at this inopportune moment because Bonaparte had been misled, first by the reports of his agents regarding the English nation's overwhelming wish for peace, second, by the ineffectiveness of the English negotiators at Amiens, and third by the weakness of the Addington Ministry in being prepared to accept so disadvantageous a peace. How could a strong Britain be prepared to give up all her conquests save Ceylon and Trinidad, while at the same time be willing to agree that France should not only be left in possession of her widespread conquests in Europe, but should also be entitled to claim back the colonies that she had lost in the war? These considerations had tempted Bonaparte to overplay his hand and had led to those provocative actions which had finally resulted in the British declaration of war. For a while, Bonaparte had tried to prevent a resumption of war at the present time through diplomatic approaches, but had abandoned these attempts once it became clear that a renewal of peace could only be secured through sacrifices on his part which he was not prepared to make.

Although he could not now avert war, he knew that its resumption was highly unpopular with his own people. Yet for the moment, it was a war against Great Britain alone, and it was in his interest to bring this war to as early a conclusion as possible, before the British had time to form a new coalition against him. The only way in which he could hope to achieve a quick victory over that maritime Power, however, was by undertaking an early invasion of England, and he now concentrated all his energies to that end. His initial invasion plan envisaged transporting some 100,000 men across the English Channel in a flotilla of unarmed fishing-boats escorted by armed craft of small size and shallow draught in the course of a single night. Perhaps this strange concept was encouraged by knowledge that the British fleet at this time was very short of frigates. The French naval commanders were understandably far from impressed by the whole project. As the months rolled by, delay followed delay; at first, it was hoped that the flotilla would be ready by November 1803, then by January 1804, and again by September. But as early as June 1803, Bonaparte seems to have come to accept the fact that the French fleet would need to play its part in the whole operation. Feverish activity followed in the French dockyards and arsenals in an attempt to rebuild France's sea power which had been so seriously undermined by the French Revolution, for Bonaparte had to face the fact that the British had a two-to-one superiority over the French at sea.

When Admiral Ganteaume was asked for his views, he suggested the possibility of a fast-sailing French fleet being used to lead the enemy astray by a series of feints, after which, by suddenly appearing in the English Channel, this force might be able to secure temporary command of that seaway for a couple of days, just long enough for the flotilla to make its crossing. But he made no secret of his scepticism regarding the flotilla and warned that the whole project would be very hazardous. Nevertheless, Ganteaume's idea took root, and after Spain had declared war on Britain on 12 December 1804, in the wake of the interception and destruction of the Spanish treasure fleet off Cadiz by British frigates, Napoleon, as Bonaparte had recently become,[1] could now plan on the basis of using the combined fleets of France and Spain; by this time, indeed, Britain's naval predominance in European waters was described as being extremely slight. But progress with the flotilla was another matter, and though Napoleon had continued to make a heavy investment in it, this was proving a very difficult force to assemble and operate. For those sections of it which were being constructed along France's Atlantic coast were finding it exceedingly difficult to get past the British fleet blockading Brest, so that of the 231 craft which were constructed in that region, only 35 were able to reach the English Channel.[2] In addition, the French feint at the West Indies failed to achieve its object, since Nelson, in his pursuit of Villeneuve, did not remain long enough in those waters to enable the French to gain the temporary command of the English Channel that they were aiming at, so as to enable the flotilla invasion to get under way.

Furthermore, Britain was no longer alone. As soon as he had resumed office, Pitt started work on building a new coalition against France. Tsar Alexander was suspicious of Napoleon's policy in the Levant, and by April 1805, an Anglo-Russian agreement had been reached, then on

9 August 1805, Austria, already allied to Russia, joined the new coalition against France, while Prussia was sympathetic. With Austria's accession, Napoleon felt compelled to disband his invasion army at Boulogne and to redirect his troops to the Germanies. In October 1805, after the Battle of Ulm, he endeavoured to divert Austria from her English alliance, but his appeal having fallen on deaf ears, the defeat of the Austrians at Austerlitz (2 December 1805) ensued, and the death of the Younger Pitt soon followed.

Napoleon now set about redrawing the map of Europe. France had already attained her 'natural frontiers,' Spain under Godoy was a subservient ally, and France also dominated Italy, where Napoleon's brother Joseph was made King of Naples (February 1806). Meanwhile Napoleon's younger brother, Louis Bonaparte, became King of Holland. These two appointments were worrying for Britain since they meant, first, that the Mediterranean route to the East was increasingly coming under French domination, and second, that the Dutch East Indies, so close to the Eastern Passage to China, and to the western coasts of the Australian continent, were being brought under direct French control. Similarly, the creation of the Confederation of the Rhine (12 July 1806), from which both Austria and Prussia were excluded, now brought a large part of Germany under French domination. Furthermore Prussia's ill-considered ultimatum to France only led to the annihilation of her armies at the battles of Jena and Auerstadt on 14 September 1806. Having thus demolished the Kingdom of Prussia, Napoleon now pressed forward to deal with Russia which, like Britain, had refused to come to terms with him. The Battle of Eylau (7/8 February 1807) was a sanguinary but inconclusive encounter, but at the Battle of Friedland (14 June 1807) the French were victorious and the Tsar was ready to make peace.

In the mean time, Nelson's victory at the Battle of Trafalgar had ensured that a French invasion of the British Isles was an impossibility for the foreseeable future, and Napoleon was forced to concentrate his full attention upon the longer-term strategy of defeating Britain by attempting to close the entire European coastline to her trade by his 'Continental System, a policy that was inaugurated by the Berlin decrees of 21 November 1806. The two stretches of coastline that he now sought to bring under his control to make this possible were those of the Baltic and Portugal, and for the former it was necessary to have Russian cooperation. Hence, when the war with Russia was brought to an end by the treaty of Tilsit, Napoleon set about the task of making Tsar Alexander an ally.

Up to this point Denmark, holding the keys to the Baltic and thus coming under pressure from both sides, had been trying her utmost to maintain her neutrality, whereas Sweden, under Gustavus IV, had been opposed to Revolutionary and Napoleonic France from the start, and had played a leading part in the formation of the Third Coalition. But now secret articles agreed at Tilsit declared that it Britain refused the Tsar's mediation, Russia would declare war upon her, whereupon Sweden, Denmark and Portugal were to be summoned to follow the same course.

When the British Government received intimation of these developments from its own secret agent at Tilsit, one immediate reaction was to check on what the effect might have on the prevailing naval balance in Europe, should Denmark, Sweden and Portugal all succumb to this pressure and be forced to join in with France and Russia. In those circumstances, it was calculated that if Denmark's reported twenty ships of the line, Sweden's eleven, and Portugal's nine were added to France's fifty-nine, then the naval forces at Napoleon's disposal would be almost equal in numbers to Britain's own. In view of this critical situation, and because Denmark's fleet, if hostile, would be in a position to close access to the Baltic to British ships, Canning, Britain's Foreign Secretary, decided that an immediate decisive, even ruthless, response was called for. By 19 July 1807, he had concluded that nothing less than the seizure of the Danish fleet would suffice, and on 26 July Admiral Gambier set sail from Yarmouth with seventeen (later increased to twenty-five) ships of the line and some 25,000 troops under Cathcart, bound for Copenhagen. This fleet arrived off Elsinore on 3 August, and after the Danes had rejected a demand to surrender their ships, or 'deposit them in pledge,' Cathcart's troops were disembarked to encircle Copenhagen, and a prolonged bombardment of the capital followed with the inevitable tragic consequences, including the death of some two thousand civilians and the destruction of the cathedral. On 7 September, the Danish Government finally agreed to surrender the fleet, including eighteen ships of the line and ten frigates.[3] By this drastic action, the British Government had ensured that the Royal Navy continued to have numerical superiority in Europe, but at the cost of throwing Denmark into an alliance with France.

Canning's action had also undermined the position at Gustavus IV of Sweden, and when he was forced to yield up both Stralsund and the island of Rügen to the French, this setback contributed to his dethronement on 13 March 1809, whereupon his uncle succeeded him as King with the title of Charles XIII. And since the latter was without an heir, the Swedes chose Marshal Bernadotte to be the Prince Royal and heir-apparent, an appointment that Napoleon agreed to, though without much enthusiasm, since he had never really trusted this Gascon. This appointment was made on 21 August 1810, and it looked as though Sweden was about to return to its traditional French alliance.

Meanwhile, Napoleon wanted to see the eastern shores of the Baltic come under Russian rather than Swedish control, since only his ally, Tsar Alexander, could be relied upon to enforce the Continental System there. Finland had once been a Russian Grand Duchy, but had been captured by the Swedes in the thirteenth century, and ever since, with two brief interludes in the eighteenth century when the Russians had recaptured it, Finland had remained under Swedish control. Now, however, Alexander had ambitions to recapture it once more, and Napoleon gave him every encouragement to do so, stating in a letter to Caulaincourt that he would be happy to see the Tsar conquer Sweden, and even capture Stockholm itself. When King Gustavus of Sweden, in the dying days of his reign, refused to abandon Sweden's alliance with Great Britain, as the treaty of Tilsit had demanded, the tsar had the excuse that he wanted to order the invasion of Finland, though its conquest proved a far more difficult undertaking than he had anticipated.

Having thus markedly tightened his hold over the Baltic, the major source of Britain's naval supplies, Napoleon now turned on Portugal and on 19 July 1807, he sent a message to Talleyrand directing him to inform the Portuguese that unless they closed all their ports to the import of British goods by 1 September 1807, 'I declare war on Portugal.' At the same time, he also ordered the massing of 20,000 French troops at Bayonne, ready to move against the Portuguese at short notice. Any French invasion of Portugal, however, would require the passage of their troops through Spanish territory. He sought to achieve this by proposing, in the secret Convention of Fontainebleau, a future partition of Portugal, in which Godoy was to be bribed by being promised the Algarve in the south, while the larger portion in the north would go to France. By a separate Military Convention, whose significance was not appreciated by the Spaniards until too late, in addition to the significant Spanish force already serving under Bernadotte in distant Holstein, Spain was also committed to furnishing another large force to support Junot in Portugal. While this appreciable number of Spanish troops were thus now serving, or about to serve, outside Spain, French troops continued to pour into Spain on the pretext of helping to defend the country against supposed British designs to invade the land. By early 1808, it has been estimated that Napoleon had some 40,000 French troops in the north of Spain, a further 12,000 in Catalonia, in addition to Junot's force in Portugal, so that, without firing a shot, his men had been able to gain access to, and take control of, the Spanish strongholds of Pamplona, Monjuik, Barcelona, St Sebastian and Figueras.[4]

Junot's invasion of Portugal began with the crossing of the Bidessoa on 19 October 1807, and both on the 17th and again on the 31st of October Napoleon hammered home the need for haste, emphasising how important it was for Junot to reach Lisbon by 1 December. 'I wish my troops to reach Lisbon at the earliest time possible,' he told

Junot, 'in order to sequestrate all the English merchandise. I wish them to arrive there, if possible, as friends, in order to seize the Portuguese fleet.' Had this happened, not only would Napoleon have substantially added to his own naval strength, but he would have had a real chance of gaining control of Portuguese Brazil, as well as of Portuguese Goa in India In fact, Junot did slightly better than he had been told, and with his weary vanguard actually reached the vicinity of Lisbon on 30 November, yet for the second time in his career Napoleon was thwarted at a vital moment by Sir Sidney Smith, for this Admiral, with the British Ambassador, Lord Strangford, on board his flagship, had persuaded a very reluctant Portuguese Prince Regent, together with his senior ministers carrying the State archives with them, to leave Portugal for Portuguese Brazil, escorted by the Portuguese navy.

It was only when they tried, in vain, to set a limit to the number of French troops pouring in over the Pyrenees, and begged, futilely, for the partition of Portugal, as agreed upon at Fontainebleau, to be put into effect, that Charles IV and Godoy came to realise that they had been duped, and that the real purpose at Fontainebleau had been to open the gates for French troops to pour into both Portugal and Spain until the whole of the Iberian Peninsula was under French control. When this grim truth struck home, the Spanish royal family and Godoy together decided to escape to Latin America, but such a move had been foreseen by Napoleon, who was determined to prevent a repetition of the recent events in Portugal, and on 21 February 1808, he sent a secret order for a French squadron to be anchored off Cadiz to prevent any such flight overseas.[5]

Napoleon was now ready for the final act in this drama, namely, his bid to gain personal control of the Spanish monarchy, and for this the Spanish royal family itself provided the means for its own destruction. After a riot had broken out, during which Godoy was mobbed and his life put in danger, a furious row had broken out between King Charles IV and Ferdinand, his heir, and the King had unwisely turned to Napoleon for advice. The latter, who in 1805 had observed that '*un Bourbon sur le trône d'Espagne, c'est un voisin trop dangereux*,' now saw his opportunity to get rid of the family altogether. After managing to entice the king and queen, Prince Ferdinand and Godoy to Bayonne, he then scared the prince into submission before compelling Charles IV to abdicate and hand over the crown of Spain and the Indies to himself. Napoleon then withdrew his brother Joseph from Naples, where he had achieved some success during his brief reign, and installed him as King of Spain and the Indies on 12 July 1808. By this move Napoleon was seeking to lay the foundations for gaining mastery of the Mediterranean on the one hand, a necessary precondition for an attack upon British influence in the Orient, and of the Spanish Empire in Latin America on the other, thus effectively extending the blockade of British commerce to that continent as well.

Even before these moves in Spain, the Emperor had sought to begin the process of dominating the Mediterranean. On 6 June 1806, he had pressed upon his brother Joseph, who had been appointed King of the Two Sicilies in 1805, that he should lose no time in gaining control of the island of Sicily, but to no avail since a British force had successfully thwarted this first attempt. In the early months of 1808 the Emperor had again raised the matter with Joseph, now styled King of Naples, urging that he should make every effort to gain control of that island whose capture, he said, 'would change the face of the Mediterranean'. He was equally emphatic upon the need to retain control of the island of Corfu.

The future oriental campaign for which this mastery of the Mediterranean was the necessary prerequisite had been dominating his thinking even before he had succeeded in bringing the tsar to the negotiating table at Tilsit. Thus, when he had met the Turkish and Persian ambassadors at Finkenstein in April 1807, in an effort to arrange for an attack on Russia from the south, he had taken the opportunity to conclude a treaty with the Shah of Persia, signed on 4 May 1807. Under the terms of this agreement, in return for a French undertaking to help the Persians in forcing the Russians to leave Georgia, the Shah would allow a French army to pass through Persian territory on its way to invade India, and would provide it with military support and help with its sustenance. To make all this possible, a team of French officers under General Gardane was to be sent to Teheran to instruct the Persians in the skills of modern warfare, and at the same time the general and his officers were instructed to examine the routes from both Egypt and Syria to Delhi as well as the harbours in the Persian Gulf. Gardane was also told to make contact with the Mahratta princes in India. And a year later, after the initiation of the Continental System, and when he believed that he had established French control in Spain, Napoleon was to inform Decrès, in a letter dated 17 May 1808, that he planned to launch the invasion of India by the close of that year.[6]

In his subsequent report Gardane expressed the view that larger forces would be needed for a successful invasion – he specified some 40,000–50,000 French troops and some 30,000–40,000 Persians – and he recommended that if it was decided to march overland from Syria to the Ganges, Cyprus would be needed as a base, and the army would need to advance on India by way of Teheran, Herat, Kabul and Peshawar.[7] The rapid conclusion of the Franco-Russian war, however, followed by the alliance between those two countries concluded at Tilsit, before the French had honoured their pledge to recover Georgia, had greatly displeased the Shah, and the position of Gardane as French ambassador at Teheran had been seriously undermined. As a result, whatever the value of the reconnaissance which he and his officers had been able to undertake, any future French invasion of India by land was now unlikely to enjoy Persian cooperation.

Meanwhile, at the same time as he had been taking measures aimed at securing for France mastery of the Mediterranean, Napoleon had also been seeking to reach an agreement with Austria and Russia over a possible partition of the decaying Ottoman Empire.

On 2 February, Napoleon corresponded with both Caulaincourt, his ambassador at St Petersburg, and with the Tsar. To the former, writing at a time when Russian troops were about to invade Finland, he stated that he would be happy to see Alexander conquer Sweden, thus making St Petersburg the geographical centre of his empire and above all he was to press for an Eastern expedition, in which between 20,000 and 25,000 Russians, some 8,000 to 10,000 Austrians, and between 35,000 and 40,000 French troops would march through Asia to India.

In view of the very poor relations subsisting between Russia and Turkey, any such joint invasion of India presupposed a partition of the Ottoman Empire, and the Tsar responded to Napoleon's approach by suggesting the need for some preliminary agreement on the subject. This was agreed to, and Caulaincourt began discussions with Romanzoff, the Russian chancellor, and with the Tsar. But in the talks that followed it soon became apparent that while much common ground existed, the fate of Constantinople posed a crucial barrier to any final understanding unless one side or the other was prepared to give some ground, and of this, there was no sign whatever. While Romanzoff was willing to concede to Napoleon Albania and much of Greece,[8] which would have consolidated his control of the Adriatic, as well as of the Aegean Archipelago, Egypt, the chief seaports of Asia Minor and perhaps a part of Syria, and Caulaincourt agreed to the Russians having Moldavia, Wallachia, part of Bulgaria and a large area around Trebizond, the discussions became tense over the question of Constantinople.

Caulaincourt tried to persuade the Russians at least to accept the earlier proposal that it should become an independent free city, which had previously seemed to hold out some hope of proving an acceptable compromise. But the Tsar now stated that the proposed joint invasion of India would benefit France much more than Russia, and that the latter must therefore take very particular care of her own interests in this case. By mid-March 1808, both Caulaincourt and Napoleon were convinced that the Tsar would only agree to take part in a joint expedition to India if the French agreed to evacuate Prussia and allot both Constantinople and the Dardanelles to Russia, for as Romanzoff said, Russia must hold both the keys to the Black Sea, not just the one.

Napoleon stated that he and Alexander had had many discussions regarding Turkey. 'At first I was pleased with his proposals,' he recalled, 'because I thought it would drive the Turks out of Europe. But when I reflected upon what a tremendous weight of power it would give to Russia. I refused to consent to it, especially as Alexander wanted to get Constantinople'. And as he remarked on another occasion, 'once mistress of Constantinople, Russia gets all the commerce of the Mediterranean, becomes a great naval power, and God knows what may happen ... Above all the other Powers, Russia is the most to be feared'.[9]

For Napoleon, the final objective in view in all this diplomatic manoeuvring regarding the Ottoman Empire and Persia remained an attack upon British influence in India and the Far East. Six months before Joseph Bonaparte's accession to the Spanish throne, Napoleon had taken advantage of the enthronement of Louis Bonaparte as King of Holland to have Daendels appointed the new Governor of the Dutch East Indies. In his native Dutch Netherlands Daendels had become an ardent member of the Patriot party, and after Sir James Harris's diplomatic victory of 1787 he had moved to France where, after the outbreak of the Revolution, he had developed into a zealous and effective military leader. He had returned to his homeland with the French invading revolutionary army in 1795, and had thereafter proved a mainstay of French influence in the Netherlands, eventually having the rank of marshal conferred upon him by Napoleon. During the course of the year 1807, as the French Emperor began to plan for his intended Oriental drive, Daendels had received his new appointment, his brief being to reform the administration of these islands and to improve their defensibility as a matter of urgency. He reached Batavia to carry out this task on 1 January 1808.

Hitherto the Dutch authorities in Java had sought to avoid giving aid to the French, in order to prevent giving the English East India Company any reason for planning an attack upon the Dutch East Indies. They had therefore been dismayed to learn that Napoleon had now converted the Dutch Republic into a monarchy, with his brother Louis Bonaparte being appointed the new King of Holland on 5 June 1806. The arrival of Daendels at Batavia confirmed their worst fears. Now, under his energetic leadership, the size of the army in Java was increased and its training improved. The defence works of Batavia itself were augmented by the construction of two new forts, while a great main road, some 2,000 kilometres in length, was constructed, stretching from Anjer in the west of Java to Panarakam near that island's eastern extremity. This great road was built to improve the army's ability to move rapidly across Java from one end to the other, and this was achieved, the time taken to complete such a journey being reduced from a matter of some forty days to one of six-and-a-half days.

This was only accomplished, however, by resorting to forced labour, and the whole undertaking involved a tremendous loss of life. His simultaneous energetic reform of the administration does not concern us here; it is sufficient to say that, like so many revolutionaries in a hurry, he felt it necessary to introduce a rapid centralisation of the administration, and was prepared to ride roughshod over everything that stood in his way. But the price he had to pay for this was the alienation of the native princes.[10]

Daendels had arrived at Batavia at the start of the very year in which, within a twelvemonth, Napoleon was planning to initiate an invasion of India itself. He was trying to interest Austria in taking a share in such a project, and was also seeking to persuade Tsar Alexander that he and Alexander should revive Tsar Paul's concept of a joint Franco-Russian invasion of India.[11] Then on 17 May 1808, he told Decrès to prepare for an expedition against India at the end of the year. 'England is in great penury there,' he informed his Minister of Marine, 'and the arrival of an expedition [from France] would ruin that colony from top to bottom'.[12]

Napoleon had, in fact, been giving a good deal of attention as to how India could best be attacked, and on 27 January 1808, just six days before writing the above letter to the Tsar, he had had an interview with René Decaen, younger brother of the Governor, who had recently arrived from the Ile de France.

During this interview, René had raised with the Emperor the question of an invasion of India, arguing that an army coming by sea would arrive sooner than one marching overland, and that the English would be unable to concentrate their forces against such an attack. And though Napoleon raised the problem of feeding such an army en route, René thought that he had answered all the points raised by the Emperor satisfactorily and left the meeting under the impression that an invasion by sea had been decided upon in principle.[13] It was however, the problem of provisioning such an army on the voyage out that had defeated the project. 'I had made several calculations about the possibility of sending so large a body of men [by sea] to India,' the Emperor was later to tell Dr O'Meara at St Helena, 'but always found that they would have been short of water for a month'. However, in the course of a conversation with Admiral Plampin at St Helena, he had learned that a 74-gun ship could carry approximately 80 tons more water by means of tanks. 'Had I known this in 1806 or 1808,' he lamented 'I would certainly have sent an army of 30,000 men to invade India [by sea].' In explaining the plan that he had had in view, he stated that he had had a fleet of line-of-battle ships ready at Brest, varying in number from forty to well over fifty at different times. 'In forty of these,' he said, '... I intended to have dispersed ... eight hundred [soldiers] in each ship, and only four hundred sailors.' Ten of these ships had been old and of little value, and 'they were also to take on board six or eight hundred dismounted cavalry and ... artillery'. After calling at the Ile de France to take on fresh supplies, the ships 'were to have proceeded to India, and to have disembarked in the nearest possible place, so as to have allowed the Mahrattas, with whom I had an understanding, to join them. They [the Mahrattas] were to form the cavalry of the army. A few of the French were also to have been mounted ... After the landing, they were to have burnt the ten old ships ... They would then proceed in different directions, and do all possible mischief in your settlements ... [But] all this plan was frustrated by the calculations I had made'.[14]

While Napoleon was thus considering the best ways in which to attack the British in India and the Far East, the Baudin expedition had also alerted him to the dangers and opportunities now lying before the Spaniards and the French in the Pacific Ocean. The *Naturaliste* and the *Géographe* had arrived back in France on 7 June 1803 and 24 March 1804, respectively, and before leaving the Ile de France on the last leg of the journey, Péron, on 11 December 1803, had submitted a report on the expedition to the Governor, telling him what some of its members had learned while at Port Jackson. He had recounted how the British, already masters of the east coast of Australia, had probably already begun to colonise Tasmania, and were intent upon expanding to and occupying 'the immense extent of the west and south-west coasts, which contained very fine harbours'. In Bass Strait, he noted how the seal fisheries were providing Britain with the very thing that the Macartney mission to China in 1792–93 had failed to find, namely a market in China for British goods which would thereby save her from having to export 'a mass of specie'. And New Zealand was especially advantageous to her, owing to its whaling industry; 'never was a fishery so lucrative and so easy,' he remarked.

But that was only a beginning, he warned. By astute policy, the British had never defined an exact eastern boundary to their claims in the Pacific Ocean, and he saw them as being in the process of founding an empire which would 'extend over the continent of New Holland, Van Diemen's Land, New Zealand and the numerous archipelagoes of the Pacific Ocean,' whereby Britain would be able to exclude her European rivals from entry to the Pacific from the west. In the meantime, aided by the westerly winds which prevailed in the higher latitudes, her privateers and fleets in wartime would be able to devastate the coasts of South America, while in times of peace Spanish authority in those regions would be further undermined by her ability to carry on an active contraband trade which, in itself, would prepare redoubtable enemies for Spain. Aware of the weakness of Spanish authority in her settlements on the Pacific coast of South America, the British were already providing Chilean insurgents with arms and ammunition, and Péron saw the archipelagoes, scattered as they were 'like so many stepping-stones between New Holland and the west coast of America,' as providing Britain with the means whereby she hoped in due course 'to be able to stretch her dominion as far as Peru'.

Péron therefore wanted to see this dangerous development of British power nipped in the bud. He pointed out that the defence of Port Jackson had never needed to be formidable in the past; the garrison there at the time of their stay had only numbered some 800 men. Furthermore, while the harbour at Port Jackson was magnificent, it did have one serious weakness from a strategic point of view; the entrance to its harbour was so narrow that 'two frigates could by themselves blockade the most numerous fleet within'. Furthermore, if the French attacked the settlement, they would find many strong supporters from within its ranks, including the transported convicts and the Irish 'whom the desire of freeing their country from the British yoke caused to arm in concert with us against the English Government'. He and Freycinet had made a particular study of the colony's vulnerable points during their stay in 1802, and in his own view France's interest demanded that the settlement 'should be destroyed as soon as possible: today we could destroy it easily; we shall not be able to do so in twenty-five years' time'.[15]

Napoleon who, as First Consul, had so eagerly backed and authorised the Baudin expedition when it was first proposed, must surely have read Péron's report with great interest and attention, not to say concern. In seeing what Péron had to say about British expansionist ambitions in the Pacific and the consequent threats to the Spanish settlements on the Pacific coast of Latin America, the French Emperor had much to meditate upon. He knew that these conclusions were based upon conversations with the leading personalities in the colony and upon months of personal observation on the spot, and must therefore be taken seriously. Some of Péron's conclusions were, of course, much exaggerated, but they were not without some substance, and they had ominous implications for the Emperor's wartime policy. His whole strategy was dependent upon his blockade of the British Isles. He was intent upon closing the European continent to British trade, knowing that at the same time the Spanish Empire was theoretically closed to British ships and goods as well. He was obviously familiar with the fact that this closure of the Spanish Empire to British trade was only theoretical, and that it was evaded in practice to a significant extent. That, however, was something that he clearly planned to put right by increasing French control over the execution of Spanish policy. He would therefore have been disturbed to read in Péron's report, how Spanish authority along the Pacific coast of Latin America was coming under increasing pressure from the British, and appeared to be in real danger of being overthrown altogether. If that were allowed to happen, it would prove a major blow to the viability of the whole Continental System. Napoleon would also have been concerned to read about the supposed British plans to take control of the main archipelagoes in the Pacific Ocean. If they were successful in achieving that end, would the Philippine

Islands themselves, ruled, as they were, by way of Mexico, fall a prey to the British?

In May 1808, Napoleon formulated what he termed his 'immense project', and on 19 May he told Murat that money must be found for naval preparations at the Spanish ports: 'I must have ships,' he told him, 'for I intend striking a heavy blow towards the end of the season'.[16] At the same time intense activity was reported in all the French ports and in those of her vassal states. The French navy, which had been decimated by the excesses of the French Revolution, was well on the way to recovery. It now possessed forty-two battleships and in a year's time this would have increased to seventy-seven, in addition to which his allies possessed a further fifty-four, which needed to be added to that total. The plan was to have large expeditions made ready at the ports of Brest, Lorient, Rochefort, Ferrol, Nantes and Tyrol, with large forces of troops being encamped close to the naval squadrons in these various ports, so that powerful expeditions would be ready to sail from these harbours at short notice, whenever the blockading English fleets slackened their hold. In this way it was hoped that the English would eventfully become exhausted and disillusioned by having to respond to these incessant alarms. But since Lorient, as its name implies, was the port specialising in France's trade with the East, its inclusion in the above list of ports suggests that Napoleon was also hoping that an opportunity might come to organise a strike at Port Jackson, in the manner suggested by Péron. Meanwhile, Péron himself, who had given an account of the Baudin expedition in a lecture at the Institut, had been appointed the official historian of that undertaking, with his friend and former colleague on the voyage, Louis de Freycinet, being made responsible for the navigational details of the expedition. Péron's first volume, describing the natural history and scientific discoveries appeared in 1807, the accompanying General Chart in 1808, then Freycinet's charts in 1811, while the second volume written by Freycinet, with its account of the nautical and geographical aspects of the expedition, did not appear until 1815, after the war had ended.

Ever since the time of its return, the Baudin expedition has been the subject of controversy, but most of the confusion has been due to a failure to distinguish between its political and scientific objectives, or even to admit that the former existed at all. From the moment of the expedition's return, efforts were being made to persuade the Government that the objects of the expedition had not been achieved, and this caused Péron to pay a hurried visit to the Ministry of Marine to give a detailed account of the great scientific work that had been accomplished during the voyage. In view of the outstandingly rich collections that had been brought back, the very fact that Péron felt a need to draw attention to what had been achieved in the way of scientific discovery only confirms his own statement that, from the viewpoint of those who had helped to launch the undertaking in the first place, 'all our natural history researches ... were merely a pretext for its enterprize.'

J. Holland Rose saw in the General Chart, with its plethora of French names and its *Terre Napoléon* evidence of a French intention to invade the continental island. This argument has not convinced many as it stands. When the timing of the General Chart's publication is taken into consideration, however, coinciding as it did with the birth of Napoleon's 'immense project' of a variety of maritime expeditions being organised in French and Spanish ports, a toned-down version of Rose's thesis becomes plausible. The whole chart, showing seven Dutch regions containing a large number of French discoveries and names, plus the land denominated *Terre Napoléon* separating the original Dutch territories from the English colony of *Nouvelle-Galles du Sud* on the eastern seaboard and its immediate hinterland, certainly suggested a French claim to the whole of the continent to the west of New South Wales. With Louis Bonaparte on the Dutch throne, Napoleon was in a position to regard the Dutch colonial empire as now constituting an extension of the French Empire, just as he believed that the same fate was soon to overtake the Spanish Empire, now that Joseph Bonaparte was enthroned as King of Spain and the Indies. Those who have regarded *Terre Napoléon* as representing a bogus French claim to a prior French exploration of that whole coast have really missed the point. In the first place, Flinders' own charts were not yet available, not being published until 1814. Second, such critics have been viewing the chart solely as part of the record of the scientific and geographical research carried out by the expedition, whereas the timing of its publication strongly suggests that it was primarily related to the expedition's political role. The appearance of the map at the very moment when all those expeditions were about to be assembled at French and Spanish ports can therefore be seen as a propaganda exercise designed to create a fear in British minds that France was indeed planning an invasion of Australia, and therefore to compel them to undertake an ever more widespread dispersal of their fleets. It is true, of course, that Péron had made it clear that he believed Port Jackson to be vulnerable to attack, and that France could capture it with ease at the present time, though she would not be able to do so later; and Napoleon may well have thought that such an attack might soon become possible, whether from the Ile de France, or from the Dutch East Indies, or from the Philippines. But in May 1808, the map of *Terre Napoléon* was probably, in the first instance, a propagandist exercise in deception.

At the same time, the *Quarterly Review* in 1810 was probably correct in surmising that one objective of the expedition was to establish some port in the vicinity of the British settlements which could play a similar role in Australia to that which Pondichéry had formerly played in India.[18] Péron's observations certainly lent themselves to this interpretation. When the French investigated Flinders' recent discovery of Port Lincoln, which they named Port Champagny, and which at 135° 52'E was on the very border that the British had originally proclaimed as marking the western frontier of their territory, Péron referred to its harbour as 'one of the finest and most secure in New Holland,' a 'magnificent port competent to receive the most numerous fleet,' and as the place 'best adapted for the establishment of a European colony.[19] Furthermore, on the west coast Péron drew particular attention to 'the extraordinary abundance of whales' in Sharks Bay, which 'cannot fail one day to render it of great importance to [a] fishery here,' while Dampier Bay was not only able to furnish wood, but provided a good stock of turtle and a 'vast abundance of whales,' which would 'render safe any extent of speculation in a [whale] fishery'.[20] The British had every reason to fear that any French settlement on this coast would endanger their use of the Eastern Passage in time of war.

Napoleon was, however, dangerously deluded as to the overall political situation that now prevailed, and was quite unconscious of the fact that his earlier good fortune was about to desert him, for on 31 May he still felt able to assure Caulaincourt that affairs in Spain were 'entirely finished,' and that the Spaniards were quiet and even devoted to him.[21] Yet nothing could have been further from the truth, with powerful opposition now beginning to manifest itself simultaneously both in the Iberian Peninsula and in the Orient.

In Spain itself, as Napoleon's faithful secretary was later to record, 'the news of the double abdication of Charles IV and of Ferdinand, and King Joseph's Proclamation brought about an explosion of ... feelings of hatred. In the space of a week, towards the end of May, the East, North, and West of Spain were on fire. The Spaniards had risen as one man. The arsenals had been ransacked, and the people had armed. Juntas had been formed, and a mass levy was being organized on every side'.[22] This was a mass movement from below, where, as Méneval noted, 'the mob took the initiative everywhere,' and it repeated many of the characteristics of the Vendée rising of 1793 during the French Revolution, both in 'the rhetorical dehumanization of the enemy and the extreme ferocity with which the war was waged'.[23] Napoleon, as a son of the Enlightenment, was as incapable of empathising with the religious beliefs and fervour of the peasantry as he was of understanding the nationalistic outrage of the Spaniards. Although, as a Corsican, he had in his youth been, for a time, an ardent follower of Paoli, and continued to hold that leader in respect in later years, that phase of his life had passed, and he had later become a convinced believer in the ideals of the French Revolution. And, thereafter, he had remained insensitive to the cause of nationalism throughout the rest of Europe.

During the winter of 1807–08 he had initially planned for what amounted to a large-scale policing operation in Spain, but he was now forced by this sudden upsurge of violent opposition to change tactics, and to attempt to suppress it by dispatching 'a few flying columns to scour the insurgent districts and to take possession of the chief strategical points'. It was in attempting to carry out this policy that one corps, commanded by Dupont, set out from the capital on 24 May 1808 with the intention of capturing Seville and then going on to the port of Cadiz, where the remnant of Villeneuve's fleet, which had escaped the disaster of Trafalgar, had taken refuge. Dupont, however, had been unable to take Seville and had begun to fall back, whereupon the officers in command of Villeneuve's remnant, losing all hope of being rescued, felt compelled to surrender to the Spaniards. Worse was to follow, for Dupont, whose soldiers were exhausted, demoralised and surrounded, was also forced to capitulate at Baylen on 23 June. Napoleon was thunderstruck by this news, which created a sensation throughout Europe, and Méneval wrote how 'this disastrous day of Bailen [*sic*], during which 20,000 French soldiers had marched past and laid down their arms before enemies who had always fled before them in the open field, was a reverse without example in the military history of the new France, [and] struck a most severe blow against our prestige in Spain'. Napoleon had already warned Decrès that his maritime plans for the year might have to be delayed.

This was not the end of French setbacks in the Iberian Peninsula at this time, for a British army under the command of Sir Arthur Wellesley, in response to Portuguese calls for help, had landed on the coast near Lisbon, and when Junot attacked this force on 21 August, together with its supporting Portuguese insurgents, he was defeated at Vimiero, and nine days later, fearing a general uprising in Lisbon, signed the Convention of Cintra with the British, whereby his 25,000 French soldiers were shipped out of the Peninsula and back to France.

It is not intended to follow the course of the Peninsular War. It is enough to emphasise that even at this early stage the upsurge of nationalistic fervour in Spain and Portugal, backed by the arrival of General Wellesley, was making it increasingly difficult for Napoleon to achieve his worldwide imperial ambitions. Yet he was always the optimist, describing the word 'impossible' as one that only appeared in the dictionary of fools, and after Austria had yet again entered the war, Vienna was in French hands by 13 May 1809, and although the Austrians fought with great bravery and resolution, and were even able to defeat Napoleon at the battle of Aspern and Essling on 21–22 May, the first time that the hitherto invincible Emperor had failed to achieve victory, the ensuing Battle of Wagram, though described as 'one of the most brilliant feats of arms in Austrian history,' was nevertheless a costly defeat, and the Austrians were compelled to agree to the terms of the treaty of Schönbrunn on 14 October 1809 which, among other things, tightened French control over the Adriatic and the eastern Mediterranean.

As the year 1810 dawned, Napoleon still had reason to feel that he was at the zenith of his power. In March he married the Archduchess Marie-Louise of Austria, and it was now that he felt ready to make a supreme effort to force Great Britain to make peace by bringing to a climax all three of his long-standing forms of attack upon her – economic blockade, expeditions against her eastern possessions, and invasion of Britain itself. He believed that if he could only force the British out of the war, opposition in the Iberian Peninsula would thereupon die away. As regards the economic blockade of the British Isles, the extent of smuggling along the Dutch coast was a cause of concern to the Emperor, and the *Annual Register* recorded how Napoleon had intimated as early as the beginning of December 1809 that he intended that Holland should become a part of the French Empire to which, he asserted, 'It naturally belonged, as it was nothing ... but an alluvium of the Rhine, Meuse, and the Scheldt, the great arteries of the Empire.' To this end, the *Register* reported, French troops had already 'begun to glide imperceptibly into Holland, till at last it was occupied by a French army of 40,000 men,' thus constituting 'a virtual or real annexation of that country to the French Empire,' even though, at first, Napoleon appeared 'to have been willing that it should possess a nominal independence, and his brother wear a nominal crown'. To this end a treaty was concluded on 1 April 1810, 'whereby Holland, on the left bank of the Waal, was to be annexed to France. An army of 18,000 men, partly French, partly Dutch, was to be distributed at all the mouths of the rivers, along with officers of the French customs, for the prohibition of all trade between Holland and England'. And though this had not been agreed to in the treaty, detachments of French soldiers, accompanied by French custom-house officers, also spread themselves over various parts of the interior. But what finally persuaded King Louis to abdicate and flee the country, on 1 July 1810, was the official information that had reached him ten days earlier that Napoleon was now insisting upon the French occupying Amsterdam and setting up their headquarters in that city.[24]

This incorporation of Holland in the French Empire was followed by Napoleon's annexation of a large part of the Kingdom of Westphalia, of the Grand Duchy of Berg, of East Friesland, and of the Hanseatic cities, so that he now controlled the entire Channel and North Sea coast and was in a position to apply his blockade of Britain with the utmost rigour. In fact, since the entire European coastline from the Adriatic to the Baltic was now under Napoleon's control, this left British traders, apart from their extensive smuggling operations, with virtually no opening into the continent of Europe save through Russia. Furthermore, not only was the English harvest of 1810 an almost complete failure, but in November of that year the number of bankruptcies was almost three times the normal figure. The blockade seemed to be coming dangerously close to achieving its objective and, all in all, Méneval was not far from the truth when he stated that at the end of 1811, 'the cries of distress and weariness heard in London, Liverpool, Bristol, and elsewhere, already announced the early and complete success of the Continental System'.[25]

In pursuit of his second line of attack, the long-planned but repeatedly postponed invasion of the British Isles, Napoleon was once again pushing ahead with vast works at Antwerp and Cherbourg, and at the same time, he was concentrating upon building ships and gunboats at every suitable port from the Texel to Naples and Trieste. By these means, he hoped to build up a fleet of 104 ships-of-the-line which could convoy transports from the Mediterranean, Cherbourtg, Boulogne and the Scheldt, thus threatening England with an invasion army of some 200,000 fighting men.[26]

The pursuit of his Oriental plans was more difficult, for the British had not been idle in defending their interests. A new Governor-General of India, Lord Minto, had arrived upon the scene, and though he had originally been anti-expansionist in his thinking, he had soon found himself compelled to bring Governor-General Wellesley's policy to fruition in a number of areas as he sought to counter the plans of the French Emperor. Thus when reports were received at Calcutta that Napoleon and Tsar Alexander had supposedly agreed at Tilsit upon a policy of concentrating their forces in Persia for an advance upon India, Minto had responded by sending missions to Teheran, Kabul and Lahore in an effort to win the cooperation of the leaders in those lands in opposing any Franco-Russian advance through their territories.

There was now a pause in the Eastern crisis as the Spanish uprising and the landing of the British expeditionary force in Portugal, followed by the war with Austria, forced Napoleon to postpone his plans for an invasion of India and for a series of maritime expeditions against Britain's overseas trade and possessions. This pause enabled the Court of Directors of the English East India Company to take a new initiative to undermine the French position in Persia. The Shah bitterly resented Napoleon's failure to honour his promise under the Finkenstein treaty to drive the Russians out of Georgia, and the Company now appointed its own 'Envoy Extraordinary and Minister Plenipotentiary' to exploit the new opportunity it saw opening. The man chosen for this role was the Company's former Resident at Baghdad, Sir Harford

Jones, who was known for his great proficiency in Oriental languages. This new envoy reached Bushire in October 1809, and early in the following year was able to travel to Teheran, which he reached just after General Gardane and his French mission had been forced to leave the city. Sir Harford Jones was able to see the Shah who, now thoroughly disillusioned with the French, was prepared, once more, to renew his contacts with the British, and in due course the envoy was able to conclude a provisional treaty whereby the Shah undertook not to permit any European force to march through his country on its way to India, while the British, for their part, promised to help the Persians with troops and money to resist any such invasion of Persian territory. The British Government thereupon decided that it was time for formal relations to be restored, and when the two countries exchanged envoys, Sir Gore Ousely became the new British ambassador, reaching Shiraz in April 1811.

French initiatives were similarly forcing Minto into active interventions both in the Indian Ocean and in the East Indies. The Cape of Good Hope had passed into English hands in 1806, and thereafter the Ile de France had been subjected to an increasingly effective blockade until, by 1808, it was in real danger of famine. Napoleon had always been surprised that the British had not made a determined effort to take it much earlier, and he had never placed too much reliance upon France being able to retain it indefinitely, but as long as it remained in French hands he was prepared to send it some assistance, and in the years 1808–09 four frigates were able to reach Port Louis where, under the command of Commodore Hamelin, they proved an effective small force. The French Navy, which had been so decimated by the French

Revolution, was now recovering, with a new generation of able officers coming to command.[27] In the course of 1809 these frigates, between them, captured five East Indiamen, a sloop and a Portuguese frigate and destroyed a small British trading settlement off the west coast of Sumatra.

In June 1809, a French agent named Col. de la Houssaye had been seized on board a native proa off Penang. In some boastful talk after his capture, he had spoken of the arrival of seven frigates at the Ile de France and of the anticipated arrival of a further seven at Batavia. He had aroused suspicion both on account of his inability to give any convincing explanation for his presence on that small vessel, and because of the large amount of ready money that was found on his person. Then, when his papers were examined, he was found to be carrying a letter to the King of Ava,[28] and other letters to various people in Calcutta and in other parts of India. Hence fear began to be entertained that an army was being trained in Burma, under the command of French and Dutch officers, together with another in Indonesia, for future use against the British.

Meanwhile it was feared that Daendels' agents were at work forming an anti-British league of Indian states. When all was ready, it was surmised that a French fleet would descend upon Bengal, its attack being timed to coincide with an uprising of these Indian states, this whole campaign being supported by the above Burmese and Indonesian armies. Minto therefore appointed Captain Canning and David Campbell to carry out investigations at Ava and at Achin respectively to discover the truth or otherwise of these rumours. They both concluded that these assertions were fictitious. Nevertheless it was suspected that Daendels had indeed been thinking along these lines, and even before Minto had received the reports of Canning and Campbell, he had requested the support of the Secret Committee and had begun to prepare for the conquest of Java.[29]

The Spice Islands of Amboina and Ternate, difficult to defend, had already been captured early in 1810, but before he was ready to tackle Java, Minto needed to deal with the Indian Ocean Islands before more damage was done to the Company's trade, and the Ile de Bourbon and the Ile de France were finally taken on 8 July and 2 December 1810. Napoleon, however, was still hopeful that Java might be saved, and having become aware, shortly after his annexation of Holland, that Daendels had made himself very unpopular with the Indonesians, he therefore arranged for General Janssens to replace Daendels as Governor, but the new man had not had time to make his mark before the British arrived off Batavia in August 1811, and the surrender of the Dutch in Java followed on 17 September.

These setbacks in Persia, the East Indies and the Indian Ocean, however, seemed only to make Napoleon the more determined to pursue his Oriental ambitions. Thus in the autumn of 1810, he again sent agents to inspect the defences in Egypt and Syria, while he also arranged for half-yearly reports to be sent back to his Government regarding the current situation in the Ottoman Empire. Finally, on 17 September 1810, he wrote to Decrès drawing attention to the attractions of making an attack upon Port Jackson, which Péron had said could easily be captured now, though not in twenty-five years' time, saying: *'On proposerait ... de faire prendre la colonie anglaise de Jackson, qui est au sud* [sic] *de l'ile de France, et où l'on trouverait des resources considérables.'* In view of the probability that the East Indies would not remain in French hands for very much longer, it seems that he must have been visualising the Philippine Islands, at the farthest reach of King Joseph's Spanish Empire, as the base for any move against Port Jackson, any such expedition perhaps comprising a mixture of French, Spanish and possibly even Dutch troops as well.

At this point, however, Napoleon's attention once again became focused upon a widening breach that seemed to be opening up in his economic blockade of the British Isles. He had extended the Continental System to the borders of Holstein along the shores of the North Sea, and to the southern shores of the Baltic, but 2,000 ships entered the Baltic in 1810, including 600 English vessels that were hoping to be able to enter Russian harbours, and all these ships carried British goods under the cover of false papers, including forged certificates of origin, and Napoleon was demanding that all such goods should be seized. It was in vain that the Tsar argued that though he remained faithful to the Continental System in principle, yet his first duty was to guard the economic interests of his Empire. The truth was that Napoleon was intent not only upon enforcing his continental blockade so as to bring about the defeat of Great Britain, but also upon preserving his own dominance over the continent of Europe, a dominance now increasingly threatened by the resurgence of Russian power. He therefore now wished to see the Russian Empire brought back to that same state of inferiority that had been her lot at the time of the signing of the treaties of Tilsit in 1807.[30] Napoleon was thus already heading for his disastrous decision, in 1812, to invade Russia, and in the intervening period his oriental ambitions remained 'on hold'. For the authorities in London and in New South Wales, however, the French plans during the Revolutionary and Napoleonic wars to establish a presence on the west coast of Australia, and to undermine both British rule in the subcontinent of India and British dominance over the China trade, were a stark reminder that further expansion and settlement over the whole continent of Australia was now becoming a matter of increasing urgency.

Chapter Seven

A RING-FENCE AROUND AUSTRALIA

In the aftermath of the downfall of Napoleon, British policy towards the island continent of Australia underwent a sea-change. Hitherto the emphasis had been upon maintaining the security of the colony of New South Wales in the eastern half of the continent, including the island of Tasmania, while the main thrust of Britain's imperial policy as a whole had been upon safeguarding the British position in India. By 1815, the latter objective had been achieved, and attention now began to be focused upon bringing about a comparable stability over the Australasian region.

The changed relationship between France and Holland made this policy both possible and opportune. The long years of French domination and occupation, and Napoleon's subordination of Dutch economic interests to the enforcement of the Continental System, had brought about so much Dutch disenchantment with the French connection that any attempt to renew the Franco-Dutch alliance in the foreseeable future appeared inconceivable. Such an eventuality was made still more unlikely by the Congress of Vienna's creation of a strengthened Kingdom of the Netherlands as a barrier against future French expansion across the continent of Europe. Hence the British Government was no longer inhibited from envisaging the annexation of parts of, or even the whole of, New Holland, whose coast had originally been discovered by Dutch navigators, by the fear of forcing the Dutch into a closer alliance with France, and thus endangering Britain's sea-links with China by way of the Malay Archipelago.

Furthermore, the British authorities became increasingly convinced that the situation would be exploited to the advantage of France, and possibly Holland as well, if they did not first undertake this expansion themselves.

Despite the final overthrow of Napoleon in 1814–15, the French did not lose interest in the Orient. While it was no longer practicable to hope for a revival of their former influence in India, after a quarter-of-a-century of war and revolution there was now need for initiatives that promised to bring economic rewards, and French attention was initially drawn to Indo-China. Vietnam had for long been considered important, not only in its own right but also in relation to trade with China, and between 1816 and 1818 French naval vessels were sent in an attempt to re-establish political contact with Annam, and to capitalise upon the privileged position which Bishop Pigneau de Behaine had formerly established at the court of the Emperor Gia Long. The latter had indeed been willing to establish trading links with France, but he had since died, and his successor, Minh Mang, was strongly opposed to all Western influence, and in particular to that of France.[1]

Though frustrated in Indo-China, the French were also showing a renewed interest in the Pacific, and at the same time as they were seeking to re-establish their influence in Indo-China, Louis de Freycinet was engaged in a voyage to the Pacific Ocean in the years 1817–20 in which the official emphasis was upon scientific observation. Such scientific voyages, however, always had a political dimension as well, and the visit to Shark Bay in Western Australia enabled de Freycinet to complete the hydrographic work of the Baudin expedition among the chain of islands guarding the entrance to the bay. This was followed by visits to the straits between Gilolo and New Guinea. Neither Britain nor the colonial authorities in Australia could overlook the fact that all this activity was in waters close to the sea-lanes employed by East Indiamen using the Eastern Passage.

The French were, in fact, thinking of following the British example in New South Wales, by themselves establishing a penal settlement as the nucleus of a new colony in Western Australia. In 1818, when the post-Napoleonic allied occupation of France came to an end, Pierre Barthélemy Baron Portal had been appointed Minister for the Navy and Colonies in France. It was his ambition to rebuild a powerful French navy, but in this he was handicapped by the fact that his department was also responsible for the criminals sentenced to transportation, and their maintenance was a costly burden. The answer seemed to lie in following the example of Botany Bay, and the publication of the second volume of the story of the Baudin expedition, followed by de Freycinet's recent voyage, focused French attention on Western Australia as the most promising location. A committee was therefore set up to investigate and make proposals, and in the spring of 1819, it presented its report. During the discussions, Western Australia had been agreed upon, with special attention being drawn to King George Sound and the Swan River, and though no definite site was specified, it was significant that Rosily was in charge of the hydrographic office which advised the French Navy on strategic bases overseas; for Rosily had himself sailed northwards along the Western Australian coastline with St Allouarn in 1772, when they had proceeded as far as Shark Bay, and he had witnessed that territory being annexed for France in the name of the Bourbons.

In the years that followed these committee meetings of 1819, Rosily prepared the instructions for a number of expeditions which were sent to investigate the suitability of south-western Australia as the site for a possible penal settlement. For the authorities in Australia, the significance of any such French base, in time of war, for the security of East Indiamen using the Eastern or Outer Eastern Passages to and from China was only too obvious, not to mention the safety of British India. Its possible value as a whaling and sealing base would also have been kept in mind.[2] Thus in 1824–25, both Duperrey and Hyacinthe Bougainville were put in command of expeditions with instructions to survey south-western Australia, paying particular attention to Rottnest and Garden Islands, so as to gain detailed information before any settlement was decided upon. Both these seamen, however, ran into difficulties in the East Indies, as a result of which both had decided to omit this part of their instructions.

Meanwhile, in northern Australia it was the Dutch rather than the French who forced the British to act. In South-East Asia Anglo-Dutch relations had become increasingly strained since the Congress of Vienna. At that Congress, the peace-makers had decided to amalgamate Holland and Belgium so as to form the new Kingdom of the Netherlands, with the Prince of Orange becoming King William, as a barrier against possible future French expansion. Since it was essential that the new Kingdom should be economically strong, it had received back all the captured Dutch colonies save the Cape of Good Hope. To the Government in London this seemed a statesmanlike arrangement that would ensure the future stability of Europe, but to British officials and merchants in the East it appeared far otherwise. Merchants who had built up valuable trading links with islands of the Malay Archipelago now faced the prospect of being excluded from those very markets, should the Dutch revert to their former monopolistic practices, nor was there any clear definition of precisely which islands and territories had been returned to Dutch control.

The fears of a Dutch return to a policy of monopoly were not without foundation. Though the Dutch themselves were divided on the issue, with some officials sympathetic to free trade theories, and others wanting a return to monopolistic measures, the wishes of their Belgian partners also had now to be taken into consideration. During the long years of war the Belgian cotton manufacturers had been able to exploit Britain's exclusion from the continent of Europe, under the Continental System, to their own advantage. They had developed markets for their products throughout the Napoleonic Empire and its satellite states. While the return of British competition after Napoleon's downfall was expected to entail the loss of much of their European business, these Belgian manufacturers now looked forward to enjoying, as compensation for that loss, similar protected markets in the

Dutch colonial empire, where they wished to see a monopoly reintroduced, and any such development would obviously constitute a severe setback for the export prospects for British textiles in South-East Asia.[3] Furthermore, there was the financial position of the Dutch East India Company to be taken into account. As a result of the disastrous Dutch participation in the American War of Independence, that Company had run deeply into debt, which had led the Dutch Government to take over its control in 1798. When the islands were returned to Dutch control in 1816 a deficit still remained, and the problem was made harder to resolve because of the need for costly campaigns in the East Indies to overcome the stiff resistance put up by some native rulers who were opposing the Dutch efforts to revive their colonial rule. Despite such opposition, the Dutch were able progressively to restore their authority over Pontianak in Borneo, Macassar in Celebes, Palembang in Sumatra, then over the island of Bangka, and finally over the islands of the Moluccan archipelago.[4] The costliness of this exercise of power, however, was another factor militating against the hopes of the free-traders.

For their part, the Dutch were incensed by the activities of Stamford Raffles, who saw his ambitions for the expansion of British trade throughout the Malay Archipelago and beyond under threat, and who, as Lieutenant-Governor of Bencoolen, was ready to challenge every Dutch move that could possibly be portrayed as being without historical justification. His various initiatives earned him a succession of rebukes both from the Government in London and from the directors of the English East India Company. In India itself, however, he won the invaluable support of the

Governor-General, Lord Hastings, whom he had visited in 1818. He had persuaded Hastings that the Dutch were intent upon achieving political supremacy in the Malay Archipelago and upon impeding the expansion of British trade in the area. In support of this contention, Hastings himself argued that 'the collection of Establishments Naval and Military at Java is far more extensive than the occupation and defence of their existing possessions [would require]'. And he drew particular attention to the vulnerability of the trade routes to China in these circumstances, since it was through the seas in which the Dutch were situated 'that our China ships whether outward or homeward bound must pass, and because both the Straits of Malacca and Sunda were in their hands, not only our Trade with the Eastern Islands, but our Commerce with China is thus at their mercy.'[5]

Hence when Raffles left Calcutta in December 1818, he carried with him qualified authority from the Governor-General to establish a fortified post to the eastward of the Straits of Malacca, and on 19 December 1819 he landed on the island of Singapore. A month later he concluded a treaty with the Sultan of Johore who agreed to the establishment of an East India Company factory there.

While Singapore, if retained, offered potential security and facilities for the expansion of British trade in the western parts of the Malay Archipelago and the neighbouring mainland, mainland, there was still no comparable British base in sight for the eastern half of that island world. Some men of vision therefore began to wonder whether the northern coastline of Australia might not be able to play this role. It was Matthew Flinders who had first realised the economic potential of these northern shores. For just after completing his careful examination of the Gulf of Carpentaria he had met up with a number of Malay praus from Macassar. Initially this had come as a great surprise, but in conversation with the leader of the Malays he learned that this was a long-established practice, and that this man himself had been engaged in the trade for some twenty years. Flinders discovered that the general pattern was for these traders to sail with the northern monsoon from Macassar to Arnhem Land, and then to work their way along the coast as far as the Gulf of Carpentaria in search of trepang or bêche-de-mer, the 'sea-slug' which the Chinese considered such a delicacy. On the present occasion, Flinders was told, there were some sixty praus present carrying a thousand men, strung out along the coast of Arnhem Land, and when their catch was complete at the end of the season, they would sail to Timor-laoet (i.e., the Tanimbar Islands), where the Chinese would buy their cargoes.

Flinders named the islands where he had met the Malays the 'English Company's Islands,' and on 28 March 1803 he wrote to Sir Joseph Banks to suggest 'that if the East India Company have had any intention of making a settlement on New Holland, the good harbours in Cape Arnhem, the wild nutmegs, and perhaps the trepang which seems to bring the Malays a good many thousand dollars annually from the Chinese, might be additional inducements'.[6]

This idea was now carried a stage further by William Barns who, after spending some four years trading between New South Wales and the Moluccas, arrived in London in 1823 and promptly wrote to the Earl of Bathurst to propose a settlement on the northern coast of Australia, to exploit the extensive trade which was being carried on between the Gulf of Carpentaria and the Dutch inhabitants of the Moluccas.

Asked to spell out his plan in more detail, Barns pointed out that in the absence of a British settlement in the Eastern Islands, the Dutch, 'having shut all their ports to the British flag' were engrossing the whole of the immensely profitable trade based upon the sea-slug. He argued that a base in the vicinity of the Gulf of Carpentaria would be well placed to trade not only with the Eastern Islands, but also to the east as far as the Solomon Islands, and in view of the fact that these seas abounded with sperm whales, might also become the centre of an important fishery. He urged the formation of an English settlement, 'especially as the Dutch are most anxious to form one themselves in the hope of shutting us out from the trade of the Eastern world'.[7]

This proposal was backed by the East India Committee, which emphasised the vulnerability of English trade with the eastern parts of the Malay Archipelago in the event of another war, so long as Britain had no base in the area. 'The establishment of the British in the proposed situation,' the Committee pointed out, 'would not only furnish the desired protection to our Trade in that quarter, but would give security to the East India Company's and the Indian Private Trade to China by the Eastern route'.[8] And John Barrow, from his office at the Admiralty, signified his strong agreement. After discussing with Captain King the surveys which the latter had made along this coast, he stated emphatically that 'we ought not in sound policy to hesitate a moment in forming a settlement on the northern part of New Holland,' in view of the Dutch determination to re-establish their dominion in the East Indies and to resort to 'their pernicious and narrow system of exclusion' there. King himself, after the completion of his survey, had also urged the British Government to establish a settlement on the northern coast of Australia, and had recommended Port Essington as the best site for this purpose.

Bathurst[9] responded to these various proposals by deciding that the time was indeed ripe for the establishment of such a settlement. It was in this same year of 1824 that the British and Dutch Governments recognised that a new diplomatic initiative was needed to avoid future friction, in view of the expansion of Dutch control in the East Indies on the one hand, and the British establishment of Singapore on the other. A new Anglo-Dutch treaty was therefore signed whereby the English withdrew from Sumatra in return for a Dutch withdrawal from the Malay Peninsula, including Dutch recognition of Britain's right to Singapore. This meant, in effect, that the Dutch now gained undisputed control of the Strait of Sunda, while the British controlled the northern and southern entrances to the Straits of Malacca, though the latter would remain a vulnerable shipping-lane in time of war, despite the fact that the port of Malacca itself was now in the hands of the British. Thus when Bathurst decided on a North Australian settlement, he did so at a moment when the Dutch were steadily expanding their control and influence over the Malay Archipelago, while the only British presence in that area was on the Archipelago's western flank. A British settlement in the vicinity of Port Essington thus promised to complement the value of Singapore, by providing a similar trading base on the eastern flank of those islands, with the added attraction of providing security for outward- or homeward-bound shipping using the Eastern Passage.

Bathurst therefore sent Captain Bremer RN in HMS *Tartar* to take possession of 'that part of the ... coast between the western shore of Bathurst Island and the eastern side of the Coburg Peninsula, including the whole of Bathurst and Melville Islands, and the said Peninsula'. This entailed an extension of the western limits of New South Wales as originally claimed by Great Britain, and when Bremer reached Port Essington by way of Sydney on 20 September 1824, he formally took possession of the northern coast of Australia between 129°E and 135°E. However, not finding any immediate source of fresh water, Bremer soon moved on to Melville Island, where a settlement was formed on Apsley Strait at a spot which was named King's Cove. Bremer saw the whole exercise primarily in naval terms, and a few years later Earl explained that Bremer had chosen this particular location because the large tidal range made it particularly suitable for the construction of dry docks, and therefore well adapted to be a naval station. But it did not prove to be well chosen for a trading post, being too far away from the fishing grounds of the Malays, who were intended to be a key element in the whole operation.

Meanwhile, early in 1826 Jules Blosseville, an influential figure who had sailed in Duperrey's expedition, had drawn up plans, at the behest of the Director General of Police (DGP), for a French penal colony in Western Australia. He envisaged a settlement stretching from the south-western corner of Australia northwards as far as the Tropic of Capricorn, and eastwards as far as 122°E, with its capital at King George Sound. Perhaps the leaking of this report, and certainly the despatch of Dumont D'Urville on a new voyage of discovery, led Bathurst, on 1 March 1826, to instruct Governor Darling to send soldiers and convicts to Shark Bay, the harbour on the west coast which had been so lauded by Péron and which was in so significant a location for ships using the Eastern Passage.

But recollecting that that area lacked water and a fertile soil, on 11 March he suggested that it might be best to start with King George Sound, this fine harbour, the site of modern Albany, being located in a more fertile area.[10] Accordingly, Major Edmund Lockyer was sent there with a body of convicts and soldiers, with instructions that stated, for the first time, that Great Britain now claimed sovereignty over the whole of Australia. This base thus safeguarded shipping approaching Van Diemen's Land and Port Jackson from possible enemy attack in time of war, just as the simultaneous (and temporary) occupation of Western Port protected shipping using Bass Strait. But Shark Bay was not forgotten, still being regarded as a port which could prove 'important to have retained'. And in a private letter accompanying his despatch, Bathurst explained that the departure of two French ships on a voyage of discovery had led the Government to ponder how far British possessions in Australia might be prejudiced by possible French plans to establish themselves in that area, and especially in the case of 'that line of coast which extends westward from the western point of Bathurst Island in 129° East Longitude where the North-Western boundary of the New South Wales Government has been lately fixed in order to comprize within its jurisdiction the newly made settlement of Melville Island'.[11]

Since Melville Island had not been living up to its commercial expectations, however, and because it was feared that the brig *Stedcomb* had been lost to the pirates who infested the Malay Archipelago, the East India Trade Committee now asked that naval protection be given to the settlement and its trade, and that a more careful examination should be made of the coast farther to the eastward, since, despite Bremer's failure to find water upon the immediate spot indicated in his Instructions, they thought it probable that if a little more time had been devoted to the search, a settlement might have been established farther to the eastward, near the western side of the Gulf of Carpentaria, which might have brought to Britain the commercial advantages that had originally been hoped for.[12]

Accordingly, James Stirling arrived at Sydney aboard HMS *Success* in November 1826 with orders either to remove the settlement at Melville Island or to found a new one on the northern coast of Australia, but as this was an unpropitious season of the year for the immediate execution of these Instructions, he left Sydney on 17 January 1827, with Darling's approval, to explore the Swan River in Western Australia. He had already come to the conclusion that this was a promising site for a settlement, in a strategically important area, and had presented the Governor with a memorandum on the subject which he had prepared on the outward voyage, and Darling had been impressed by his arguments.

Meanwhile, Maj. Campbell wrote from Melville Island to say that the navigational hazards of the area militated against the present site, whether viewed as a commercial or a military post, whereas 'all the accounts I receive from Timor represent that the Malays repair to the coast of New Holland during the months of December, January, February and March, and that their fishing ground is from the Gulf of Van Diemen's to that of Carpentaria'. He therefore planned to run down to Port Essington to see if he could find trace of their presence, as it would be useful to be armed with positive intelligence before the arrival of the *Success*.

Stirling himself arrived back at Sydney in April 1827, and a month later he left for the north with orders to maintain the original settlement at Melville Island and at the same time to found a new one to the eastward. The area around latitude 11° South and longitude 132° East Croker Island had been recommended as the area that held most promise, but when Stirling reached there he found that this island was unsuitable during the north-west monsoon, whereas Raffles Bay on the mainland, a few miles away, not only provided a safe anchorage for vessels of all descriptions at all seasons of the year, but was also known to be 'a haunt and fishing station of the Malays'.

It was not to be expected, of course, that the Dutch would remain passive in face of these developments in such close proximity to their own settlements. Having so recently won recognition for their own predominance in the Malay Archipelago in the Anglo-Dutch treaty of 1824, they had no intention of seeing that position eroded by the establishment of a new British base in northern Australia. In earlier times the Dutch themselves had had small military posts on all the islands lying between the Moluccas, the centre of the spice trade, and the northern coast of Australia. These posts had been established to protect the Dutch monopoly of the spice trade, by eradicating the spice trees that grew on islands which were outside their immediate control, and by preventing rival European nations from establishing settlements of their own in the area. As the fortunes of the Dutch East India Company had declined during the second half of the eighteenth century, these posts had had to be withdrawn on the grounds of expense.

In 1824, however, a new Dutch company had been formed, which enjoyed a virtual monopoly of the trade of the East

Indies, and in which the King was the principal shareholder with power to appoint the company's directors. In face of English activity on the north coast of Australia, therefore, the Dutch prepared a brig-of-war named the *Dourga*, which sailed from Amboina and visited all the islands lying between Timor and New Guinea. Some of these islands had not been visited by a Dutch vessel for half-a-century, but an effort was now made to rekindle friendly relations with the islanders who were invited to visit Banda to trade. The *Dourga* also visited the western coast of New Guinea from Cape Valsch, the south-western extremity, to the coastline nearest to the Molucca Islands. And following this reconnaissance, a proclamation on 24 August 1828 announced that the Dutch had formally taken possession of the west coast of New Guinea, a claim that was given added weight by the establishment of Fort du Bus at Merkus Oord.[13]

Stirling, however, was already convinced of the superior attractions of Western Australia. As he had argued in his original memorandum, this location enjoyed great advantages with respect to speed of communication with Europe, with the Cape of Good Hope, with Mauritius, with the subcontinent of India, and with the East Indies, and it was close to the track followed by ships using the Eastern Passage to and from China. This was in sharp contrast to New South Wales and its subordinate establishments in Tasmania, which were cut off from commercial communication with those same places for much of the year. As soon as he had returned from his short reconnaissance, Stirling had submitted a further report for Governor Darling, in which he had been able to announce the excellent anchorage for ships-of-war provided by Cockburn Sound and to point

out that the neighbourhood of Swan River provided the
only known port between Cape Leeuwin and Shark Bay,
which greatly enhanced its significance; it was the key to
that whole coastline. In face of the fact that the French also
had a 'shadow of a right' of their own to that coastline,
based upon their own exploration, he urged that French
claims could not be too speedily extinguished by a British
occupation. In addition, he recommended the occupation
of Geographe Bay and the establishment of a settlement at
Shark Bay, so as to exclude all foreign intrusion on the west
coast of Australia.[14]

After establishing the new settlement at Raffles Bay and
spending some three months on the northern coast, Stirling
had sailed back to England, and it was in the following year,
while he was out of regular employment in the Service, and on
half-pay in London, that he submitted a further memorandum
on the subject of the Swan River. With first-hand experience
of both the west and north coasts of Australia, he was now
able to write with added authority, and he was able to
assure the Government that the Swan River area was not,
as previously reported, sterile and inhospitable, but was in
reality well adapted to cultivation and abundantly supplied
with fresh water. Since there was a safe anchorage in the
vicinity of Swan River, which could easily be developed into
one of the finest harbours in the world, this, he stated, was
a potential settlement which could not remain unoccupied
for long. It was not only well located for carrying on trade
with India and the Malay Archipelago, but would provide
cruisers with a convenient base 'for the annoyance of trade in
those seas,' and if the British Government failed to act, then
some foreign Power was likely to see the advantage of taking

possession of it; and there was scant reason to doubt which particular Power he had in mind.

This memorandum and Stirling's subsequent drive for the establishment of a settlement in Western Australia attracted considerable interest, and eventually the Government decided to plant a Crown Colony there so as to ensure that the French did not get possession of that coast. As a consequence, on 5 November 1828, Captain Fremantle was sent out to take formal possession of the west coast of Australia, and after reaching Cockburn Sound on 27 April 1829, on 2 May he took possession, as ordered. Thus, for the first time, Great Britain had formally laid aside all Dutch or French claims to any part of New Holland, and had annexed the whole continent herself.

Actual settlement was still needed to make the claim a reality according to the concepts of the age, and a month later Stirling arrived with officials, soldiers and settlers to found the new British colony of Western Australia, which officially came into existence with the further proclamation of 18 June 1829. Two years later, this new colony also incorporated the former military settlement at King George Sound.

The strategic significance of the new colony was underlined by John Barrow in a paper read before the Royal Geographical Society on 1 January 1830. Mentioning the capacious anchorage in Cockburn Sound, which Stirling dramatically described as being capable of containing in safety a thousand ships, he pointed out that vessels in this Sound would be safe from an enemy squadron stationed outside, 'as the middle part of it is out of mortar range, either from the sea or land side. Such a port, situated as this is,' he went on, 'in the hands of an enemy might become, in any future war, ten times more destructive to British trade than ever the Isle of France was in the last'.[15]

On the north coast of Australia, however, all was not well. Port Essington at Raffles Bay had been abandoned in 1829, a hasty decision which had been based, as Barrow said, on misrepresentations made to the Governor by the military commanding officers who, with the exception of Captain Barker, had disliked the place. 'The alleged causes which led to the abandonment,' Barrow wrote a decade later, 'were first, the unhealthiness of the climate. Second, the hostility of the natives. Third, the non-visitation of the Malays. Now every one of these allegations was proved to be utterly without foundation'. In the case of the Malays, he stated that between 23 March and 10 May 1829 'thirty-four prahus arrived, manned by one thousand and fifty-six persons ... and their captains all said that a much greater number would arrive in the course of the next season'. As Barrow remarked, 'the main commercial objective had been to allow the Malays ready access to British articles of commerce and manufacture, instead of having to purchase these through the Dutch at inflated prices.' But Barrow was still more interested in the strategic value of the settlement, which he described as follows: 'a coast so situated in relation to the Dutch Archipelago and to the shores of India ought not to be left open to any European or Asiatic power that might find it convenient to avail themselves of our absence and establish a settlement there that in a little time might prove another Singapore.

'Contemplating the future destiny of Australia, it is most desirable that the whole of this great continent should be held under one undivided power, and that Great Britain, which first planted colonies on its shores, should be that power; and that, to keep it in secure possession, she ought to draw a ring-fence round its whole coast.'

It was not long after the abandonment of Port Essington that officials in London became aware that this decision had been reached too hastily, and by April 1836 rumours were current that a new settlement was to be established at Raffles Bay. G. W. Earl therefore wrote to the Colonial Secretary to ask whether these rumours were true. Earl was a man of adventurous and enterprising spirit, who had been fascinated by the possibilities that were opening up for a promising career in the East. He had spent some time travelling around parts of South-East Asia, and had also spent several months at Fremantle during its formative stages. Initially he had experimented with opening up a trade between the western coast of Borneo and Singapore, but it was the possibility of developing a settlement on the north coast of Australia which attracted his keenest interest. When he was in Singapore he began to consider a project for opening up trading links between that port and northern Australia, and some Chinese merchants at that settlement tried to get him to lead an expedition for that purpose in 1834. Their idea was that he could return with a cargo of sea-slug and tortoise-shell, but Earl declined the offer since he was convinced that a permanent settlement needed to be established in northern Australia first, before that type of trading venture could be set up on a firm and stable basis.

The rumours that Earl had heard were indeed well based. Such a settlement was now under consideration, and Lord Glenelg, the Colonial Secretary, was at that moment seeking the advice of John Barrow and Captain Beaufort RN Barrow, in addition to being Secretary to the Admiralty, was also

President of the Royal Geographical Society, while Beaufort was hydrographer to the Royal Navy, and the two men now prepared a joint memorandum on the subject. They stressed that 'the mere fact of taking or resuming formal possession ... of any territory, unaccompanied by actual occupancy, would not be sufficiently valid to prevent any other power from seizing and forming a settlement on such territory,' and if it was the Government's intention to resume actual possession of the original settlements, they strongly advocated immediate action. They also argued that 'the time will come, and has perhaps already arrived, when we ought ... to plant our standard on ... Cape York, This point is the key to Endeavour Passage and indeed to the whole of Torres Strait, the direct line of communication between Sydney and India. If this point, or the adjacent islands, were in the hands of an enemy the communication with India by this route would be completely shut out, and the consequences must be most pernicious'.[16]

Glenelg, who had regretted the original decision to withdraw from Raffles Bay at the very moment when circumstances seemed propitious for a successful expansion of commerce, endorsed the Barrow-Beaufort memorandum, and agreed that it might be wise to think of two settlements, one in the vicinity of the Coburg Peninsula and the other at Cape York, since it seemed probable that Torres Strait would become a regular route to India once its hazards were better known. But the first necessity was speedy action, since both the French and the Americans were even now fitting out expeditions to that part of the world, where the Dutch, too, were also actively engaged in establishing new mercantile stations. Glenelg stressed that he was 'fully impressed with the paramount importance of retaining permanent possession of the entire coasts of Australia,' and realised that no time must be lost in considering what measures needed to be taken.[17]

Earl added his own support to this campaign by publishing his book on *The Eastern Seas* in this same year of 1838. Pointing out that few parts of the world presented a fairer field for British commercial enterprise than the Malay Archipelago, he complained that nevertheless no place had had to sustain such deplorable neglect. In the western parts of the archipelago, British merchants had had to bear the costs of arming their vessels on a scale more suited to ships-of-war than to merchantmen, while pirates had even been allowed to swarm in the immediate vicinity of Singapore. With the eastern half of the archipelago the British had had no commercial intercourse at all, yet British cottons were highly prized and, he wrote, 'A very lucrative and extensive traffic might be carried on with these islands, since they are annually visited by fifteen or sixteen American traders for the purpose of obtaining articles for the Canton market, in exchange for American goods.' The Aru Islands had become the emporium of the south-eastern corner of the archipelago, and the north coast of Australia was the best site for a British emporium for trading with the eastern half of the Malay Archipelago.

Both Earl and the Royal Geographical Society were also calling for an exploration of the north-western coast of Australia. Ever since the time of Dampier there had been puzzlement over the large rise and fall of tides in Buccaneers Archipelago. By the close of Captain King's survey, the fifteen hundred miles of coastline between Dampier's Archipelago in latitude 20° South and Cape Hay in latitude 14° South still remained largely unsurveyed, and this was the only place left where large rivers running from the interior of the continent into the sea might yet be found. Ever since the time of Flinders, a theory had prevailed that a great inland sea existed in the interior of Australia. In the words of Eyre, 'It is generally believed that the vast continent of Australia is ... little more than a narrow crust or barrier intervening between an inner and an outer sea, and that the great mass of the area which is thus enclosed consists of water.'[18]

Some thought that this great inland sea was an enclosed one, like the Caspian Sea, others, including both Earl and John Barrow, thought that rivers flowed from it into the ocean. As Earl put it, there was at least a probability that a vast inland sea occupied the interior part of the continent, and that this sea communicated 'with the main ocean, by a strait only three hundred and fifty miles from the southernmost islands of the Indian Archipelago.' He then went on to spell out the political implications of such a conjecture. 'The shores of this sea,' he wrote, '... would present a field for European colonization unequalled in any known part of the world, and it should be an object of the British to take possession of them, were it merely to prevent any European nation from posting themselves at the back of the settlements which we already possess in Australia.'[19]

The Royal Geographical Society, too, in detailing the alternative versions of this theory of an inland sea, expressed its opinion 'that in the undiscovered portion of the North-West will be found the great drain of waters from the interior' If that proved to be the case, it pointed out, a settlement at the mouth of a navigable river on the north-west coast would be of incalculable value, both from its connection with India and, still more, 'from its power of extension inland by water communication, the real cause of the prodigiously rapid growth of our North American settlements'. The Society considered it surprising that after half-a-century of British occupation neither the whole of the continent's coastline nor the interior had yet been fully surveyed, and as an immediate contribution it called for a survey both of the north-western coast of Australia and of Torres Strait. Finally, as a means of riveting the Government's concentration upon this problem, it drew attention to the fact that both France and the United States of America were sending out splendidly equipped surveying expeditions to the Pacific Ocean, adding that 'it would be a most humiliating mortification to witness the tricoloured flag, or that of the stripes and stars [*sic*], waving in Dampier's Land'.[20]

According to Earl, it was while the Government was considering the problem created by the great amount of shipping that was now passing through Torres Strait, and the need for a port of refuge in the vicinity, in view of the loss of life which was occurring through shipwreck, that 'it was discovered that a French expedition was preparing at Toulon for the express purpose of taking possession of some post on the north coast of Australia'. He did not specify where this piece of intelligence came from, but added that it was the danger of a French station 'midway between our Indian and Australian possessions [which] tended to precipitate matters, and the immediate occupation of the coast became a matter of importance'. As a result, HMS *Alligator*, commanded by Sir Gordon Bremer, and the *Britomart* under the command of Lieutenant-Commander Owen Stanley, were chosen for this service. Captain John MacArthur was appointed to command the marines who were to form the garrison, while Owen Stanley's specific task was to examine 'the seas and islands contiguous to the north-west of Australia, which had hitherto been very imperfectly explored'.

This expedition left Plymouth on 10 March 1838, eventually reaching its destination, in company with the *Orontes* in the following October.[21]

Meanwhile, the exploration of the north-west coast was undertaken by a combined sea-and-land expedition, HMS *Beagle* under the command of Captain Wickham carrying out the survey by sea, while Grey and Lushington worked their way along the coast by land.

At this same time, the New Zealand Association had been founded in Britain to colonise that land on the principles laid down by Edward Gibbon Wakefield, and in 1838 the British Government decided upon at least a partial annexation of New Zealand. From June 1839 to May 1841, New Zealand remained a part of New South Wales. Then Hobson, as Governor, having already negotiated the treaty of Waitangi with the northern Maori chiefs, declared the annexation of the whole country.

However, as Britain was thus consolidating her hold over the Australian continent and the islands of New Zealand, the particular circumstances which had led to the attempts to establish a settlement on the northern shores of Australia were changing. In 1842, the French established a Protectorate over Tahiti, and this led John Barrow to express the opinion that the French focus of attention appeared to have shifted from the Australian continent to the Pacific Ocean, and that in the future the French would probably be satisfied with the latter.[22]

Second, as a result of the 'Opium War', the British had acquired the island of Hong Kong as a base from which to trade with China, and with the supposedly vast potential of the Chinese market now at hand, the relative importance of the East Indies trade was likely to decline and to receive less attention than had been the case hitherto, Moreover, the ready market for opium lessened the need for the marine and jungle products of the Malay Archipelago to pay for the purchases of Chinese teas and other luxury goods. Another negative influence derived from the serious problems which had been experienced with fever at Victoria, Port Essington.

The original strategic significance of Port Essington in relation to the Eastern Passage was rapidly disappearing. In the first place, the South China Sea was now likely to be available to British ships in time of war, since the British settlements at Penang, Malacca and Singapore now controlled the Straits of Malacca, while James Brooke had become the Rajah of Sarawak, and Labuan, near Brunei, was about to become another British base. Second, sail was being progressively replaced by steam at sea, and when steam eventually came to predominate, the Eastern Passage would lose its significance. On the Indian and Far Eastern routes, regular services by steam had begun in 1834, with ships sailing from England to Alexandria, where passengers and cargo were transported overland to Suez, whence East India Company steamers then conveyed them to their destinations in India and also, after 1842, to Hong Kong and Shanghai. A little later, in 1852, the first steam mail services to Australia were inaugurated. Furthermore, even in the case of the sailing ships themselves, technological advances were changing the situation, since the old square-rigged sailing ships, which had been slaves to the prevailing monsoon winds, were now giving way to clipper ships, whose sails and hulls were designed to enable them to beat against the prevailing monsoon winds when necessary.

In these changed circumstances, the Government began to question whether the correct location had been chosen for Port Essington, which was failing to pay its way. The Colonial Land and Emigration Board therefore began to consult various authorities, including John Crawfurd, a man of long experience of South-East Asia. After several years' service in India and Penang, Crawfurd had then held office in Java under Raffles, after which he had carried out diplomatic missions to Siam and Cochin China, and had then succeeded Raffles as administrator of Singapore. A final diplomatic mission to Burma had ended his direct involvement with the region, but on his return to England he had thereafter published various important and authoritative works on South-East Asia. He was therefore particularly well qualified to express an opinion, and when he was consulted he stated that while he did not disagree with the idea of establishing a commercial emporium on the north coast of Australia, he did not consider that Port Essington was well adapted either for a commercial emporium or for an agricultural settlement. Instead, he favoured Cape York.[23] Bremer, on the other hand, disagreed, perhaps not unexpectedly in view of his long personal association with the venture, and expressed the opinion that Port Essington 'was eminently suitable, and Cape York eminently unsuitable for a naval port and commercial emporium'.

In coming to a final conclusion, the Colonial Office rejected the Colonial Land and Emigration Board's old argument that abandonment of the settlement would once more attract foreign Powers to the north coast by insisting that such a withdrawal could not be construed as a repudiation of British sovereignty. After all, they pointed out, the Dutch themselves had set a precedent by abandoning their unhealthy West Irian post without renouncing their claims to that territory. Earl Grey, the Colonial Secretary, was also probably influenced by Barrow's change of opinion on this subject, and his belief that the French were now more interested in the Pacific Ocean than in Australia. Furthermore, Grey had also been advised that the settlement was not needed as a coaling station for ships sailing between Singapore and Sydney by way of Torres Strait. Hence on 8 June 1849, orders were sent for the final withdrawal of the settlement. It had served its purpose in ensuring that no foreign intrusion had taken place on the north coast of Australia at a critical time, and now it was no longer needed.

Two decades later, not far distant from those pioneer settlements of Melville Island and Port Essington, Darwin was finally established as the terminus of the overland telegraph. Thus was fulfilled the dream of John Barrow who, when contemplating the future destiny of Australia, had called upon his countrymen to draw a ring-fence round the whole coast of the continent so that it was held under one undivided power.

Chapter Eight

OPENING THE CHINESE EMPIRE TO THE TRADE OF THE WORLD

With the return of peace after the prolonged Revolutionary and Napoleonic Wars, Great Britain was subjected to a period of economic dislocation and social distress, the large-scale augmentation of the labour force following upon the demobilisation of the armed forces having coincided with the sudden cessation of Government orders for munitions and weapons of war, as well as for clothing and supplies for the armies and fleet, and all this at a time when no new markets for British industry were in sight.

These conditions gave added attraction to the supposed great potential market offered by the Chinese Empire. It was therefore particularly unfortunate that Anglo-Chinese relations were subjected to new strain at this critical time as a result of naval operations connected with the Anglo-American War of 1812–14 having spilled over into Chinese waters. Lord Amherst was accordingly despatched in an effort to defuse this crisis and to seek, as Lord Macartney had vainly tried to do a quarter-of-a-century earlier, permission for a British diplomatic representative to be allowed to reside at the Chinese capital. The British saw such an appointment as the best way to deal with such problems in the future, but for the Chinese such an innovation was unacceptable since it would imply that the British were on an equal footing with the Chinese, and not tributaries as tradition demanded. As a result, Lord Amherst was not even granted an audience with the Emperor, and so achieved nothing.

An even greater misfortune was the fact that the East India Company, after searching in vain over the course of the previous century for any product that the Chinese wanted to buy, apart from silver, in exchange for their exports of tea, silk, porcelain, and other luxury goods, finally found the answer in opium, a product of their Indian Empire. Both the importation and domestic production of opium had been forbidden by the Chinese Government in 1796, but the East India Company found a simple means of getting round this restriction. In its guise as the Government of British India, and with a monopoly of the production of opium in its own part of the subcontinent, it forbade the shipment of the drug in its own ships while promoting its carriage in 'country ships'[1] and in vessels sailing under foreign flags, while relying on the corruptibility of Chinese officialdom to get the opium into the Chinese market. To begin with, the Company did seek to restrict the sale of the drug, and to extract the maximum revenue from this traffic by charging high prices, with the result that in the period from 1800 to 1821 the average annual exportation to China was restricted to approximately four-and-a half chests. But as the cost of governing British India rose, and the 1824–26 Anglo-Burmese War had to be paid for, an increase in revenue was needed. Hence the Company now changed its policy and began to promote the large-scale export of opium, with the result that by 1838 the annual exportation had reached the astronomical figure of some forty thousand chests.

Furthermore, the enormous profits to be made from smuggling opium into China were attracting lawless adventurers of every nationality, and no early amelioration of this demoralising trade was to be looked for in face of the fact that the administration of British India was now dependent upon it for between 5 per cent and 10 per cent of its annual revenue.[2]

While foreign and especially British trade was thus forcing its way into an unwilling Chinese Empire, in England itself the industrialists and merchants, faced with social tension at home, were desperate to find new markets abroad to replace those that had been lost on the continent of Europe as a result of the war.

In order to exploit Britain's advantage as the leading industrial Power in the world at that time, they were also seeking to get the Free Trade doctrines of Adam Smith adopted by the British Legislature. In pursuit of this aim a delegation of London merchants, led by Thomas Tooke, called upon the Prime Minister, Lord Liverpool, in 1820, to drive home their free trade convictions. As it happened, Lord Liverpool did not need convincing, as he had been proclaiming the same message in public on a number of occasions. His room for manoeuvre, however, was strictly circumscribed by the fact that that he had to deal with a Parliament in which the landed interest was dominant, while the mercantile and industrial interests were unrepresented. Hitherto the industrialists and merchants had not wished to involve themselves in politics, which they had viewed as a potential distraction from the effective management of their various enterprises, but they were now coming to see that they urgently needed to have a direct influence over policy-making. This belated desire to win representation in the Legislature finally achieved success with the passage into law of the Parliamentary Reform Bill in 1832. The enactment of this Bill gave direct representation both to the mercantile and industrial classes and also to such important industrial cities as Birmingham and Manchester.

As part of the campaign for seeking new markets, the Manchester Chamber of Commerce set up a committee, in February 1827, to enquire into 'the state of our trade with the East Indies', and its report stressed that in consequence of the ongoing industrialisation of other European nations and of the United States of America, Britain needed to make up for their lost custom by exploiting 'the vast field for commercial enterprise which the East Indies offer to us'. But it was the Chinese Empire above all that these cotton manufacturers wished to reach. For, as readers of the *Oriental Herald* were told, 'The provinces of China, which carry on foreign trade, are Canton, the island of Hainan, Fokien, Tchekaing and Kianan [and these] four provinces are alleged to contain fifty million inhabitants, but if they contained [only] half [that number], they are upon a level with the first Kingdoms of Europe; and this may afford an index of the amount of foreign trade which they are capable of conducting, without reckoning that they are channels for a trade with the provinces of the interior, which are still more populous and extensive than themselves.'[3]

With these heady prospects in view, the industrial and mercantile interests in Britain now exploited their newly won control of parliament to bring about the immediate abolition of the East India Company's monopoly of the China trade in 1833–34.[4] In bringing this about, no attention was paid to the fact that the Chinese authorities themselves wished to see the Company's monopoly continue, since its mode of carrying on its business in Canton fitted in very well with the traditional Chinese way of trading with foreigners. Since the year 1757, apart from a few Spanish ships still allowed to visit Amoy, all foreign trade had been confined to the port of Canton. Here British trade predominated, and the Chinese had come to regard the East India Company's senior representative at the port, the President of the Select Committee, as the headman, or *taipan*, with whom they could deal when problems with foreign trade arose. Nevertheless, because the Chinese still regarded all foreign nations as being in a tributary relationship with the Manchu Emperor, the President of the Select Committee was not permitted to address the Viceroy or even the hoppo[5] directly. Instead, all communications had to be passed through the Cohong, the guild of those Chinese merchants who were alone authorised to trade with Western merchants at Canton. But under the new arrangement that Parliament instituted in the wake of the abolition of the East India Company's monopoly, Lord Palmerston, as Foreign Secretary, appointed Lord Napier to the new post of Superintendent of Trade at Canton. He was to replace the former President and Select Committee, and was instructed by Palmerston to report to the Viceroy at Canton upon arrival. It is doubtful whether Palmerston appreciated the full significance of this change of routine which the Chinese immediately regarded as an entirely unacceptable ending of their traditional tributary system. Hence, when Lord Napier wrote to the Viceroy upon his arrival, as instructed, his letter was promptly returned unopened. From this initial rebuff, the dispute rapidly escalated. The confiscation and destruction of twenty thousand chests of opium brought in by foreign traders was quickly followed by a British refusal to hand over, for execution, a sailor chosen at random, in retaliation for the death of a Chinese at the hands of an unknown assailant. This British refusal was the immediate cause of the outbreak of the first Anglo-Chinese 'Opium War'.

Their victory in that war enabled the British to dictate the terms of the subsequent Treaty of Nanking (1842) whereby the island of Hong Kong was ceded to Great Britain and five treaty ports were opened to British residence and trade.[6] These ports had all been *entrepôts* of foreign trade in the past, and they were spaced at approximately equal intervals along the one thousand miles of coastline between Canton and Shanghai. And it was in the exuberant belief that the ending of the East India Company's monopoly and the opening of these treaty ports would now make available to British industry the vast Chinese market, that Sir Henry Pottinger, who had negotiated the treaty, was led to make an ill-judged prophecy, boastfully telling the people of Manchester that he had opened to them a market so vast 'that all the mills of Lancashire could not make stocking-stuff sufficient for one of its provinces'. Though this prophecy soon proved to be wildly misplaced, nevertheless the signing of the Treaty of Nanking signalled to the world at large that a new era was dawning in the China trade.

With the supposedly illimitable Chinese market now seemingly in the process of being opened up to world trade, the United States of America, France and Russia lost no time in signing similar treaties with China to that just negotiated by Great Britain.

Hitherto, in the post-1815 period, much of the French exploration in the Pacific had seemed to be primarily concerned with forwarding the interests of the French whaling industry. The close attention paid by the French to New Zealand could be viewed as being aimed at supporting both trading and whaling in the Pacific, but Louis de Freycinet's examination of Shark Bay on the western coast of Australia, during his voyage of 1817–20, was clearly motivated by the observation of his late colleague Péron, during Baudin's voyage, that this bay was of potential promise for French whalers. This was followed by an examination of the islands off the western coast of New Guinea, the all-important task which Baudin had not lived to complete, and shortly afterwards Duperrey, in the course of his 1822–25 voyage, after traversing the north coast of New Guinea, spent a further two weeks at the island of Waigeo, off north-western New Guinea, investigating the anchorages and studying the people. Admittedly, this had been a region of particular interest to France ever since Pierre de Poivre had smuggled spices from islands in that region in the mid-eighteenth century, but these new surveys were sure to raise suspicions in British and Australian minds. While the French might view such exploration as a search for a potentially valuable port-of-call for shipping returning to France from the Pacific either by way of Torres Strait and the northern coast of Australia or via the northern coast of New Guinea, to many Australian and British observers, in that age of sail, all this activity was bound to be suspected as constituting a search for a French foothold in the most vulnerable portion of the Eastern Passage. For this, of course, was still the age of sail, and the Eastern Passage was to remain of vital strategic significance as long as that era lasted.

The possibility of a French base being established in New Zealand led Governor Darling of New South Wales to appoint James Busby as British Resident in New Zealand in order to keep an eye on French activity there, and in 1835 the latter had become concerned on learning that a Frenchman named Baron du Thierry was planning to establish a 'sovereign and independent state' in the Hokianga, in the interior of the Bay of Islands, but it was the involvement of European riff-raff in some inter-tribal fighting in the Bay of Islands which finally persuaded the Colonial Office to intervene. In 1839 Captain William Hobson, in command of HMS *Rattlesnake*, who was already in the area, was appointed Governor, whereupon he negotiated the Treaty of Waitangi in 1840 and then annexed the whole of New Zealand.

At the very time that their ambitions in New Zealand were thus being brought to naught, the French became aware that the benefits and practicality of constructing a canal across the isthmus of Central America were being hotly debated in the Unites States, and they were quick to appreciate that if such a project came to fruition, it promised to bring about a great increase in trade between the western coasts of the American continent and the great markets of mainland Asia. Any such development would greatly benefit some of the islands located in the middle of the Pacific Ocean, which could provide safe harbours, coaling stations and facilities for refitting and provisioning both ships trading with Asia and the whalers operating in that ocean. As Guizot, the French Prime Minister, told the French Chamber of Deputies on 31 March 1843, France needed "points on the globe destined to become commercial centres of trade and navigation, which will prove secure and strong maritime stations, affording harbours and shelter for our shipping, without our being compelled to resort to foreign port.This was precisely what du Petit-Thouars had had in mind during his Pacific voyage of 1836–39, when he had visited the Marquesas and had advocated a French occupation of those islands in order to provide a convenient port-of-call on the route from Chile to China, the French Pacific fleet then being based at Valparaiso in Chile. When he had returned to the Pacific Ocean in 1841, now as an Admiral, he had been instructed to establish a French settlement there as a port-of-call 'for our commerce and above all our whalers'. Having carried out that task he had gone on to Tahiti, where he arrived just after Dr Pritchard, the British missionary and consul, had left for a visit to England, whence he was expected to return with a British guarantee of protection for the island kingdom. The Flemish missionary Moerenhout, his rival for influence on the island, exploited the opportunity afforded by Pritchard's departure to persuade the local chiefs to request the French king to take them and their islands under his protection. Du Petit-Thouars reached Papeete from the Marquesas on 30 August 1842, the day after the signing of the Treaty of Nanking, and he immediately took advantage of Moerenhout's move to pressurise the Tahitian chiefs into signing a document giving France 'external sovereignty' over the islands, and when Pritchard returned in early 1843 and refused to recognise this *fait accompli*, the French expelled him from the archipelago. The French Government accepted their Admiral's unauthorised act, and a dangerous crisis in Anglo-French relations ensued, but the British Government, not wishing to risk war over the issue, was finally compelled to accept the situation.

In 1853 Louis Napoleon expanded upon these gains by annexing New Caledonia, adding the small Isle of Pines the following year, and the Loyalty Islands a decade later. It was these moves that first alerted the Australian colonists to the fact that their days of geographical remoteness from Britain's European rivals, which had hitherto done so much to ensure their security, were now coming to an end. Governor Hobson's annexation of New Zealand had narrowly forestalled the French in those important islands, but in New Caledonia they were there to stay, and the fact that this was soon to become a penal colony made this development doubly unwelcome in Australia.

While the French were thus establishing their own trans-Pacific line of communication between Valparaiso and China, the Americans were busy making a reality of John L. O'Sullivan's call to his countrymen to fulfil their 'Manifest Destiny' by expanding westward to the Pacific Ocean; and soon some Americans were interpreting that slogan to embrace the Pacific Ocean as well. And on 20 March 1838 Lieutenant Charles Wilkes received orders to take command of an expedition that was required, among other things, to survey the Samoan and Fijian archipelagoes, and to make a thorough examination of the Sulu Sea 'to ascertain if there might be a safe route through it that would shorten the passage of American ships going to China'.[7]

Meanwhile, after gaining economic dominance in the Hawaiian Islands, the Americans gave a warning, at the very time that China was being opened to world trade, that they would not accept the annexation of those islands by any other Power. The islands' strategic location on the route to China was too significant for that to be allowed to happen. Then, in 1852, Commodore Perry was ordered to take a squadron of four ships to Japan, which he himself had earlier described as being on 'a route of commerce destined to be of great importance to the United States'. His instructions had noted how the discovery of gold in California had led both to the development of rapid communication across the isthmus of Central America and to the fast settlement of the Pacific coastline of the United States, which had been followed by the introduction of steamships to the trans-Pacific routes, and he was told to seek from the Japanese, who had hitherto excluded themselves from the outside world,[8] the opening of one or more ports for provisioning and trade and the establishment of coaling depots.[9]

In China itself, however, the initial euphoria created by the Treaty of Nanking and the similar treaties that followed between China and the other Western Powers, and by Pottinger's speech at Manchester, soon began to fade, for when the manufacturers and merchants, quite carried away in their enthusiasm, caused cotton piece-goods to pour into the newly opened treaty ports in China, they were shocked to discover that these goods only sold very slowly, causing a disastrous glut, and this was to bring ruin to not a few. For what these traders had overlooked was the fact that China had been self-sufficient in the production of cotton textiles for centuries. The Chinese peasants were satisfied with the local product, and found some of the foreign imports ill-suited to Chinese conditions. It was found, for instance, that the British manufacturers would have to double or treble the amount of cotton in their heaviest products to clothe the Chinese masses according to their needs, in which case these textiles would no longer be competitive in price with the local product.[10] Furthermore, the Chinese peasants were too poor to be able to afford these foreign imports. The East India Company had repeatedly warned that the market for British manufactures in China was a limited one, and those words of caution, regarded as special pleading at the time, were now found to be verified. The truth of those earlier warnings, however, was too much for the traders to accept, and they continued to seek local explanations for the failure of this supposedly limitless market to materialise. One hoped-for remedy was the opening of still more treaty ports, while, from 1851 onwards, the new *likin* system of taxing the inland trade was seized upon as an explanation for the failure of the inland trade to increase.

The Treaty of Nanking was due for revision in 1854, and the mercantile community accordingly pressed not only for the opening of new treaty ports, but also for a footing inland, either on the banks of the Yangtze, or upon the Grand Canal, or both. Hangchow and Soochow, both great centres of consumption, and Chinkiang, located at the crossing of the Yangtze and the Grand Canal, were foremost in their minds. But Palmerston, sensing that the merchants on the spot were showing dangerous signs of frustration, warned that any proposal must be made diplomatically, and must not be accompanied by a naval demonstration which, while it 'might be proper for the purpose of supporting a demand for a redress of a breach of treaty,' would not be justified 'in support of an application for that which her Majesty's Government do not demand as a right, and which the

Chinese Government is at liberty to withhold without giving thereby to this country any just cause of war'.[11]

However, when Sir John Bowring, the Governor of Hong Kong, travelled north with his French and American colleagues to negotiate with the Chinese Government for a revision of the 1842–44 treaties, in accordance with the terms of the Treaty of Nanking, the Chinese refused to respond. And from this point on, the British and French officials on the spot began to believe that a new collision with the Manchu Government was inevitable, The incident which provided the British with the excuse for war was the seizure by the Canton police of the *Arrow*, a Chinese-owned but British-registered vessel flying a British ensign, and the arrest of members of the Chinese crew on charges of smuggling and piracy. The French excuse for war was based upon the arrest and execution of a French missionary bishop in Kwangsi Province. The war coincided with the outbreak of the Taiping rebellion (1850–64), as well as with the 1855–73 Panthay (Mohammedan) revolt in Yunnan Province and the 1855–83 revolt of Miao tribesmen in Kweichow Province. The paradoxical result was that an Anglo-French attack on the Manchu Government's forces, with the implied support of the American and Russian governments, coincided with Anglo-American support for that same Manchu Government's armies in their war against the Taiping rebels.

After the allied Anglo-French forces had seized Canton in June 1858, negotiations for a new peace settlement followed. The ensuing Treaties of Tientsin, in addition to opening eleven new treaty ports and giving foreigners the right to travel in the interior under passports, also allowed foreign ships to trade and patrol on the Yangtze River. For the

British these were crucial concessions, for their great aim was to be able to trade with Szechuan, the richest and most populous province in the Chinese Empire, which was located far in the interior and to which the Yangtze gave direct access through the interior port of Chungking. In addition, the Yangtze was also the artery of the economic life of ten of the eighteen provinces of the Chinese Empire. But these treaties also declared that British and French ministers could reside at Peking on terms of diplomatic equality, and this was something that the Manchu authorities were extremely reluctant to concede, since the presence of Western legations at the capital would bring to an end the ancient Chinese tradition of conducting that Empire's foreign policy on the basis of a patron-client relationship. The Manchus feared that if they agreed to such a humiliating concession, this was likely to be seen by their subjects as a sign that the dynasty no longer enjoyed the 'Mandate of Heaven', and it required further fighting before this demand was finally agreed to by the conventions of Peking (1860). Meanwhile the American and Russian plenipotentiaries who had been accompanying the Anglo-French forces as 'observers' had been able to negotiate almost identical treaties with the Manchus to those concluded by the British and French.

As the Anglo-French armies advanced on Peking, and internal rebellion was rife in various parts of the Chinese Empire, the Manchu Government found itself facing fresh challenges on every side, including pressure from the Russians in the north and north-east, and from the French in the south-west, thus placing China, in the words of a contemporary, 'between the Russian and French upper and nether millstones'. To concentrate on the Russians first, in

1847 the tsar had appointed the young General Muraviev
Governor-General of Eastern Siberia, and the latter quickly
appreciated that the limits imposed by the earlier Treaty of
Nerchinsk (1689) greatly complicated his task. That treaty
had obliged the Russians to relinquish all claims to the river
Amur and the surrounding districts, and this had deprived
the Russians of their easiest means of communication with
their Pacific port of Kamchatka. Those original terms had
been negotiated at a time when the forces of the new Manchu
dynasty in China had been strong in this region and those
of the Russians weak. Now the situation was reversed and
Muraviev was determined to take full advantage of his
opportunity. He began by authorising a naval reconnaissance
of the neighbouring seas, a reconnaissance which revealed
the insularity of Sakhalin, hitherto thought to be a peninsula.

This meant that the Amur could now be reached not only
from the Sea of Okhotsk, ice-bound for several months of
the year, but also from the ice-free waters to the south. This
prompted the Russians, after developing a winter station
at Nikolayevsk on the Amur itself (1850), to establish the
port of Alexaandrovsk (1853) on the west coast of Sakhalin,
commanding the whole lower course of the Amur, while the
tsar also authorised Russian occupation of the whole island
of Sakhalin. Muraviev then established Russian posts along
the northern bank of the upper reaches of the Amur as far
as Khabarovsk, where the Ussuri flows into the Amur. When
Muraviev had opened negotiations with the Chinese in
September 1855, the latter were not only battling with the
advancing Anglo-French armies, but were confronting
the three widespread internal rebellions already referred to.
The Chinese therefore felt compelled to sign the Convention

of Aigun on 16 May 1858, which ceded the north bank of the Amur to Russia, while the region between the Ussuri and the sea was left under joint Sino-Russian possession, pending a definitive decision upon its future status. In the meantime General Nikolai Ignatiev, who was accompanying the advancing Anglo-French armies as an official Russian observer, saw an opportunity, in 1860, to mediate between the two sides. His reward for these services was a Chinese agreement not only to confirm the concessions they had made at the Convention of Aigun, but also to cede to Russia the Maritime Province between the Ussuri and the sea.

Anticipating this outcome, Muraviev had already founded the port and naval base of Vladivostok in this very region.[12]

At the same time as the Russians were thus strengthening their position along the north-eastern frontier of the Chinese Empire and in the neighbouring waters of the Pacific Ocean, they had also been expanding into Central Asia, and after establishing the Russian province of Turkestan in 1865, had then moved into the territory bordering the northern frontier of Afghanistan. As a result, this whole process of Russian expansion now began to worry the British too. In the first place, the establishment of Vladivostok as a base for Russia's Pacific fleet was but the prelude to a search for a port that, unlike Vladivostok, was ice-free all the year round, and this led the Russians to take a close interest in Korea. That interest worried not only Japan but also Great Britain, since it constituted a potential challenge to British predominance in the China trade, as well as to the security of British territories in the Pacific Ocean, including Australia and New Zealand. Likewise, Russian expansion to the borders of Afghanistan was also seen as a potential threat to the security of British

India. Hence from this time onwards, and until the beginning of the twentieth century, Russia was increasingly regarded by the British as their most dangerous rival in the Far East.

The Russian expansion along China's northern and north-eastern frontiers took place at the same time as the French were becoming established to the south-west of the Chinese Empire. This process had begun in the closing decades of the eighteenth century when the French missionary Bishop Pigneau de Béhaine had helped Nguyen Anh to overcome the Tay Son rebellion and establish himself as Emperor Gia Long of Vietnam. That earlier French initiative, however, had come to naught as a result of the outbreak of the French Revolution, whose principles were of no appeal either to Gia Long or to the bishop, and then because of the early death of Pigneau himself from dysentery. In 1858, however, Louis Napoleon had exploited a new opportunity to allow the French to become established in Indo-China. As a result of the Anglo-French campaign against the Manchus, the French Emperor found himself in possession of a fleet in the China Sea at the very moment when the Spaniards in the Philippines were planning an expedition to bring relief to the Christians suffering from persecution at the hands of the Emperor of Annam.[13] French missionaries, too, had been suffering similar persecution in that land, and Napoleon III now saw his opportunity to help the Spaniards to bring this persecution to an end and, in the process, to re-establish a French bridgehead in Annam.

The early loss of Tourane[14] persuaded the Annamese Emperor Tu Duc to agree to a treaty granting religious toleration in his dominions. This satisfied the Spaniards, who thereupon withdrew. But in the same treaty Tu Duc also ceded to France the three eastern provinces of the Mekong delta, where continued resistance then gave the French an excuse to occupy and annex the western provinces as well. What the French were hoping to achieve was to gain commercial access to western China in general, and to Yunnan province in particular, by way of the Mekong River, an ambition that made Anglo-French rivalry in the region certain, since the British, too, after gaining possession of Lower Burma as a result of the Anglo-Burmese War of 1824–26, were also seeking access to that same Chinese market from the west were also seeking access to that same Chinese market from the west. Thus in 1860 the Manchester Chamber of Commerce, backed by Liverpool and Huddersfield, was pressing for surveys to be carried out in order to reveal the various available routes from the west to China, especially by way of Bhamo.[15]

Thus by the 1860s and early 1870s the Chinese Empire was surrounded on every side by nations anxious to have their share of the China trade, and seeing in the supposedly limitless Chinese market the most promising remedy for the insatiable demands of their growing manufacturing industries. And one who was worrying over the implications of all this was Rutherford Alcock, then at the start of what was to prove a distinguished career in the British consular service in the Far East. He was beginning to feel apprehensive as to the likely outcome of the international rivalry that was just starting to become evident in the Orient. He was particularly concerned lest the clash of rival 'commercial and political schemes' should end up in 'attempts at territorial possession' in the Chinese Empire and 'a struggle for superiority on the soil of China for exclusive or predominant influence in

Peking', which might 'embroil the whole of Europe in hostile relations'. In view of developments a generation later, this was indeed a perceptive observation.[16]

In the wake of the discoveries of gold in California (1847) and Australia (1851), as a contemporary observer noted, 'the whole world, industrial, commercial, and financial, beat with one pulse,' and by making money plentiful this sudden influx of gold 'stimulated production in every department of agriculture and manufacture'. This made the potential market of the Chinese Empire still more attractive to the Western Powers, including the United States of America whose shipbuilding industry was making 'the most gigantic advances', its interest being 'particularly directed towards China'.[17] As a consequence of these developments, in Australia itself it was becoming ever more obvious to the people at large that as the world Powers were closing in on the Chinese Empire, so was their own isolation from world affairs increasingly becoming a thing of the past. For the defence of the continent's security from outside interference, the need for a federation of the separate colonies was therefore becoming ever more obvious. The attempt by Earl Grey to hurry on the process in the mid-nineteenth century, however, did not go down well, and it was evident that any successful move in that direction would have to come from within Australia itself. Yet progress to that end was slow.

During the 1860s, however, the international situation became increasingly tense. First, the American Civil War broke out, and Anglo-American relations were put under severe strain, initially as a result of the *Trent* affair,[18] and then over the Confederate Government's being allowed to build or purchase in England six vessels designed to prey upon the sea commerce of the North. Then, in Europe itself Bismarck's intricate stratagems to bring about the unification of Germany were not only threatening to upset the balance of power on the continent, but were also serving to heighten dangerously Franco-German tension. As a result the British Government became increasingly concerned regarding the security of the British Isles, and as part of its countermeasures it recalled the last British garrison to be stationed in Australia, the soldiers concerned sailing from Sydney on 23 August 1870.

One Australian who was similarly worried about the implications of these developments for the safety of his own continent was Charles Gavan Duffy, the Premier of Victoria, but it was indicative of Australian perceptions at that time that he believed that the chief threat to Australian security came from France and the United States of America. 'Britain might still be "mistress of the seas" and able to protect her commerce and ours,' he told a Royal Commission in 1870 when the question of Australian Federation was once more coming to the fore, 'but France and America have been making enormous expenditure and immense exertions for years past so as to be in a position to compete for this supremacy'.[19] He suggested that the need for federation was beginning to become urgent, and in view of recent French and American expansion in the Pacific Ocean this Australian suspicion of those two Powers was understandable, but in reality a new and as yet unperceived source of danger and rivalry was about to be revealed.

Chapter Nine

THE GERMAN EMPIRE BECOMES A FACTOR IN FAR EASTERN POLITICS

What Charles Gavan Duffy, the premier of Victoria, had not anticipated – and who had? – was the sudden appearance of Germany as a new world power. Even as Duffy spoke, the political environment was undergoing further drastic change, in a series of short successful wars against Denmark (1864), Austria (1866) and France (1870–71) Prussia, under Bismarck's leadership, had brought about the unification of Germany and the formation of the German Empire. This entailed a drastic change in the balance of power in Europe, and the world had to become accustomed to long-lasting Franco-German hostility as a result of Germany's acquisition of Alsace-Lorraine in the wake of the late war. This latter circumstance meant that for the rest of his political career, Bismarck's foremost preoccupation was his continuing attempt to prevent Germany's eastern and western neighbours, Russia and France, from overcoming their present mutual antipathy and agreeing to form an anti-German alliance. He had seen an initial chance to gain Russian goodwill when, in the aftermath of France's defeat, Russia had seized her opportunity to announce the abrogation of the Black Sea clauses of the Treaty of Paris of 1856. Bismarck had thereupon signified his support of Russia, had encouraged her to concentrate upon her eastward expansion into Central Asia and the Far East which was already under way, and had then consolidated the advantage thus gained by initiating the formation of the League of the Three Emperors[1] in 1873.

Russia's eastward expansion, however, was bound to arouse British fears over the future security of her Indian empire and her dominant position in the China trade, for how could a sea power like Britain defend her interests against a land-power colossus like Russia? There were other reasons, too, for British concern over recent developments in Germany, In the immediate aftermath of the 1870–71 war there had been a wild and dramatic economic boom, but at the end of 1873 this boom had been followed by an equally dramatic collapse, and by 1875–76 economic stagnation had intensified to the point where there was almost a complete paralysis, a situation made still worse by a series of poor harvests followed by the crop failure of 1876. A generation earlier the German economist Friedrich List, in his book *The National System of Political Economy*, first published in 1841, had challenged the worldwide applicability of the free trade doctrines which were then taking root in England, and which, in view of Britain's great lead in industrial development, were being widely seen as the secret of her success, and therefore widely copied. Cobden, the leader of the so-called Manchester school, had believed that free trade was of worldwide relevance, and that its adoption everywhere would bring in its train general prosperity and international peace. List, however, stressed that Britain had only achieved her world dominance in industry and commerce by having earlier relied upon monopolistic trading companies, protective tariffs and protective navigation laws. It was only when a nation 'by means of protective duties and restrictions [had] raised her manufacturing power and her navigation to such a degree of development that no other nation [could] sustain a competition with her' that she could then afford 'to throw away those ladders to her greatness, [and] preach the benefits of free trade,' he argued. Prussia, while still 'imperfectly prepared for manufacturing industry,' had achieved national prosperity by following 'the prohibitory system so condemned by theorists,' and List prophesied that it would be centuries hence before 'universal association and absolute free trade may be realised.'[2] These ideas of List came to seem increasingly attractive to Germans in the late 1870s, and in 1879 Bismarck himself changed tack by abandoning the free trade policies that he had hitherto followed in favour of a protective tariff on agricultural and industrial products.

For some years hitherto colonial expansion had been out of favour, overseas possessions having come to be regarded as entailing the assumption of new and expensive responsibilities without any commensurate reward, but the less favourable international climate now evident was bringing about a change of attitude, and both France and Germany, in 1873, were seeking to expand their interests in the Orient. That was the year that the French, after ascertaining that the Mekong river was unnavigable in its upper reaches, switched their attention to the Red River as a means of reaching China's south-western province of Yunnan, and had begun the process of conquering the Red River delta area. As for the Germans, who had been actively trading in the Pacific since the 1850s, in March 1873 a German warship, the *Nymphe*, on its way to the island of Sulu (modern Jolo), had called in at the island of Labuan, off the north-western coast of Borneo, a British possession since 1846 when it had been ceded by the Sultan of Brunei as a base from which to suppress piracy. The German commander was visiting the island in order to ask the Governor whether Great Britain could be relied upon to support a German challenge to Spanish claims of sovereignty over the Sultanate of Sulu. No answer was forthcoming, as the governor was in no position to speak for the Foreign Office, but it would have been highly unlikely for a German naval officer to ask such a question on his own authority. After leaving Labuan, the *Nymphe* sailed on to Sulu and on 9 June 1873 the acting British consul in Manila was reporting that the Sultan of Sulu had offered to place his dominions under the German flag in return for German protection against Spain.[3] It is no wonder that notwithstanding Bismarck's oft-repeated assertion that he was 'not a colonial man', there were strong suspicions in Britain that he was contemplating the establishment of a German settlement in that region.

In the event, it was not the Sulu Archipelago but the region of New Guinea that was to become the focus of German attention. German planters and traders were already active in north-eastern New Guinea which was an area not yet claimed by any Western Power, and Australians in general, and Queenslanders in particular, began to feel increasingly uneasy over this situation. The last British garrison had been withdrawn from Australia in 1870 with little publicity, but now the Australians, like the British, denials notwithstanding, began to suspect that Bismarck was beginning to harbour colonial ambitions in the area. When the British Cabinet decided, on 6 August 1884, to meet Australian concern over eastern New Guinea by making that region a British Protectorate, Granville, the Foreign Secretary, decided to get the German ambassador to confirm that the projected British move would not clash with German claims.

Lord Derby, the Colonial Secretary, rightly judged this to be a false move. 'If Bismarck objects and we don't give way,' he observed, 'we are in an awkward position with him; if he objects and we do give way, the rage of the Australians will exceed all bounds. If he does not object, have we gained much?.'[4] Granville, however, had his way and thus played into Bismarck's hands. The German *chargé d'affaires* duly protested against Britain's proposed move, whereupon Granville came up with a compromise whereby the British protectorate was to be limited to the south-eastern portion of New Guinea, and this was proclaimed on 6 November 1884, with the German protectorate over the north-eastern regions following shortly afterwards. The Australians were, as predicted, furious, as was the Colonial Office, and Joseph Chamberlain, in a speech in Birmingham on 5 January 1885, noted how the German move had 'produced feelings of the deepest irritation and alarm' in Australia, adding, 'it does not need a prophet to predict that in the course of the next half-century the Australian colonies will have attained such a position that no Power will be strong enough to ignore them, and that they will have a supreme authority in the Pacific seas, and, for my part, I cannot look with any confidence on any settlement which may be made in those regions in defiance of their united opposition'.[5]

Growing hostility did not deter the Germans, however, who rounded off their acquisition of north-eastern New Guinea and the Bismarck Archipelago[6] by further annexing, in 1885, the western part of the Solomon Islands[7] and, to the north-east of the Solomons, the Marshall Islands; and they even made an unsuccessful bid for the Carolines. Nevertheless, this short phase of German colonial expansion was coming to an end, for Bismarck was discovering that he had been misinformed when he had been led to believe that he could pursue a colonial policy without adding to the financial burdens of the State.

There had already been signs of increasing Franco-German friction, with the French ambassador warning Paris of his belief that in order to complete her industrial development and her continental policy, Germany would inevitably be led to absorb Holland and the Dutch Empire, bribing France with Belgium as her own prize. This not only echoed similar warnings sent back to London from Lord Lyons, the British ambassador at Paris,[8] but was like the policy advocated by List a generation earlier when he wrote, 'Holland is, by her geographical position, by her commercial and industrial relations, by the origin of her inhabitants and their language, a German province ... which needs now to reincorporated ... Holland belongs to Germany as much as Brittany and Normandy belong to France.'[9]

For Australians, however, a new shock was in store, the Anglo-German tension over New Guinea being immediately followed by an acute Anglo-Russian crisis that had its origins in the Russian expansion into Central Asia. In February 1884 the Russians had occupied Merv, a territory that was supposedly under the suzerainty of the Amir of Afghanistan. Both the Russians and the Afghans wanted the relatively fertile Pandjeh valley, and it was here that they came into collision in March 1885, when the Russians expelled some Afghan troops with heavy losses on the Afghan side. Hitherto people in London had joked about 'Mervousness', but this military clash suddenly changed everything. Now there was a widespread fear in England that the Russians intended to advance on Herat, which had long been regarded as of key strategic significance for the defence of India. 'Near Herat,' said Sir T. H. Holdich, a frontier surveyor, 'there exists the only break in the otherwise continuous and formidable wall of mountains which traverse Asia from the Bering Strait to the Caspian Sea. Near Herat it is possible to pass from the Russian outposts ... to India without encountering any formidable altitude – and this is possible nowhere else'.[10] The fear in Britain was not of a full-scale invasion, but of an incursion sufficiently powerful to encourage dissident elements in the subcontinent to rise up and endeavour to overthrow British authority, confident that they could be assured of large-scale Russian support. The Gladstone ministry therefore instructed Governor-General Lord Dufferin to make ready a military force to march from India to the relief of Herat, and at the same time promised him further reinforcements. In Britain, where there was much talk of a European war, the reserves were called up, while the Admiralty, in anticipation of such a war, established a naval base, Port Hamilton, on an island off the south-west coast of Korea, in the Korea Strait, which would be valuable in any operations against the Russian fleet in Vladivostok. And Australians were well aware of the fact that Vladivostok was within fourteen days' sailing time of their own country. They could now see that the danger of war was coming ever closer to their own shores.

At the same time, trouble was also brewing in south-western China and in the neighbouring regions. During his time as Prime Minister of France, Jules Ferry was an enthusiast for colonial expansion, while the new monarch of Burma, King Thibaw, was a man anxious to develop closer ties with Europe, and especially with France, as a means of countering Britain's dominating influence over his country's affairs. In May 1883, Thibaw therefore sent a mission to Europe, and this mission headed straight for Paris, where its stay was a prolonged one. This prompted the British to warn Ferry that though Upper Burma was an independent country, it was, in their view, located within the British sphere of influence, and that no interference in that kingdom from any other European Power would be tolerated. Ferry was therefore asked to give assurances that if a Franco-Burmese treaty was concluded, no facilities would be granted for the purchase of arms, and this he readily agreed to. Yet in January 1884, the mission was still in Paris, and four months later a French consul arrived in Mandalay, and it became obvious that very extensive concessions had been granted to the French. It was even believed that these were designed to give the French a dominating position in the Kingdom's economy, and though Sir Charles Bernard, the Chief Commissioner, was sceptical about this, he did tell the Viceroy, 'I believe this much, that French agents are trying to establish themselves strongly at

Mandalay with a view to joining hands at some future time with the French possessions on the upper reaches of the Red River.'[11]

In August 1885, the text of a secret letter, which had been signed in Paris in January and then handed by Ferry to the Burmese envoy during the signing of the commercial treaty, was leaked in Mandalay. This contained a cautiously worded promise that arms and military stores of all kinds would be delivered to Upper Burma from Tongking, once the latter province had been pacified.

Meanwhile, Ferry had fallen from power on 31 March as a result of a sharp reverse for French troops in the course of an unofficial war with China, and though the succeeding French Government inevitably claimed complete ignorance of the whole affair, the British authorities decided to wait no longer, but to annex Upper Burma in January 1886.[12] Burma might seem a long way away, but those Australian leaders who were particularly focused upon their continent's future security could not fail to sense that these developments in the years 1884–86 suggested that Britain might well be facing sharp rivalry from Russia, France and Germany in the Far East and the Pacific in the near future.

It was therefore clearly time to begin paying much closer attention to the matter of defence. In Britain itself, the *Pall Mall Gazette* ran a series of articles designed to awaken its readers to the inadequacies of the Royal Navy. With a national growth since 1870 of 40 per cent in trade and wealth, and 30 per cent in shipping, as well as an enormous extension in the area of her colonial possessions, it reported, Britain was spending less on the Navy than she had spent in 1868. In the meantime the expenditure of other countries, and especially of France, had greatly increased. On the China station Britain was immeasurably weaker than France. On the Pacific station she was weaker than either Chile or Brazil. Some of her most important home ports could be destroyed immediately upon war being declared.' And the journal went on to assert that not only did France have more sailors and a far larger naval reserve than Britain, but whereas 'at the end of the year our 24 first-class torpedo boats would be scattered all over the world, France would have 50, a large portion of which she could concentrate in Far Eastern waters, while Germany was building 70.'[13] These were startling assertions and the debate on the Navy Estimates in 1886 showed that there were real grounds for concern, when Lord Charles Beresford provided Parliament with a factual analysis of the state of the Royal Navy and agreed that France was moving ahead of Britain. In detailing the number of ships that he believed were required at the main naval stations, he recommended that 12 cruisers be allotted to the China station, which 'sounded a great many', he agreed, 'but the French had 17 vessels in Chinese waters.' For Australians, whose security was dependent upon Britain's maritime supremacy, this was a stark warning that the whole basis of their continent's future development had to be thought about anew. The world around them was rapidly changing, and if their future was to be secured, their parochial attitudes would have to change too.

While the British were thus beginning to worry about their navy, the Germans were likewise becoming concerned about their army. Moltke, Chief of the German General Staff until 1888, had been watching the military revival of France with concern, particularly her construction of a great belt of fortifications along her north-eastern frontiers which would make it impossible for the German army to repeat the tactics that had given it rapid victory in 1870. Like Bismarck, Moltke was very concerned that the German Empire might find itself confronted by a Franco-Russian alliance and a war on two fronts, and it was very disturbing that, since the late 1870s, Russia had been maintaining in her western military areas an army which the German and Austrian staffs, who, since 1882, had been unofficially coordinating their plans to deal with this threat, calculated to number some 600,000 men.[14]

It was just a year later that Lord Wolseley decided to speak out and to stress that Great Britain herself was as unprepared militarily as she was with her navy for self-defence in an increasingly threatening world. Back from the Sudan and now Adjutant-General, his speech at a public banquet was a deliberate breach of protocol. He suggested that 'the long statements made from time to time by the gentlemen in power' had more to do with 'the party exigencies of the moment' than with the real opinions of the First Lord of the Admiralty and the Secretary of State for War. 'We see,' he warned, 'all the great nations of Europe – with the one exception of England – armed to the teeth, [and] as you look around on the political horizon of Europe, you can gather nothing promising from it. Storms threaten.' The current state of Britain's army, he warned, was very unsatisfactory, and he concluded by suggesting that 'if a hostile force of, say, 100,000 men were to land upon our shores, there is no reason why that force, properly led, should not take possession of London'[15]

The ominous political landscape to which General Wolseley had referred was highlighted in the following month, when the completion of the final section of the Trans-Caspian Railway to Samarkand was made the occasion for the publication of some articles aimed at the British. One by M. Valzlik saw the Russian Colossus encircling Central and Eastern Asia and posing a threat to India. 'This great enterprise,' he wrote, 'called into existence by military requirements, affords the means of rapidly transporting Russian troops into the heart of Central Asia.' And operating from half-a-dozen bases, among which Merv and Pendjeh were specifically mentioned, he stressed how resources and supplies could be stored and rapidly pushed on from all sides in the direction of India, Afghanistan or Persia. 'Thus in a comparatively short space of time,' he wrote, 'an army of 100,000 men could be concentrated at the scene of action.' Another writer was General Soboloff, formerly Russian Prime Minister of Bulgaria, who thought it very possible that the Hindu Kush and Herat would soon become Russian possessions. To prevent a Russian invasion of India, the British would be compelled to maintain a permanent army of some 500,000 men in the area.

A far better solution for both sides, he suggested, was for the Russians to enter into an understanding, whereby Russia would be left free to pursue her policy in Eastern Europe, in return for a Russian engagement not to attack the British in India.[16]

It was against this increasingly ominous political background that General Edwards reached Australia in 1889 to carry out his inspection of the defences and defence plans of the Australian colonies. When this work had been completed he submitted separate reports to each of the Australian colonies, with his conclusions regarding the defence measures of each, together with an overall report in which he made it abundantly clear that the situation in Europe demanded that Australia's defence forces be put on a proper footing, which was 'quite impossible without a federation of the forces of the different colonies'.[17]

While the Australians were thus taking hesitant first steps towards Federation, the situation in Europe continued to deteriorate, with France and Russia slowly drawing closer together, while Bismarck, who shared Moltke's forebodings, and was worried by the growing political influence of the rabidly anti-German French nationalism of General Boulanger, was seeking, at one and the same time, to assure his own political future and to add to Germany's already formidable military might. In order to protect himself from the liberal views of the Crown Prince, who was shortly expected to succeed the ailing Emperor William I, then nearing his ninetieth birthday, Bismarck planned to bring about an early election, relying on the electors to vote down his liberal opponents, but in the event both the old Emperor and his successor died within weeks of each other, thus bringing to the throne the youthful and ambitious William II, usually known to the British as the Kaiser, who soon dismissed Bismarck. At the same time Bismarck's Army Bill, which provided for a huge increase in the number of men to be put under arms in the event of war, caused alarm both in Paris and at St Petersburg, and in time was to pave the way for the very Franco-Russian alliance which Bismarck had always dreaded more than anything else. Another factor which was drawing those two countries closer together was the fact that at the very time when the German banks were cutting down on loans to Russia, the French were investing heavily in the Russian army, the Russian railways, and in Russian development in general.[18]

The British, too, were worried by the tightening Franco-Russian bonds. Russia was not only building up a considerable fleet, but was, above all, a land-power which possessed immense sources of manpower and was essentially impervious to sea power. This situation was to lead Sir Halford J. Mackinder, a little later, to produce his influential paper entitled 'The geographical pivot of history', in which he argued that the age of dominant sea power was over, while that of land power had arrived. The vast area embracing the interior of Asia and eastern Europe, an area he called the Heartland and one which was now covered by railways, was about to become, he believed, the pivotal region of world politics. The French, for their part, had not forgotten their eviction from the government of Egypt in 1882, and in January 1893 Théophile Delcassé, the newly appointed Under-secretary of Commerce, Industry and Colonies, had attended a lecture given by a French hydrologist who argued that the construction of a great dam at Fashoda, some 500 miles south of Khartoum on the Upper Nile would be the key to the mastery of Egypt, for whoever controlled the dam would be the master of the Nile, and able to flood Egypt or deny it water at will.[19] This was a concept which both the French and the British came to believe to be practicable, and henceforth Delcassé was determined to put it to the test. Four months later an acute Anglo-French crisis erupted over Siam. For years, the French had been trying to extend their dominions in French Indo-China westward to the Mekong River, but this was a region over which the Siamese had traditionally claimed suzerainty, whereas the French claimed that it had formerly been under Vietnam, and was therefore now rightfully theirs. Britain supported Siam, which she wanted to remain as a buffer between British Burma and French Indo-China. However, border clashes in May 1893 had led the French to send gunboats to Bangkok, and when the Siamese fired upon these the French issued an ultimatum. A short but severe Anglo-French crisis ensued before the British Government decided to let the French have their way. As a result, France signed a treaty with Siam on 3 October 1893, and thus acquired a Protectorate over Laos.

The ever-closer ties between France and Russia were epitomised by the visit of a French fleet to Kronstadt on 24 July 1891, when 'frantic demonstrations' of Franco-Russian friendship were reported, which was followed by the visit of a Russian squadron to Toulon, on 13 October 1893, when 'wild demonstrations of affection for Russia' were reported to have taken place in various parts of France. The Russian crews, it was stated, 'became the objects of unceasing fêtes and ovations,' and 'enormous crowds assembled in Paris, Lyons, Marseilles, and Toulon' to greet them. In view of Britain's poor relations with both these Powers, these events were viewed with unease across the Channel.[20] In a debate on 19 December 1893 on a motion demanding that 'a considerable addition should be made to the Navy', Lord George Hamilton stated that Britain's 'command of the sea was in jeopardy, not immediate, but prospective, with France and Russia combined having under construction

17 first-class battleships, with a total tonnage of 196,000 tons ... as against 3 for England with a total displacement of 42,000 tons ... [and] so enormous had been the progress of France and Russia, that in the course of next year they would have 21 armoured ships under construction, or half the available navy of Great Britain.' Joseph Chamberlain, for his part, asserted that 'for the first time we were putting our national life at the mercy of a combination between France and Russia.'[21]

Germany, too, was showing signs of apprehension, and in 1892 Caprivi, who had succeeded Bismarck as Chancellor in March 1890, introduced a new Army Bill to boost the strength of the German army, arguing that France and Russia were each able to put very large armies in the field, and that 'in all probability, a military arrangement existed between them.' The long eastern frontiers of the German Empire, Caprivi told the Reichstag, 'could only be protected by offensive tactics. Good policy meant short wars, with quick victories and lasting results. All this could only be attained by assuming the offensive.' This Bill was finally passed on 14 July 1893.[22]

Although these developments were occurring in far-away Europe, they could not fail to be of concern for thoughtful citizens in Australia. For all these countries were also their powerful neighbours in China and the Pacific, and these large-scale military and naval rearmament programmes threatened a major war in the not-too-distant future. But for the moment the Australians themselves were soon to become obsessed by the great economic and financial crisis which had been seriously affecting the economies of the leading Powers of the Western world since the mid-1870s, but whose full impact only began to be felt in Australia itself in 1893 as it began to spread throughout all the Australian colonies, 'shaking the public credit,' wrote one observer, 'dislocating trade and industry, disturbing the calculations of the Treasurers, and seriously affecting all the producing interests'. No such calamity had occurred in the colonies for half-a-century, and the widespread banking failures were 'bringing incalculable loss and distress to nearly every class and every household. Some adventurous spirits, knowing that gold had been discovered at the Witwatersrand in the Transvaal in 1886, decided to try their luck in that Boer republic. Some one thousand mostly young Australians are estimated to have been involved in that move which resulted in many Australians back home coming to visualise the new city of Johannesburg as though it were almost another Australian city.[23]

The outbreak of the Sino-Japanese War on 25 July 1894 and the rapid series of Japanese naval and military successes that followed took all the Western Powers by surprise, and the immediate fear was that the Chinese Empire might be on the verge of breaking up. As all the major Western Powers trading in China except Great Britain followed protectionist economic policies, and were industrialising fast, from a British perspective the fear was that the Chinese Empire might be divided up between these protectionist Powers, with the British, still the leaders in the China trade, suffering the greatest loss of potential markets. The war, however, had come to an end in February 1895, to be followed by the signing of the Treaty of Shimonoseki on 17 April, and a mere six days later Russia, France and Germany had intervened to 'advise' Japan to relinquish her acquisition of the Liaotung Peninsula, in southern Manchuria, in return for an increased war indemnity. Japan had felt compelled to agree. It may well be, of course, that Germany's decision to join in this Intervention had more to do with her desire to remain on good terms with her powerful eastern and western well-armed neighbours in Europe than with the situation in China itself, nevertheless it marked the moment when Germany ceased to be essentially a nation of traders operating among the various island groups of the Pacific Ocean and henceforth became a powerful player in the politics of the Chinese Empire.

The recent war had dramatically exposed China's increased vulnerability through her lack of railways. In earlier days British traders had tried to interest the myopic Manchu dynasty in this development of the Industrial Revolution, but to no avail. Shortly before the war Li Hung-chang, as Viceroy of Chihli province, had exploited the fear of the court for its own safety to get something done. On 15 March 1887, he had submitted a Memorial to the throne in which he had stated, 'The northern and southern garrisons are too widely separated, and it would be difficult to come to the rescue in time of need. On the portion of the seacoast nearest to Peking, from Taku and Pehtang northwards for a distance of 500 *li*[24] the garrisons are few in number, and the gaps between them are a great source of danger. If they were united by a line of railway, in case of emergency troops despatched in the morning could arrive at their post in the evening, the soldiers of one garrison would suffice for the protection of several places, and the cost of maintaining the army could be greatly reduced.' Li Hung-chang knew the panic-stricken temper of his court, and the necessary sanction soon followed![25]

Now in the aftermath of the disastrous Sino-Japanese War, Chang Chih--tung, the Viceroy of Hunan-Hupei, felt emboldened to go much further. 'The powerful foreign nations stand armed,' he warned, 'watching for their opportunity, and making use of trivial pretexts ... swiftly despatch their warships from one end of the empire to the other. It is impossible to say when our communication by sea may be blockaded, and the establishment of internal communication by railway has become a necessity.'[26]

France and Russia were the first to exploit this new opportunity. In June 1895 they supplied China with a loan wherewith to pay the war indemnity to Japan, and on 25 June 1895, the new Franco-Chinese Convention gave first preference to French commerce and engineers for the development of Yunnan, Kwangsi and Kwangtung, and of the mines therein. It was also agreed that railways which were already in existence or were planned in Annam, which was now a French Protectorate, could be extended into Chinese territory.[27]

It was Russia's turn next. Hung-chang had gone to Russia to represent China at the coronation of Tsar Nicholas II, and the Russians took the opportunity to negotiate an agreement with him, on 3 June 1896, whereby, in return for a fifteen-year secret military alliance between the two empires against Japan, China granted Russia the right to build and operate the Chinese Eastern Railway across northern Manchuria, as a link connecting with Russia's Trans-Siberian Railway to Vladivostok. This would not only reduce the distance from Moscow to Vladivostok by some 350 miles, but would also save the Russians from having to undertake the construction of many expensive tunnels and bridges across difficult terrain. In preparation for the conclusion of such an agreement, Witte, the Russian Finance Minister and the force behind the construction of the Trans-Siberian Railway, had given a charter, in December 1895, to the Russo-Chinese Bank, whose capital was, significantly, largely supplied by French banks, and which was given unusual authority, being empowered to collect taxes, finance local government, and secure commercial and industrial concessions.

The gathering German challenge to Britain's position in the world was, at this very time, given great publicity by the publication of a series of articles in *News Review* in England in the course of the first six months of 1896, articles that were later to appear in book form under the title *Made in Germany*. The author, Ernest Williams, was determined to awaken his countrymen to the need to abandon *laissez-faire*, as Germany had done, in order to maintain Britain's position in world business. The book was very well researched, powerfully argued and well written, and the author's theme was that almost everywhere in the world German business was menacing British trade. By the summer of 1896 the British press was full of the book.[28] Was it mere coincidence that it was at this very moment that in Australia the Mayor of Bathurst was establishing the Bathurst Federation League and arranging for the convening of the Bathurst Federal Convention?[29] Australians could not overlook the fact that their own security was dependent upon British naval supremacy which, in turn rested, in the last resort, upon Britain's industrial supremacy in the world, a supremacy which, it could now be seen, was under a real and growing challenge.

Then, as the year 1897 dawned, a new German threat was brought to light. On 1 January 1897, the *Sydney Morning Herald* published extracts from an article that was both from an authoritative source and deeply worrying. The author, Baron Lüttwitz, was an officer on the German General Staff, and the original article had appeared in what was described as 'a semi-official paper'. The baron was emphasising the great opportunities that awaited Germany with 'the opening of China' But to take advantage of these new opportunities, Germany would need colonies and a fleet with which to defend them. This would inevitably entail rivalry with Great Britain, and his proposed strategy for tackling Britain's worldwide naval supremacy was very similar to that of Napoleon in 1805, when the latter had sought to wrest temporary control of the English Channel for long enough to enable him to land his projected invading army on English soil. In the present case, argued Lüttwitz, Germany would need to possess 'a strong fleet of battleships, able to protect our North Sea ports from blockade,' and at the same time capable of going 'in quest of the enemy and [keeping] them in check while the conveyance of the transport fleet to the Island Kingdom is proceeded with'. To make the scheme work, he argued, 'Our navy must be of sufficient strength, after allowing for our cruisers on foreign shores, to cope successfully with those English squadrons which are in their own home waters ... England cannot, under present political conditions, altogether leave her other spheres of interest to take care of themselves, and ... there will, at the beginning of the war, be rapid and probably decisive actions, in which distant fleets will not be able to take part.' That this was indeed a part of official policy was made evident when the Kaiser, in that same year, stated that Germany needed a strong battlefleet based on Heligoland which at any moment could leave its base for the Channel and threaten English coastal towns, while British sea power was busy in the Mediterranean or perhaps simultaneously against Russia in Far Eastern waters.[30]

The Sino-Japanese War had radically altered the situation in China. Not only was the China trade ceasing to be primarily a trade dominated by the Western Powers, but the rapid defeat of China had unexpectedly opened up the prospect of the possible falling apart of the Chinese Empire. Hence there soon began an international scramble for concessions, beginning with the German seizure of Kiaochow Bay with its port of Tsingtao in November 1897, followed by the Russian occupation of Port Arthur and Talienwan (or Dairen) in the Liaotung Peninsula in March 1898, as well as her gaining the right to construct a railway linking those ports with the Chinese Eastern Railway at what was to become the city of Harbin. This meant that for the first time Europe was linked to China by rail, thus offering a serious challenge to all the shipping companies connecting Europe with the Far East. Then the British leased Kowloon, opposite Hong Kong, as well as Wei-hai-wei, which they intended to hold as long as the Russians occupied Port Arthur, and they also forced the Chinese to recognise the Yangtze Valley as a British sphere of influence. Finally, France leased Kwang-chou-Kwang Bay, and marked out China's three south-western provinces as her own special sphere of influence.

While the European Powers were thus seeking to protect their economic interests in the region, should the Chinese Empire break apart, a Chinese reformer named K'ang Yu-wei was making a desperate effort to bring about the reforms that China so urgently needed, and having managed to win over the young Emperor to his ideas, on 10 June 1898, a programme of hasty radical reforms began, On 20 September, however, when the conservatives learned of a plot to remove the Empress Dowager, the arch conservative, they decided that the moment for counteraction had arrived, and on the following day the Emperor was detained and the Empress Dowager took over the control of the administration. The so-called One Hundred Days of Reform were over, as was the last chance of the Manchu dynasty to save itself from ultimate destruction.

The Associated Chambers of Commerce of Great Britain had become worried over recent events in China and decided, on 1 August 1898, to invite Lord Charles Beresford to undertake the task of preparing a comprehensive report on the situation there. This was a good choice, for after a distinguished naval career he had taken to politics, his Irish title enabling him to sit in the House of Commons, and it was felt that his standing would give him ready access to all likely sources of information, while his naval past would help him in assessing how far British merchants could rely on adequate protection being given by the Chinese authorities. Beresford arrived in Hong Kong on 30 September 1898 and spent October in visits to Shantung province and the Peking area, November in visiting Manchuria, Wei-hei-wei and Shanghai, and early December in touring the lower Yangtze valley, and the latter part of the month in visiting the treaty ports of Kowchow,

Amoy, Swatow, Hong Kong and Canton. In the course of this three months' tour he came across further worrying evidence of French activity and ambitions. To treat the three south-western provinces of China as a French sphere of influence ignored the fact that the trade of Kwangsi consisted mainly of British, German and American products.

Furthermore, the French were very active in surveying for a railway in Szechuan province, 'and these surveyors have openly declared,' he wrote, 'that if the spheres of influence policy is adopted, they would certainly regard Szechuan as within France's sphere of influence.' Yet this populous and prosperous province had long been the ultimate goal of the British traders working their way up the Yangtze. More worrying still was the fact that the French had a perfect pretext for intervention. For a brigand leader in that province named Yu Mau Tsu had 'come home with his bands, totalling some 10,000 men laden with the spoils of all the rich Catholics of Central Szechuan, after having burned down some 4,000 houses, including some 30 mission chapels, and after having left some 20,000 Catholics homeless and destitute. All the property thus destroyed belonged to the French Catholic mission'.[31]

Apart from the rivalry with the French and the Russians, both for Great Britain and for Australia, the challenge posed by the Kaiser's Germany was more acute than had been the case with Bismarck's German Empire, for the Kaiser, an avid reader of Mahan's works on sea power, intended that Germany should become a major player on the world scene, backed by a navy powerful enough to challenge the Royal Navy of Great Britain. Furthermore. a more aggressive nationalism was now being displayed, though even as early as 1875

Sir Robert Morier, an English diplomat, had been warning his friend, the Crown Prince, about the dangerous new German chauvinism that was already in evidence, describing it as 'methodical, calculating, cold-blooded and self-centred'. Twelve years later these sentiments were echoed by Austen Chamberlain, the eldest son of Joseph Chamberlain and the future Foreign Secretary who negotiated the 1925 Treaty of Locarno. He attended Treitshke's lectures as a student in the winter of 1887–88, and he described them as revealing 'a narrow-minded, proud, intolerant, Prussian chauvinism'.

For the future of Anglo-German relations, it was ominous for contemporaries to know that Admiral Tirpitz, who was appointed Secretary of State of the Imperial Navy Department in June 1897, and von Bülow, who simultaneously became Secretary of State for Foreign Affairs, were both devotees of Treitschke, who had just died the year before. Tirpitz remembered him as that 'wonderful man whose lectures I attended at the university from 1876 onwards and who allowed me to seek his advice privately'. These lectures had become famous and were attended by students from all the university's faculties, as well as by members of the general public from all walks of life.

Though almost totally deaf, Treitschke had been a member of the Reichstag from 1871 to 1884, and it was there that he had been disheartened to observe the decline of the patriotic movement. It was to rectify this that he wrote his major publication, the five-volume nationalistic and unfinished *History of Germany in the Nineteenth Century*. He wanted to see Germany become a great colonial power, and, like Friedrich List before him, is reported to have suggested in one of his lectures that Germany would be compelled to annex Holland, which would, of course, also entail the acquisition of the Dutch East Indies. He had concluded that for success in such a struggle Germany would have to destroy Britain's naval supremacy, and he believed that this would only be attainable if Germany was under authoritarian rule. His emphasis on the need for the strong state echoed, in the political sphere, the stress of the philosopher Nietzsche upon the need for a superman. 'It is the highest duty of the State to increase its power,' wrote Treitschke. 'Every person ought to be prepared to sacrifice himself for the State because it is more enduring than himself ... Only great and powerful States ought to exist.' He also glorified war, decrying calls for perpetual peace as an illusion supported by those of weak character. 'God will see to it that wars always recur as a drastic medicine for the human race,' he chillingly declared, further stating that 'Our age is an age of iron; if the strong vanquishes the weak, it is the law of life.'

A further ominous ingredient was about to be added to the German nationalism of the late nineteenth century when Houston Stewart Chamberlain published his *The Foundations of the Nineteenth Century* in 1899, a work that quickly became favourite reading of the Kaiser himself, who arranged for its widespread dissemination among army officers, and its issue to many public libraries. This work sought to interpret European history as one of racial struggle, and he promoted the doctrine of Aryan supremacy, though not confining the Aryan race to those of German descent.[32]

Britain's struggle to keep the sea-lanes to the Orient free from intervention by potentially hostile forces was far from over.

In the meantime a crisis over the control of Samoa had erupted between the USA, Britain and Germany, which eventually led to the USA taking control of eastern Samoa, with its harbour of Pago Pago, and an Anglo-German treaty, signed on 14 November 1899, whereby the British, a month after the outbreak of the Boer War, withdrew from the area, leaving Western Samoa to the Germans, in return for a British takeover of the Solomons, less the islands of Buka and Bougainville, which remained under German control, being the islands closest to the Bismarck Archipelago. The Tonga group and Savage Island (Nieue) also went to Britain. These changes had been brought about to counteract the German presence in islands close to the sea-lanes between Australia and China. Joseph Chamberlain told the Australian colonies that this Protectorate had been undertaken 'to prevent the injury to Australian interests that would have resulted from their 'passing under the control of a foreign Power,' and that these islands would now be dependent upon Australian capital and enterprise for their development, adding that it was desirable, therefore, 'that the responsibility for administration should rest with the Australian colonies and should be conducted in accordance with Australian rather than English ideas.'[33]

Then, in the aftermath of her loss of the Philippine Islands, Spain sold the Caroline Islands together with the Palau Islands and the Mariana (or Ladrone) Islands to Germany on 2 June 1899. By gaining control of these island groups which were, once again, close to Australia's main line of communications with China, Germany was more than making up for what she was giving up in the Solomons. This was occurring at the very time when Australian voters were about to decide upon the question of Federation and it is reasonable to conclude that the subsequent large majorities in favour of Federation that were recorded in most of the participating colonies were at least partly attributable to this increasing German threat to Australia's sea-lanes to China.

Another area of concern was the northern entrance to the Straits of Malacca. Both the French and the Germans were interested in that region. The French, backed by the Russians, were hoping to get permission from the Siamese government to construct a canal across the narrow Kra isthmus, which promised to be good for the economy of French Indo-China, but at the expense of Singapore. The Germans were at the same time pressing the Siamese government to sell to them Langkawi Island to the north of Penang, where they planned to construct a naval dockyard and a coaling station. This would have been very dangerous to British interests in the Malay Peninsula, and to her naval control both of the Straits of Malacca and of the Bay of Bengal. These dangers, however, had been foreseen and guarded against by the secret Anglo-Siamese Convention of 1897 whereby the Siamese government agreed not to cede territory south of the 11th parallel of north latitude or to grant special privileges in that region without British approval, while Britain promised to support Siam against any third party which sought to gain influence there. The focus now shifted to South Africa The discovery of gold in the Transvaal in 1886 had led to the inevitable huge influx of foreign adventurers seeking to make their fortune, and to the rapid growth of Johannesburg into a major city far outstripping the Boer capital city of Pretoria. President Kruger's efforts to shelter his Boer compatriots from the effects of this massive foreign influx inevitably caused much friction, leading to the Jameson raid, when Dr Jameson with a force of 470 men, sought to cross the Transvaal to Johannesburg in order to join a force that was planning to overthrow Kruger's government. The conspiracy failed and Jameson was captured, leading to the ill-judged telegram of congratulations sent by the Kaiser to President Kruger. No other country was prepared to support the Boers, and the only result of the telegram was to cause long-lasting antagonism in Britain, while misleading the Boers into expecting German support in any future war with the British. When imperial defence had been discussed at the Colonial Conference in 1897, Joseph Chamberlain, the Colonial Secretary, had suggested the need for some form of military cooperation between the colonial militias and the permanent forces of the British army. George Reid, the premier of New South Wales, had reacted to this suggestion by saying that only the outbreak of a just war threatening the security of the Empire would prompt the Australians to active partnership in its defence. Nevertheless, the Australian premiers did agree to the exchange of units for training purposes. When the war did break out on 9 October 1899 it called forth, as one observer noted, 'an extraordinary amount of sympathy for the mother country from all classes of the colonists,' who saw the Boers as being engaged in a bid 'to usurp the dominion of South Africa, and thus break one principal and necessary link in the chain of the British Empire'. The Canadians and New Zealanders similarly responded loyally by sending troops to serve in this war, but what particularly surprised those best acquainted with colonial sentiment was 'the ardour and enthusiasm with which the call to arms was responded to throughout Australia'.[34] The war was clearly bringing home to them the new and increasing vulnerability of their continent as nothing else had done.

The public at large in Australia could feel that their soldiers were fighting not only to defend the interests of their compatriots in the Transvaal, but were also helping to ensure that the Cape, the stronghold on the route from Britain to Australia, did not fall under Boer and Afrikaner control, possibly supported by German South-West Africa. But for those who were well informed and historically minded there was also a deeper cause for concern, the fear that the war might unite the Germans and the Dutch in their opposition to Great Britain. The outbreak of the war had evoked worldwide sympathy for the Boers, and in both Germany and Holland the attitude of the press towards Britain was extremely hostile, with public opinion among the Dutch being described as 'very excitable'. What if this mutual hostility towards Britain brought about some kind of union? Half-a-century earlier Friedrich List, who did so much to influence the formation of the *Zollverein,* had written: 'Holland is, by her geographical position, by her commercial and industrial relations, by the origin of her inhabitants and their language, a German province, separated from us ..., and which needs to be reincorporated ... Holland belongs to Germany, as much as Brittany and Normandy belong to France.'[35] This concept had more recently been taken up by Treitschke, the German nationalist historian, and what Treitschke said had to be taken seriously, since he was the mentor of both Tirpitz and of von Bulow.

Any such annexation of Holland by Germany would have created an impossible situation both for Britain and Australia. It had always been a basic tenet of British foreign policy to ensure that the Netherlands never fell into the hands of a major continental Power, not only because this would increase the vulnerability of the British Isles to invasion, but also because control of the mouth of the Rhine would enable a major Power to hinder British trade from having direct access to continental markets. But German annexation of the Dutch Netherlands would also entail annexation of the Dutch East Indies, and one who quickly realised what was at stake was George Reid, who had just been superseded as Premier of New South Wales. Speaking to a reporter of the *Sydney Morning Herald*, Reid pointed out that just as France was said to have cast a covetous eye on Belgium, 'so Germany is considered with regard to Holland'. He was worried that if Germany absorbed Holland, and with it the Dutch East Indies, she would then rule all of New Guinea apart from the British Protectorate in the south-east corner. That was why he was so anxious, when the war ended, that some arrangement would be reached that would 'take German interests away from New Guinea, which is just outside or own gates'.[36] Two more decades would have to pass, however, before that dream became a reality.

Chapter Ten

THE INTERNATIONAL
TURMOIL LEADING TO
AUSTRALIAN FEDERATION

It was Bismarck's brief spell of colonial expansion in the Eastern seas that made it clear beyond all question that Australians could no longer rely upon their distant location for their security, for the Germans in north-eastern New Guinea were now Queensland's quite close neighbours, while Germany's annexation, in 1885, of the Bismarck Archipelago and part of the Solomon Islands posed a potential threat to Australia's most direct line of communication with China. It was the Gladstone ministry's lack of an immediate response to the German intrusion into New Guinea that led Thomas McIlwraith, the Premier of Queensland, to take the dramatic step of annexing eastern New Guinea 'on behalf of Great Britain'. Not surprisingly, the British Government promptly declared this action to be null and void, nevertheless it prompted Lord Derby, the Colonial Secretary, to suggest the calling of an Intercolonial Conference. This was an opportune initiative, for apart from widespread Australian concern over developments in New Guinea, the Australians were also becoming increasingly worried regarding the adequacy of

Britain's naval defence of the Australian continent and of its trade routes, including those with Great Britain itself.

There was much to discuss, and at the end of this Conference, which met in Sydney in November and December 1883, the delegates from all the Australian colonies unanimously resolved 'That further acquisitions of dominion in the Pacific, south of the equator, by any foreign Power, would be highly detrimental to the safety and well-being of the British possessions in Australasia, and injurious to the interests of the Empire.' They further resolved 'That having regard to the geographical position of the island of New Guinea, [and] the rapid extension of British trade and enterprise in Torres Straits, this Convention ... is emphatically of the opinion that such steps should immediately be taken as will ... secure the incorporation with the British Empire of so much of New Guinea and the small islands adjacent thereto, as is not claimed by the Government of the Netherlands.'[1]

To meet Australian concern over the situation in eastern New Guinea, the British Cabinet decided, on 6 August 1884, to make that region a British Protectorate, but Granville, the Foreign Secretary, insisted that before this was done he should first get the German ambassador to confirm that the projected British move would not clash with German claims. Derby rightly judged this to be a false move. 'If Bismarck objects and we don't give way,' he observed, 'we are in an awkward position with him; if he objects and we do give way, the rage of the Australians will exceed all bounds. If he does not object, have we gained much?' Granville, however, had his way and thus played into Bismarck's hands. The German *chargé d'affaires* duly protested against Britain's proposed move, whereupon Granville came up with a compromise whereby the British

Protectorate was to be limited to the south-eastern portion of New Guinea, and this was proclaimed on 6 November 1884, with the German Protectorate over the north-eastern regions following shortly afterwards. The Australians, as predicted, were furious, as was the Colonial Office. Furthermore, both the French and British ambassadors were warning their home governments of their suspicion that in order to complete her industrial development and her continental policy, Germany would inevitably be led to absorb Holland and the Dutch Empire. This was, indeed, akin to the policy advocated by List a generation earlier when he had written, 'Holland is, by her geographical position, by her commercial and industrial relations, by the origin of her inhabitants and their language, a German province, which now needs to be reincorporated. Holland belongs to Germany as much as Brittany and Normandy belong to France.'[2] If this policy were to become a reality, as was seen in the last chapter, it would pose a deadly threat to both Great Britain and to Australia.

In the years 1884–86 Anglo-French tension over Burma and the Anglo-Russian crisis over Russia's occupation of Merv, together with the rearmament programmes of both those Powers and of Germany, made a European war seem a very real possibility, and Britain's acquisition of Port Hamilton off the coast of Korea, as a counter to Russia's naval base at Vladivostok, signified that the Far East would inevitably play a key role in any such European war. It was therefore doubly disturbing for Australians to read articles appearing in the *Pall Mall Gazette* outlining disturbing deficiencies in Great Britain's Royal Navy, Australia's first line of defence.

All those circumstances meant that Australians were beginning to experience a new and increasing sense of vulnerability, and to feel the need for a greater emphasis to be placed upon Imperial defence, and an opportunity for making this a reality was at hand. For in the spring of 1887 the Australian premiers were due to visit London to take part in the celebrations marking the Golden Jubilee of Queen Victoria's reign, and these celebrations would provide the opportunity for holding an Imperial Conference to discuss this whole question of Imperial defence.

This Imperial Conference duly met at the Foreign Office from 4 April to 9 May 1887, and in his opening address Lord Salisbury stated that 'so great was the advance in the power of making distant combinations, owing to the progress of modern science, that even if the colonies were independent States, they would not be safe. They occupied some of the fairest and most desirable portions of the earth's surface, while the desire for colonies among the nations of Europe had greatly increased and, unless defended, they might be menaced with sudden attack'. Lengthy discussions ensued, and the Australian colonies were so concerned at their own lack of military preparedness that they asked the British Government to send out an expert to examine and advise upon the problem of defending the Australian continent. As a result Major-General Sir T. Bevan Edwards, the newly appointed Governor of Hong Kong, was selected to undertake the task on his way out to take up his new post at Hong Kong.

He reached Australia in 1889, and when he had completed his examination he submitted separate reports to each of the Australian colonies, together with an overall report outlining his proposed organization of the military forces of the Australian colonies. His overall conclusion was stark: 'If the Australian colonies had to rely at any time solely upon their own resources, they would offer such a rich and tempting prize that they would certainly be called upon to fight for their independence, and as isolated as Australia would be, without a proper supply of arms and ammunition, – with forces which cannot at present be considered efficient in comparison with any moderately trained army, and without any cohesion or power of combination for mutual defence among the different armies – its position would be one of great danger. Looking to the state of affairs in Europe ... the defence forces should at once be placed on a proper footing, but this is ... quite impossible without a federation of the forces of the different colonies.'[3]

When the premiers returned to Australia from their visit to London, they had had plenty of opportunities to study the deteriorating situation in Europe, but it was Parkes, who had not attended the Colonial Conference in the spring of 1887, who seized upon the publication of the Edwards report to make the case for Federation. He had spoken on the subject several times before in the course of the year 1889, and in October of that year, at Tenterfield, he made his famous speech in which he pointed out that if they were to carry out the recommendations of General Edwards, it would be necessary for them to have one central authority which could bring all the different forces of the various colonies into one army. The existing Federal Council did not have the necessary authority or executive power to do this. What they had to consider was whether 'the time had not now arisen for the creation on this Australian continent of an Australian Government, as distinct from a local government, and an Australian Parliament.[4]

Following correspondence with Duncan Gillies, premier of Victoria, an informal meeting of delegates from the Australian colonies and New Zealand was held in Melbourne from 6 to 14 February 1890 to consider, in Parkes' words, whether 'the best interests and the present and future prosperity of the Australasian Colonies will be promoted by an early union under the Crown'. This was the first meeting in Australia called specifically to discuss whether the colonies should federate, and the meeting closed with the unanimous adoption of Parkes' resolution, but with an amendment that the word 'Australian' should be substituted for 'Australasian'. This conference also agreed that its members 'should take steps to induce their colonies to appoint delegates to a National Convention' to consider and report on an adequate scheme for a Federal Constitution. The result was the holding of the Federation Convention which met in Sydney from 2 March to 9 April 1891, which did indeed produce a draft Federal Constitution, and although this failed to be implemented, nevertheless it was highly influential and became the basis for all future deliberations on the subject.[5]

Tension in Europe was continuing to build up. France, Russia and Germany were all in the process of rearming on a very large scale, while in Germany itself the ambitious Kaiser Wilhelm II had succeeded to the throne and had dismissed the redoubtable Bismarck. Furthermore, in addition to other sources of tension there was the Anglo-French struggle over the Fashoda dam, where the future control of the Suez Canal was ultimately at stake. However, the attention of the Australian public at large tended to be distracted at this critical time by the world economic crisis which had been affecting the Western world since the mid-1870s, but whose full impact only began to be felt in Australia in 1893. It now spread throughout all the Australian colonies, disturbing trade and industry. No such calamity had occurred in the colonies for half-a-century, and the widespread banking failures were bringing incalculable loss and distress to nearly every household. It was not surprising that the people at large became inward-looking and parochial once more, and that the colonial parliaments failed, one by one, to pass the Constitution Bill drafted at the Federation Convention in 1891.

Not all Australians, however, were unmindful of developments in the outside world which, year by year, were undermining the assumptions upon which Australia's security had hitherto been based. Federation Leagues began to be formed early in 1893 to ensure that the politicians were not allowed to lose sight of this central issue, and it was the pioneering leagues along the Murray River border of New South Wales and Victoria which organized a conference that met in the border town of Corowa on 31 July 1893 to discuss how to keep the Federal cause alive, despite the failure of the various colonial parliaments to follow up the 1891 Convention. It was from this meeting that the 'Corowa Plan' emerged, widely recognized as the turning point in the movement for federation, under which the voters of each colony were to appoint representatives to draw up a new draft federal constitution. The politicians having failed to complete the work, the task was now to be undertaken by the people at large.

It was the outbreak of the Sino-Japanese war on 25 July 1894 and the rapid series of Japanese naval and military successes that followed which gave the necessary sense of urgency to propel the Australians into renewed activity in the quest for Federation. The successive Japanese victories had taken all the world leaders by surprise and the immediate fear was that the Chinese Empire might now fall apart and be divided up between the major Western Powers. When the Australian premiers met at Hobart in January 1895, the result of the war was no longer in doubt, and even though John Forrest of Western Australia and Hugh Nelson of Queensland were reluctant federationists, at this critical junction all the premiers were united in accepting that Federation was a 'great pressing issue' for Australia. They were not united, however, as to how this issue was to be addressed, and though the majority favoured going ahead with a modified version of the Corowa Plan, Forrest and Nelson, the premiers of Western Australia and Queensland, held back. The majority, however, decided to go ahead with their modified version of the Corowa Plan, and Kingston, the Premier most dedicated to the Federal cause, undertook the task of drawing up an Enabling Bill to prepare the way for the election of delegates to the Convention, a task which he had completed by 1 February 1895.

The war, however, came to an end in that very month, to be followed by the signing of the Treaty of Shimonoseki on 17 April, and a mere six days later Russia, France and Germany had intervened to 'advise' Japan to relinquish her acquisition of the Liaotung Peninsula, in southern Manchuria, in return for an increased war indemnity. Japan had felt compelled to agree, and from an Australian viewpoint something like stability seemed to have been restored to the Far East. As a result, complacency returned, and two years were to pass before the Federal cause gathered momentum once more, It was not until December 1895 that New South Wales, together with South Australia, Victoria and Tasmania at last passed their Enabling Acts. But Western Australia remained aloof, and no such move followed in Queensland, either, where internal problems were absorbing all her attention. Sir Hugh Nelson himself had never been regarded as an enthusiastic advocate for Federation, and his lack of enthusiasm had been shared by Anderson Dawson the Labour leader, who remarked on 8 July 1896, that while no-one denied the profound importance of the Federal issue in Australia, he was 'doubtful about the urgency of it'. Nelson himself agreed, saying 'I do not think it is right yet.' Hence, by the end of 1896 it was clear that Queensland would not be represented at the forthcoming Convention.[6] Forrest, on the other hand, though likewise regarding Federation premature; nevertheless ensured that his colony was represented at the Convention, so that it could exert its influence on the framing of the constitution. Thus once again, while the politicians dragged their feet, it was left to a popular assembly to keep the Federal cause alive in people's minds. In mid-1896, when momentum was clearly being lost, the Mayor of Bathurst called a public meeting not only to establish a local Federative League, but also to arrange for the election of a committee to organize a public meeting for later in the year at which the ideas and principles of Australasian union might be fully discussed. This latter meeting took place in November 1896, and one of its moves was to prepare a report to be published as a manifesto to the Australian people on a scheme of Federation. When the meeting closed, the *Sydney Mail* considered that the event had 'done more to popularize federation than anything which had occurred to this time'.[7]

The growing challenge to Great Britain's dominant position in the China trade from the French in the south and from the Russians in the north was occurring at a time when the British were becoming increasingly concerned over their country's political isolation. It was not, however, in the

Far East, but most unexpectedly on the American continent that they were suddenly reminded of this. There had been a long-standing boundary dispute between British Guiana and Venezuela which had suddenly been given a new importance by the discovery of gold in the hinterland of both countries. On 20 July 1895 the United States Government had decided to intervene, and Secretary of State Olney had invoked the Monroe Doctrine, boastfully adding that 'today the United States is practically sovereign on this continent, and its fiat is law upon the subjects to which it confines its interposition'. It took Lord Salisbury some time to respond, and when he did so it was to deny the applicability of the Monroe Doctrine in this case and to oppose the American suggestion of arbitration. This led President Cleveland to inform Congress, on 17 December 1895, that he therefore proposed to fix the line himself, and to declare that any British attempt to assert jurisdiction beyond that line 'should be resisted by every means in the United States' power'.[8] The result of the extreme language used was an outburst of jingoism in the United States, and it was reported at the time how 'in the Western and Southern States especially a feeling of bitter hostility towards Great Britain was suddenly brought into evidence, and but for the more reasonable bias of the leaders of public opinion, the Washington Government might have been hurried into a position from which the only issue would have been an appeal to arms'.[9] Finally, Britain and Venezuela submitted the question to an arbitral tribunal, which largely supported the British position.

These developments were quickly followed by the Jameson raid, the crucial precedent to the Boer War, and the Kaiser's ill-judged telegram of congratulations to President Kruger on

2 June 1896. Germany quickly found herself isolated on this issue, with France, Russia and the USA all declining to follow her initiative, while in Australia that telegram had been sure to cause growing unease, since there were many Australians based in the Transvaal, some one thousand having joined the Uitlanders in the early 1890s in order to escape the economic crisis in Australia, and hoping to find some of the gold that had been discovered in the Witwatersrand in 1886.

In the Diamond Jubilee year of Queen Victoria's reign, 1897, Joseph Chamberlain, the Colonial Secretary, took the opportunity to invite all the Australian premiers to attend. Thereupon, in the words of the Annual Register, 'one and all the Prime Ministers began by declaring they could never be able to accept Mr Chamberlain's invitation. They could not be spared from their duties at home. Then all, one after another, found reasons why they were compelled to go. So, vowing they would never consent, they all, with one mind, consented, and the second and third weeks of May witnessed a general procession of Prime Ministers with their wives and families along the ocean highway to London.' In London, they would have had ample opportunities, from studying the newspapers and journals and from conversations with those who were best informed, to learn more about the Franco-Russian challenge to British interests in China and the Far East; about the looming German naval challenge; about Spain's deteriorating position in Cuba, which might have a knock-on effect in the Philippine Islands on Australia's route to China; and about the increasingly dangerous Anglo-French crisis over the Fashoda dam issue in the Sudan.

This was the time, too, when all the Western powers trading in China were preparing for the possible break-up of the Chinese Empire, with Germany seizing Kiaochow Bay, together with its port of Tsingtao, on 14 November 1897, and the arrival of a Russian fleet at Kinchan near Port Arthur on 18 December, followed by the seizure of the southern portion of the Liaotung Peninsula, including Port Arthur and Talienwan, the very area from which they had forced Japan to withdraw in 1895.

Meanwhile a powerful German naval squadron commanded by Prince Henry, the Kaiser's younger brother, left Kiel for China. The *Sydney Morning Herald*, on 29 December 1897, concluded that the situation 'at present seems almost grave enough to be described as critical,' while the Annual Register saw the political atmosphere at the opening of 1898 as being 'so charged with electricity that it seemed possible for war or revolution to break out on the flimsiest pretext'.

Then on 1 January 1898 the British ambassador at St Petersburg informed Lord Salisbury of a disturbing interview that he had had with Sergei Witte, the Russian Finance minister and the man behind the construction of the Trans-Siberian Railway.

Witte, he reported, considered the Russian move unnecessary, dishonourable in view of the understanding reached at the time of the Triple Intervention of 1895, and a step likely to cause serious trouble in the future. To emphasise how unnecessary he felt the move to be, Witte, with a map spread out before him, drew his hand over the provinces of Chihli (modern Hopeh), Shansi, Shensi and Kansu, and prophesied that sooner or later Russia 'would probably absorb all this territory'. Since the province of Chihli incorporated both Peking and the port of Tientsin, this meant that Witte was anticipating that Russia would in due course gain control of the whole of northern China, including Peking.

It was against this menacing and sombre background that the delegates to the 1897–98 Australian Federation Convention had been meeting in Melbourne for their third and final session. Their first meeting was on 20 January 1898 and they continued their work until 17 March, when they sent forth the Constitution Bill to its fate at the Referendum in June. The debates, of course, centred upon the details of the Bill, but the international rivalry for concessions that was in full swing in China throughout the period of their meetings meant that the delegates, and the voters whom they represented, could not remain indifferent to the overwhelming need for the Australian continent to have an adequate means of defence, and the Edwards Report had left no room for doubt as to what that entailed.

Meanwhile the USA, the last major Power with an important stake in the China trade, had been unable to partake in the scramble for concessions because of the Cuban crisis, but after her declaration of war upon Spain on 24 April 1898, Admiral Dewey's squadron entered Manila Bay on 1 May 1898 and sank the antiquated Spanish warships there, thus gaining control of the city of Manila. A potential German challenge was abandoned when the British naval commander at the scene declared his support for Dewey, realizing that the likely loss of a valuable British market in the Philippines was better than allowing the Germans to acquire the Philippine Islands, which, in addition to their bases in the Bismarck Archipelago and the Solomon Islands, would have given them complete control of Australia's main line of communications with the Chinese Empire. But as the *Sydney Morning Herald* reminded its readers on 20 June 1898, while it was very important to have a friendly Power controlling the Philippines, the attitude of the Americans was as yet uncertain. The USA was 'a nation with which at present we have the most friendly relations, but which,' it recalled with reference to the recent Venezuelan boundary dispute, 'was fulminating threats of war against Britain not many months ago'.

On 31 May a new crisis loomed when the London *Times* printed a despatch from the Australian journalist Dr Morison, its reporter in Peking, who was renowned for the accuracy of his reports. This related to an apparently innocuous concession that had been granted in 1897 for the construction of the important railway which was to run from Peking to the treaty port of Hankow, and thence to the cities of Hanyang and Wuchang on opposite banks of the Yangtze, these three cities together forming the industrial centre of China.

Morison's despatch now revealed that the construction of the line from Peking to Hankow was being financed by the Russian-Chinese Bank, the bank that Witte had founded, with very unusual powers, to finance construction of the Trans-Siberian Railway, and which had originally been established with funds supplied by the great banks in Paris. But Morison further reported that negotiations were now said to be under way for the line to be completed by a Russo-French-Belgian combination, again with the Russian-Chinese Bank playing a prominent role.

Furthermore, he reported, 'the whole northern section of the line will be mortgaged to the great Russian State institution (i.e., the Russo-Chinese Bank), and may, conceivably, pass by foreclosure into its possession. If the southern sections are to be constructed on the same facile terms, the whole great trunk line from Peking to the Yangtze Valley will pass practically under Russian control.' This showed that it was Paris, whose banks largely financed the Russians, rather than Brussels that was really in charge, and as Morison observed, 'the prospect is interesting when we recollect the avowed desire of France to join hands from the south with Russia in the north.'

Two months earlier, as the national debate on the draft constitution got under way following the ending of the Australian Federation Convention, the *Sydney Morning Herald*, in its issue of 24 March 1898 (p. 4), had warned its readers to pay careful attention to the deteriorating situation in the Pacific region in general, and in China in particular, as this was a time when 'the world's peace was never in greater danger of being broken on a gigantic scale.' In the first place there was the growing industrial, naval and military threat posed by the German Empire, as described in the last chapter. Then there was the fact that while British traders were concentrating on the Yangtze river, with the province of Szechuan as their ultimate goal, the railway-building plans of France[10] and Russia posed another serious threat to Britain's hitherto dominant role in the China trade. 'What Russia is aiming at in the north,' the paper warned, 'is being imitated by France in the south from Tonquin ... French and Russian railways will eventually enclose China with a ring of iron impervious to outside competition.' All of a sudden Morison's report made it look as though this 'ring of iron' was no mere figment of the imagination, but was a development in the very process of becoming a reality.

When the Australian referenda on Federation were held in the four participating colonies, the voters in general were well aware that the centre of gravity in world affairs had now shifted to Chinese waters, and that Australia was no longer an isolated naval station, hundreds of miles away from the probable scene of naval operations in the event of war, but might now find herself in the very centre of such operations.[11] Hence there were substantial majorities in favour of Federation in Victoria, South Australia and Tasmania. The much smaller vote in favour in New South Wales, which prevented the motion passing in that colony, was due to the very ambivalent stand that had been taken by George Reid, the premier, not because he doubted the need for Federation, but because he wanted it on more favourable terms for his own colony. These he very largely got at a further conference of the premiers held in Melbourne from 29 January to 3 February 1899.

In the meantime, the Anglo-French crisis over Fashoda had been coming to a head. The origin of this dispute had been the lecture given by a French hydrologist in January 1893 attended by Théophile Delcassé. As mentioned earlier, the lecturer had argued that if a great dam were to be constructed there, whoever constructed it would thereby become the master of Egypt, since he could either flood or parch the country at will.[12]

Both French and British experts believed that this was practicable, and Delcassé persuaded his government to adopt the idea. The French had never come to terms with the ending of the Anglo-French Condominium in Egypt, whereas for the British the vital point at issue was the control of the Suez Canal, and thus of the shortest route to the Orient and Australia. As a result of Delcassé's initiative, a French expedition, bound for Fashoda, landed at Loango in West

Africa on 8 July 1896, and when it was known to be nearing Fashoda two years later, Lord Salisbury ordered Kitchener, the commander-in-chief in Egypt, to lead his army up the Nile. The crisis was coming to a head when the Australians held their first referendum in June 1898. Marchand reached Fashoda on 10 July. After Kitchener had learnt of Marchand's arrival at Fashoda, the two men eventually met on 19 September and amicably agreed to leave the solution to their respective governments, and there was ironic poetic justice in the fact that Delcassé, who was now French Foreign Minister, was left to find a solution to the crisis of which he had been the original cause. Since France's Russian allies had no intention of becoming involved, and France, wracked by the Dreyfus affair, was unprepared for war, Delcassé was compelled to give way and to order Marchand to withdraw from Fashoda in November 1898, while the Anglo-French agreement of 20 March 1899 excluded France from the valley of the Nile, thus assuring Britain's position in Egypt and her control of the Suez Canal.

The voting for the second Referendum on Australian Federation took place between 24 April 1899, when South Australia went to the poll, and 2 September 1899 when the voters of Queensland at last took part, New South Wales, Victoria and Tasmania having voted on 20 June and 27 July. All recorded favourable verdicts.

This was not surprising, for as they cast their votes the crisis in the Boer Republics was rumbling on until, on 31 May 1899, Alfred Milner, the Governor of the Cape Colony and High Commissioner for South Africa, met President Kruger in conference at Bloemfontein in an effort to sort out the growing crisis in the Transvaal, where Kruger had disenfranchised the

Uitlanders, at least for a time. Unfortunately, Milner had not
heeded the advice of Joseph Chamberlain to take along with
him Prime Minister Schreiner of the Cape Colony, who was
not only an outstanding and fair-minded lawyer but, as the
DNB put it, 'understood and could rival Boer methods of
arguing almost interminably round a question before coming
to a decision,' an approach that Milner, with his clear-cut and
decisive frame of mind, found intolerable.

Hence the conference was a disaster, and on 5 June 1899,
Milner broke off the discussions with the fateful words: 'The
conference is absolutely at an end, and there is no obligation
on either side arising out of it.' He was later to admit that he
thought that he had been wrong in breaking off the talks so
abruptly, but the die was cast and the two men did not meet
again. The Australian voters in the participating colonies
therefore knew, as they cast their votes, that there was every
possibility of war soon breaking out, thus placing the Cape
route to Britain and Europe in jeopardy, and war became a
reality after Kruger had issued an ultimatum to the British
Government on 9 October 1899.

Then, after the Boxer Rebellion had broken out in China
and the siege of the foreign legations was in full swing, in
the early summer of 1900 the people of Western Australia
also finally voted in favour of Federation, reportedly 'with a
mixture of excitement, trepidation and hope'.

Almost five years earlier, at a banquet given in honour of
Colonel Gerard Smith, the Governor Designate of Western
Australia, Joseph Chamberlain had expressed confidence
that the Australian colonies would soon agree to unite, and
had forecast that this would result 'in the foundation of a
mighty commonwealth, which – in a time that is historically

visible is – destined to outstrip the waning greatness and the lagging civilization of the older countries of Europe'.[13] These were prophetic words, and the foundations for a great Pacific Power of the future were indeed now in place.

NOTES

Chapter One

1. The modern Jakarta.

2. For fuller details of the discovery and significance of this new route, see Sir H. E. A. Cotton and Sir C. G. H. Fawcett, *East Indiamen: The East India Company's Maritime Service* (London, 1949); Crowhurst, 'The Voyage of the *Pitt*: A Turning Point in the East Indian Navigation,' *Mariner's Mirror*, 55 (1969), 43–56; H. T. Fry, 'The Eastern Passage and Its Impact on Spanish Policy in the Philippines, 1758–1790,' *Philippine Studies*, 33 (1985), 3–21.

3. See H. T. Fry *Alexander Dalrymple and the Expansion of British Trade* (London and Toronto, 1970), Chapters 2 and 4.

4. Kempenfelt to Admiral Pocock, 1 April 1762. The original is in the *Pocock Papers* in the National Maritime Museum, Greenwich, with copies in the *European Magazine*, 42 (1802), 321–22; and in the *Orme Mss.*, India Office Library (British Library), vol. 52, f. 25, p. 183.

5. Secret Committee to Earl Halifax, 14 January 1764, Dutch Records A, vol. xvii, India Office Lbry. Three East India Men, the *Caernarvon*, *Princess Augusta*, and the *Warwick* attempted to follow the *Pitt's* route in September 1760, but only the *Warwick* – the ship stopped by the Dutch – was successful. See Crowhurst *op. cit.* and Fry *op. cit.*

6. C. N. Parkinson, *War in the Eastern Seas, 1793–1815* (London, 1954), p. 43.

7. E.g., John Campbell's edition of John Harris's *Navigantium atque Itinerantium Bibliotheca; or A Complete Collection of Voyages and Travels*, 2 vols. (London, 1744–48); and C. de Brosses, *Histoire des Navigations aux Terres Australes*, 2 vols. (Paris, 1756), translated by J. Callander as *Terra Australis Cognita* (London and Edinburgh, 1766).

8. A. Dalrymple, *An Historical Collection of the Several Voyages and Discoveries in the South Pacific Ocean*, 2 vols. (London, 1770–71); See also H. T. Fry, *Alexander Dalrymple and the Expansion of British Trade*

(London and Toronto, 1970), Chapter 5; and 'Alexander Dalrymple and Captain Cook: The Creative Interplay of Two Careers' in Robin Fisher and Hugh Johnston (eds) *Captain James Cook and His Times* (Vancouver and London, 1979).

9. V. T. Harlow, *The Founding of the Second British Empire*, vol. 1 (London, 1952), p. 28; he covers the whole crisis in detail on pp. 22–32. Egmont's letter to Grafton was written on 20 July 1765.

10. In addition to Harlow *ut supra* see G. J. Marcus, *A Naval History of England*, vol. 1 (London, 1961), p. 421 and G. R. Barnes and J. H. Owen (eds), *The Sandwich Papers*, vol. LXIX (London: Navy Records Society, 1932), pp. xix–xx.

11. Admiral Sir Herbert W. Richmond, *The Navy in India 1763–83* (London, 1931), pp. 120–21.

12. This was not immediately a universal practice, but seven used variants of the Eastern Passage in 1780, three in 1781, four in 1782, five in 1783 and five in 1784.

13. (1) The 'Direct Passage' to the west of Halmahera. (2) The 'Pitt's Passage,' i.e., every route to the south of Halmahera and to the north of Australia. (3) The 'New Zealand Passage,' including all routes to the east of Australia. (4) The Passage to the south and east of New Zealand. (5) The Passage round Cape Horn.

For security reasons, only a few copies of this Memoir were printed at the time, and these were issued by the Secret Committee to the commanders of China-bound East Indiamen.

14. See Holden Furber, *Rival Empires of Trade in the Orient 1600–1800* (Minneapolis, 1976), pp. 156–57, 177.

15. Bernard M. Vlekke, *Nusantara: A History of the East Indian Archipelago* (Cambridge, Mass, 1943), p. 217.

Chapter Two

1. *The Annual Register for the years 1784 & 1785* (London, 1787), pp. 9–11. During his visit to Antwerp, the Emperor made a personal reconnaissance of the river Scheldt 'as far as the first of those Dutch forts, which have been established to secure to the [Dutch] states the exclusive navigation of that river, [and] all those obstructions which tried to impede its navigation, and to shut up the port [ofAntwerp]'.

2. Ibid.

3. *The New Cambridge Modern History*, vol. VIII (Cambridge, 1971), p. 273.

4. Keith to Carmatthen 17 July 1784 FO 7/9.

5. Carmarthen to Keith 23 January 1784 FO7/. This was a time of acute

Russo-Turkish tension after Russia's 1783 annexation of Crimea. Austria was supporting Russia, whereas France had ties with Turkey.

6. Keith to Carmarthen 19 May 1784 FO 7/8.

7. Carmarthen to Pitt 23 June 1784, Pitt to Carmarthen 24 June and 10 September 1784 Egerton Mss. 3498.

11. Hailes to Carmarthen 7 and 10 June and 2 September 1784, Dorset to Carmarthen 1, 8, 22 and 29 July 1784. *Despatches from Paris, 1784–1790*, selected and edited by Oscar Browning, vol. 1 (London, 1909), pp. 8–12 and 19. An alternative interpretation was that France was planning 'an attack upon Jamaica and a descent on England as near the same time as possible. The works now going on in Cherbourg – they will be completed in about 3 years – are principally contracting with a view to favour a future invasion of England,' report from M. Simolin, 12 August 1784, who further noted how de Segur, the French Minister of the Army, on his way to Brighton had been observed taking frequent notes of different positions which the country afforded, and which might be of great consequence on a future occasion. Egerton Mss. 3504.

8. Nathaniel Smith to Carmarthen, 9 April 1784, Egerton Mss. 3505 f.13.

9. Oscar Browning (ed.), *Dispatches from Paris 1784–1790*, vol. 1 (London, 1909), pp. 2–3.

10. Torrington to Carmarthen 14, 16 and 20 September 1784, Add. Mss. 28, 06 off 140–63. Torrington admitted that when he had written to Holland for copies of the secret articles of the projected alliance, his correspondents had exploited the prevailing air of mystery 'to enhance the value of their intelligence'. Torrington to Carmarthen 25 August 1784 FO26/6.

11. What had aroused suspicion was 'the difference of style and language in the last eleven articles from what appears in the nine preceding ones,' and Carmarthen asked Torrington to communicate in the strictest confidence the source of his information. This the latter refused to do, pleading that his word of honour and the lives of his agents were at stake. Carmarthen to and from Torrington 21 September, 7, 13 and 19 October and 10 December 1784, FO 26/6. Regarding the build-up of the French fleet and the rumours regarding Trincomali, see Torrington to Carmarthen 19 August 1784, FO26/6.

12. Hailes to Carmarthen 7 May 1784 in O. Browning (ed.) *Dispatches ...* vol. 1, p. 6; Pitt to Carmarthen 7 June 1784 Egerton Mss. 3498; Harris to Carmarthen letters dated 6, 16 and 23 October, 28 November, 2 December 1784.

13. Dundas to Sydney 2 November 1784 PRO 30/8/157:7.

14. Memoen closed in a letter from Harris to Carmarthen 25 January and 1 February 1785, Add. Mss. 28,060. He was very surprised that neither Keith at Vienna nor Fitzburgh at St Petersburg had got 'wind of this extraordinary treaty'.

15. Dorset to Carmarthen 13 January 1785 in Browning *op. cit.* and 3 February 1785 FO27/16. It may be added that France's ally, Spain, was soon to do likewise with the formation of the Royal Philippine Co.

16. Dorset to Carmarthen, letters of 3 February and 3 March 1785 in Browning *op. cit.* and Harris to Carmarthen 28 January 1785 *Add. Mss.28,060f.241.*

17. *The New Cambridge Modern History* vol. VIII, p. 273.

18. Dorset to Carmarthen, letters of 3 February and 3 March 1785 in Browning *op. cit.* and Harris to Carmarthen 28 January 1785 *Add. Mss. 28,060f.241.*

19. *Diaries and Correspondence of Sir James Harris*, vol. II, pp. 151–52 'What the King of Prussia said to Lord Cornwallis,' sent by Ewart to Harris from Sans Souci, 17 September 1785.

20. Harris to Carmarthen 15 November 1785 FO37/925.

21. Dorset to Carmarthen, 22 July 1784 Browning, *Dispatches ...* vol. I, pp. 15–6. He had expressed the conviction that France was bound to remain at peace for the time being because of the very deep wounds that she had suffered during the recent war in her 'navy, Commerce and Finance,' as evidenced by the many post-war bankruptcies in Bordeaux, Marseilles and other French ports. This was a conviction shared by Harris.

22. Harris to Carmarthen 20 January and 24 February 1786 FO 37/10.

23. For details see H. T. Fry, 'The Eastern Passage and Its Impact on Spanish Policy in the Philippines, 1758–1790,' *Philippine Studies,* 33 (1985), 3–21.

24. *Annual Register for 1786*, pp. 34 *et seq.*

25. The Dutch determination to resist this Spanish claim, which they insisted was a breach of their treaty rights, simmered on throughout the whole of that year. On 8 December 1786, Harris was still reporting that 'Spain even insists on a right of sailing through the Molucca Islands, and this is refused in a still stronger manner by the Dutch than that round the Cape,' while on 19 December 1786, he reported that the Dutch Ambassador at Madrid 'understands the Dutch East India Company was preparing to oppose by force the passage of the Spaniards round the Cape (the fact is true), and that if this happened Count Florida Blanca declared that his Catholic Majesty would consider every act of the East

India Company as acts of the Republic, and immediately give orders for reprisals to be made on the ships of the States'. Harris to Carmarthen 19 December 1786 FO37/12.

26. Hailes to Carmarthen 27 July 1786 Browning *op. cit.*, vol. I, pp. 126 and 131–32.

27. Harris to Carmarthen 11 March 1785 FO37/6. He described the Dutch answer as 'a very idle one,' since it was impossible for 'anything like a fleet being requisite to keep these petty sovereigns in order'. Alan Frost, *Convicts and Empire*, p. 100.

28. Add. Mss. 38,409ff103 *et. seq.* In a postscript dated 12 April 1786, the writer notes that he had 'this day [seen] a paper drawn up by the late Lord Clive' which put forward almost identical arguments, and in which it was suggested that while the Bengal river did not admit ships of such a large size, 'the trade to the coasts of Coromandel and Malabar, to Sumatra and China etc. may be carried on with more advantage in ships of a great size'. This was soon to happen.

29. Harris to Carmarthen 13 January 1786 FO37/10.

30. Harris to Carmarthen letters of 27 January, 3, 14 and 24 February 1786 FO37/10. 'India' and 'East Indies' were used interchangeably at this time. Harris's own view was that the time for conciliation was past, and that 'we must awe them into respect, by making them feel our power and weight in the East'. He even favoured a preemptive strike against the Dutch East Indies and taking possession of their spice trade.

31. Harris to Carmarthen 7 March 1786 FO37/10. On 21 March, he pointed out that whereas formerly 'no increase either of the naval or of the military force, could take place in India without previously consulting the Directors, the new regulations which have taken place in the Direction have put an end to this communication.'

32. Harris to Carmarthen 2 May 1786 Add. Mss. 28,061.

33. Harris to Carmarthen 5 and 9 May 1786 FO37/10.

34. Harris to Carmarthen16 and 20 June 1786 FO 37/11.

35. Harris to Carmarthen 15 and 22 August 1786 FO37/11; and 'Private' Add. Mss. 28061f266.

36. Harris to Carmarthen 1 January and 27 March 1787FO37/13, and 13 April 1787 *Diaries* ..., vol. II, p. 289.

37. Harris to Carmarthen 12 September 1786 FO37/12, and 1, 4 and 5 May 1787 FO37/14, and *Diaries* ..., vol. II, p. 295.

38. *Diaries*, vol. II, p. 305.

39. Harris to Carmarthen 22 June 1787.

40. For a fuller account, see Ehrman *op. cit.*, pp. 528–36.

41. Quoted by N. Tarling *Anglo-Dutch Rivalry in the Malay World 1780–1824* (Cambridge, 1961), p. 45.

Chapter Three

1. Harris to Carmarthen 10 December 1784 FO37/5.
2. Ainsley to Carmarthen 10 and 11 March 1785 FO78/6 and Dorset to Carmarthen 21 April, 2 and 30 June 1785, FO27/16.
3. 'Speculations on the Situation and Resources of Egypt, 1773–1785' Add. Mss. 38, 346, pp. 237–57. In this document, they gave a detailed description of how the Marmalukes had gained power in Egypt, and of their form of government. For the Board of Control's approach, see Rouse to Fraser 23 April 1785 FO 78/6.
4. Carmarthen to Ainsley 10 and 19 May 1785, Ainsley to Carmarthen 9 and 23 July 1785, FO78/6.
5. Ainsley to Carmarthen 10 and 25 November 1785 FO78/6, Harris to Carmarthen 13 December 1785 FO37/9.
6. See H. T. Fry, 'Early British Interest in the Chagos Archipelago and the Maldive Islands,' *Mariner's Mirror* (1967), 53, no. 41967, pp. 343–56.
7. Modern Atjeh.
8. Carmarthen to Hailes 23 December 1784 Egerton Mss. 3499. Carmarthen added that if the report proved groundless it 'would not be in our interest to give the slightest idea of the importance in which the subject appears to us'.
9. Le Baron Hulot, *D'Entrecasteaux* (Paris, 1894), p. 271.
10. Harlow *op. cit.*, vol. 2, pp. 349–50; D. J. M. Tate, *The Making of Modern South-East Asia*, vol. 1 (Kuala Lumpur etc., 1971), pp. 106–07; D. G. E. Hall, *A History of South-East Asia*, 4th ed. (London, 1981), pp. 539, 543–44.
11. Log of the *Antelope*, India Office Library (in the British Library), Marine Records L/MAR/B57A.
12. This monopoly had in fact already been breached, since Pierre Poivre, in the 1740s, had managed to bring in 400 plants of nutmeg trees, 10,000 nuts, ready for germination, as well as 70 clove plants and a large collection of clove seeds from the outer islands of the East Indies to the Ile de France and Bourbon. See Sonia E. Howe, *In Quest of Spices* (London, n.d.), pp. 257–58. Thomas Forrest, when navigating through East Indian waters in the *Tartar* galley, reported French ships having been active collecting spices from islands in the neighbourhood of the island of Gebe; V. T. Harlow and F. Madden, 'Orders from the Court of Directors of Lord Cornwallis Relative to the Strait of Malacca,' *British Colonial Developments 1774–1834* (Oxford, 1952), pp. 52–4.

13. See A. Frost, *Convicts and Empire* (Melbourne, 1980), pp. 10–14.
14. Frost Ibid., pp. 10 and 14, citing CO201/1 and 57–61.
15. The Rt. Hon. William Eden, *The History of New Holland from Its First Discovery in 1616 to the Present Time*, 2nd ed. (London, 1787), p. v.
16. Dorset to Carmarthen 28 April, 5 May and 9 June 1785; Lord Dalrymple to Carmarthen 8 June 1785 Egerton Mss. 350, British Library.
17. Cobbett's, *Parliamentary History*, vol. 25, p. 906.
18. Frost *op. cit.*, pp. 86–7.
19. J. Ehrman, *The Younger Pitt* (London, 1969), p. 460.
20. See Robert H. King, 'The Territorial Boundaries of New South Wales in 1788,' *The Great Circle*, 3 no. 2 (Oct. 1981), 70–89.
21. Eden *op cit.* p. 12.
22. D'Entrecasteaux to Maechal de Castries 28 September 1786 and 8 February 1787 Hulot *op. cit.*, pp. 284 *et seq.*
23. Eden *op. cit.*, p. 36.
24. R. W. Giblin, *The Early History of Tasmania 1642–1804* (London, 1928), pp. 123–24.
25. For the aftermath of the expedition and the British capture of its charts, and the subsequent events leading to Dalrymple's dismissal and death, see H. T. Fry, *Alexander Dalrymple and the Expansion of BritishTrade* (London and Toronto, 1970), pp. 261–66.
26. This was stated in his *Memoir concerning the Passages to and from China*. For a fuller account, see H. T. Fry, 'Alexander Dalrymple and New Guinea,' *Journal of Pacific History*, IV (1969), 83–114.
27. Jan Huygen van Linschoten (1563–1611) was a Dutch traveller and explorer who, having spent four years in Portugal, in 1583 sailed to Goa where he spent the next five years as the archbishop's secretary. On his return to Holland, he published two works which provided a great fund of practical information regarding the trade and navigation of the Indian Ocean.
28. 11, 23–25 March 1790, paras. 18–49.

Chapter Four

1. J. Dunmore, *French Explorers in the Pacific*, 2 vols., vol. 1 (Oxford, 1965–69), pp. 288–89.
2. See *The Cambridge Modern History*, vol. IX (Cambridge, 1906), p. 363; and Simon Schama, *Citizens* (New York and London, 1989), p. 687. Kersaint himself was soon to be guillotined, having had the courage not only to oppose the execution of Louis XVI, but also to resign from the Convention in protest against its bloodthirsty policies in France.
3. S. G. Rainbow, *English Expeditions to the Dutch East Indies During the Revolutionary and Napoleonic Wars* (London University,

MA thesis, May 1933), pp. 73–4, quoting from the translation of the Stadtholder's orders in the Bengal Secret and Political Consultations, vol. 32 Consultation of 17 July 1795, and vol. 33, translation of thePrince of Orange's letter to Van Nerburg in the Consultation of 11 September 1795.

4. The fall of Colombo and of the whole island of Ceylon was to follow on 16 February 1796. The defence had been the responsibility of a Swiss Regiment (Regt) of which the Comte de Meuron was the proprietor, but the Comte and his regt transferred to the British side, and the expected French reinforcement failed to arrive. Ibid., pp 90–1.

5. Modern DaNang.

6. National Libray of Scotland, The Melville Papers, ms 1069, f.180, 11 June 1801.

7. I. o. Lbry. *Board's Collections* vol. 49, Paper 1109.

8. Thomas E. Ennis, *French Policy and Development in Indochina* (Chicago, 1936), Appendix App. 194–95. In April 1799, Mr Berry, returning from Saigon, reported, having seen there a large armament of some 80,000 and more than a thousand vessels being fitted out.

9. C. Northcote Parkinson, *War in the Eastern Seas 1793–1815* (London, 1954), pp. 118–19 quoting Rainier's letter in the Public Record Office Adm1/168.

10. A. Wellesley to Dundas Fort William 25 October 1800 Private no. 31 (secret) in E. Ingram (ed.) *Two Views on British India* (Bath, 1970), p. 309.

11. Sloane *op. cit.*, vol. I, p. 38; Rose *op. cit.*, vol. I, p. 178.

12. V. Cronin, *Napoleon* (London, 1971, reissued 1979), pp. 37–8.

13. Rose *op. cit.*, vol. I, pp. 175–76.

14. Rose *op. cit.*, vol. I, pp. 175–76.

15. Moon *op. cit.*, pp. 280 *et seq.*

16. Sloane *op. cit.*, vol. II, p. 35.

17. C. Breasted, *Ancient times: A history of the Early World,* 2nd ed. (Boston, Mass. Etc., 1944), pp. 100–02.

18. See Cronin *op. cit.*, p. 155. The whole of Chapter 10 gives an interesting account of Napoleon's time in Egypt.

19. Rose *op. cit.*, vol. I, p. 200.

20. Rose *op. cit.*, vol. I, p. 200 and vol. II, p. 582.

21. Bonaparte had begun his Syrian campaign with 13,000 soldiers and 900 cavalry. At this battle he had 8,000 men against 9,000 Turks, but in the outcome 5,000 Turks were drowned and 2,000 captured.

22. Great Britain, Turkey, Naples, Austria and Russia.

23. Sloane *op. cit.*, vol. II, p. 35.

Chapter Five

1. The Annual Register for 1800.

2. Sir John T. Pratt, *The Expansion of Europe into the Far East* (London, 1947), pp. 63–4.

3. *The Cambridge Modern History* [hereafter CMH] vol.ix (1906) pp.42, 47

4. Ibid., pp. 47–8 and B. E. O'Meara, *Napoleon in Exile*, vol. 1 (London, 1822), p. 80.

5. *The New Cambridge Modern History* [hereafter NCMH] IX. 262. See also *The Cambridge Modern History* [hereafter CMH] IX. 76–7.

6. J. Holland Rose, *The Life of Napoleon I*, vol. I (London, 1904), p. 357.

7. At the beginning of the American War of Independence Baudin had been relieved of his command through the intrigues of aristocratic officers, because he was not of noble birth. He had thereupon been appointed captain of a ship of the line in the Austrian navy. He had returned to France in 1793 and had become a respected figure in the Museum National, which was closely linked to the Institut National. See the Foreword by Jean-Paul Faivre in Christine Cornell, *The Journal of Post-Captain Nicolas Baudin, Commander-in-Chief of the corvettes Geographe and Naturaliste* ... (Adelaide, 1974).

8. I.e., Tasmania.

9. This was actually at the eastern end of the Louisiades. One of La Pérouse's unfinished tasks had been to establish the relationship of the Louisiades to New Guinea.

10. See H. L. Hoskins, *British routes to India* (New York, 1928, repr. London 1966), p. 84.

11. James D. Mack, *Matthew Flinders* (Melbourne, 1966), pp. 43, 97.

12. E. Scott, *Flinders*, pp. 180–81 and Cornell *op. cit.*, p. 19 quoting *Historical Records of Australia*, vol. III, p. 698.

13. For correspondence on this, see India Office Library, *Board's Collections* F/4/159 Political letter from Fort St George 22 February 1803 and extract of letter from Colonel Oliver to Court of Directors 9 March 1803; see also Nicholas Tarling, *Anglo-Dutch Rivalry in the Malay World 1780–1824* (St Lucia: UQP, 1962), p. 63 quoting Edmonstone to Farquhar 15 March 1803, *Bengal Foreign Consultations* 165/80 31 March 1803.

14. This abdication coincided with the outbreak of a rebellion led by the White Lotus Society which it took the Chinese government seven years to bring under control.

15. I.e., South Vietnam.

16. (Or Turon), modern DaNang.

17. Under the terms of this treaty France undertook to dispatch to Cochin China four ships carrying 1,200 infantry, 200 artillery, and 250 'Kaffirs' complete with arms and ammunition.

18. Luconia was Luzon, the large northern island of the Philippines. *The Melville Papers* MS1069f. 18011 June 1801, National Library of Scotland. See H. T. Fry, *Alexander Dalrymple and the Expansion of British Trade* (London and Toronto1971), Chapter VII for fuller details.

19. H. Compton, *Particular Account of European Military Adventurers of Hindustan 1784–1803* (London, 1889–1803), pp. 248 *et seq.*, 284 *et seq.*, 294–96, quoting Wellesley's *Own History of the Mahratta War.*

20. O'Meara *op. cit.*, vol. II, p. 199. The remnant of the expedition was eventually forced to surrender on 9 November 1803 and to withdraw.

21. Rose *op. cit.*, vol. I, p. 411.

22. J. Marlowe, *Perfidious Albion: The origins of Anglo-French Rivalry in the Levant* (London 1971), pp. 95–6 quoting Stuart to Hobart 18 October 1802 in WO1/346 in the Public Record Office.

Chapter Six

1. On 16 May 1804 he was declared Emperor Napoleon I; in that same week Pitt returned to power as Prime Minister.

2. It was now realised, too, that a surprise invasion could be carried out successfully only if the boats involved were kept outside the basin at Boulogne, where the main invasion force was assembled, since only 100 boats could get out of the basin in one tide. Yet once outside they were vulnerable to attack and were at the mercy of the elements; Napoleon saw for himself five boats wrecked in November 1803, and another thirteen in July 1804 in storms during visits he paid to Boulogne.

3. Rose said there were fifteen of each – see his *Nap.* III., p. 143.

4. Rose *Nap. I*, vol. 2, pp. 160–61.

5. Ibid., p. 163.

6. See J. H. Rose, *Life of Napoleon I*, vol. II, p. 117 and *The Cambridge Modern History*, vol. IX, p. 311.

7. Sloane *op. cit.*, vol. III, pp. 23–4 and Rose *op. cit.*, vol. II, pp. 117–18.

8. Thessaly, Epirus, the Moreau.

9. O'Meara *op. cit.*, vol. I, p. 382; vol. II, p. 69

10. See D. G. E. Hall, *A History of South-EastAsia* 4th ed. (London, 1981), pp. 515–19.

11. His interview with Ambassador Metternich on 22 January 1808, and his letters to Caulaincourt and Tsar Alexander dated 2 February 1808, *CMH*, vol. IX, p. 310.

12. Ibid., p. 311 and Rose, *Napoleon I*, vol. II, p. 176. Upon taking over from Wellesley as Governor-General in India in 1805, Cornwallis had indeed drawn attention to the critical state of the finances there, a problem that had continued under his immediate successors.

13. C. Northcote Parkinson, *War in the Eastern Seas, 1793–1815* (London, 1954), p. 310.

14. O'Meara *op. cit.*, vol. II, pp. 196–98. He stated that his communication with the Mahrattas was *via* Bussorah, Baghdad, Mocha and Surat, adding: 'I had frequently earlier intelligence from India than you had in England.'

15. E. Scott, *The Life of Captain Matthew Flinders R. N.* (Sydney, 1914), pp. 436 *et seq.*

16. Rose *op. cit.*, vol. II, p. 176.

17. *Terre de Nuyts; terre de Leuwin; terre d'Edels; terre d'Endracht; terre de Witt; terre de Carpentarie;* the southern island of *terre de Diemen* (Tasmania).

18. See J-P Faivre, *L'Expansion Française dans le Pacifique de 1800 a1842* (Paris, 1953), pp. 145–46.

19. *Historical Relation of a Voyage Undertaken for the Discovery of Southern Lands,* English translation from French of M. Peron in John Pinkerton *A General Collection of Voyages and Travels* vol. XI (London, 1812), p. 885. 'We did not find fresh water at the port,' wrote Péron, 'but the vigour and liveliness of the vegetation were certain indices of the existence of some rivulets, or at least of some copious springs.'

20. Ibid., pp. 787, 830. He noted how Captain Hamelin, at SharksBay, in answer to the lack of water, was able 'with a single still to obtain daily eight pints of soft water.'

21. *CMH*, vol. IX, p. 315.

22. Baron Claude-Francois de Méneval (translated and annotated by Robert H. Sherard), *Memoirs to Serve for a History of Napoleon I,* 3vols. (London, 1894), vol. II, pp. 116–17.

23. S. Schama, *Citizens: A Chronicle of the French Revolution* (London, 1989), p. 694, who writes: 'What began in Western France in 1793 was repeated in the northern Italian *Viva Maria* riots, the Calabrian *Sanfedista* and Belgian peasant revolts, all in 1799, as well as in Spain in 1808. In each case the authority of republican government was embodied in townsmen, often professionals, and in a minority of ardent politicians whose rhetoric was the more shrill for being isolated in regions largely unsympathetic to their doctrine.'

24. *Annual Register for the Year 1810*, p. 233.

25. *CMH*, vol. IX, p. 241 and Méneval *op. cit.*, vol. II, p. 459.
26. Rose *op. cit.*, vol. II, pp. 228–29 quoting a letter of 17 September 1810.
27. See C. Northcote Parkinson, *War in the Eastern Seas 1793–1815* (London, 1954), pp. 365,368.
28. Ava was the former capital of Burma.
29. Rose *op. cit.*, vol. II, pp. 228–29, quoting a letter of 17 September 1810, and C. Cornell, *Questions Relating to Nicolas Baudin's Australian Expedition, 1800–1804* (Adelaide, 1965), p. 15.
30. Rose *op. cit.*, vol. II, p. 235.

Chapter Seven

1. See John F. Cady, *The Roots of French Imperialism in Eastern Asia* (Ithaca, N. Y. rev. ed. 1967), pp. 15–16.
2. See L. Marchant, *France Australe* (Perth, 1982), pp. 225–29.
3. See *The New Cambridge Modern History*, vol. IX (Cambridge, 1969), pp. 468, 472–73.
4. See D. Howard. *The English Activities on the North Coast of Australia in the First Half of the Nineteenth Century* (London University. MA thesis 1924), pp. 48–53.
5. Quoted in N. Tarling, *Anglo-Dutch Rivalry in the Malay Archipelago, 1780–1824* (Cambridge & St Lucia, Queensland, 1962), p. 89.
6. Quoted in K. A. Austin, *The Voyage of the Investigator* (Adelaide, p/b ed. 1968), pp. 168–70.
7. Barns to Bathurst, 23 July 1823, and to Horton 15 September 1823, CO201/146.
8. Larpent to Bathurst 23 December 1823 *Historical Records of Australia* Series II, vol. 5, p. 745. Hereafter *HRA*.
9. Henry Bathurst (1762–1834), styled Lord Apsley 1775–94, 3rd Earl Bathurst 1794, was Secretary of State for War and the Colonies 1812–27.
10. See G. Blainey, *The Tyranny of Distance* (Melbourn ed. 1966), pp. 89–93.
11. Bathurst to Darling 1 and 11 March 1826, *HRA* Series I vol. 12, pp. 193–94. This longitude still agreed with the original Portuguese interpretation of the Papal line of demarcation, and so did not yet breach the Dutch claims in Western Australia.
12. Begbie to Hay 18 March, Hay to Barrow 6 April, and Bathurst to Darling 7 April 1826, *HRA* Series I vol. 12, pp. 224–26.
13. The Dutch claimed the territory west of long. 141° East of Greenwich. Owing to the unhealthiness of the location, this fort was withdrawn after

the British had withdrawn from Port Essington and Melville Island, but, ironically, just before the British decided to renew their presence there.

14. Stirling to Darling *HRA* Series III vol. 6, pp. 552, 557–58.

15. J. Barrow, 'State of the Colony of Swan River,' 1 January 1830, chiefly extracted from Captain Stirling's Report, *Royal Geographical Society Journal*, 11831, pp. 7–10.

16. Barrow and Beaufort to Glenelg, 10 April 1837, CO 201/264.

17. Glenelg to Wood, 10 May 1837 and Stephen to Spearman, 28 July 1837, CO 202/34.

18. E. J. Eyre, 'Considerations Against the Supposed Existence of a Great Sea in the Interior of Australia,' a paper read on 23 June 1845 and published in the Society's *Journal*, 16 (1846), 200–11.

19. Earl *op. cit.*, pp. 447–61.

20. Royal Geographical Society to Lord Glenelg, forwarded by John Barrow on 13 December 1836, CO201/256.

21. For a history of this enterprise, see Peter G. Spillett, *Forsaken Settlement* (Melbourne, 1972).

22. Dora Howard *op. cit.*, pp. 134–37.

23. Elliot, Wood and Rogers to Stephen 22 January 1847 CO201/389.

Chapter Eight

1. These vessels were sometimes owned by English free merchants or even by servants of the East India Company, or might be chartered from native shipowners, and were not subject to the supervision of the East India Company. See Serafin D. Quiason, *English 'Country Trade' with the Philippines 1644–1765* (Quezon City, 1966).

2. Sir John T. Pratt, *The Expansion of Europe into the Far East* (London, 1947), pp. 80 *et seq.*; and John K. Fairbank and Edwin O. Reischauer, *China: Tradition and Transformation* (Sydney etc., 1979), pp. 273–76.

3. *Oriental Herald*, vol. 31824, pp. 437–38.

4. Its monopoly of the trade with India had been terminated in 1813.

5. The name given to the Imperial Superintendent of the Maritime Customs for the Canton region.

6. These ports were Canton, Shanghai, Ningpo, Amoy and Foochow.

7. Ernest S. Dodge, *Beyond the Capes: Pacific Exploration from Captain Cook to the Challenger 1776–1877* (London, 1971), pp. 336–37. This search for a short route through the Sulu Sea to China was precisely the task that Alexander Dalrymple, hydrographer of the East India Company, had entrusted to the *Antelope* half-a-century

earlier; this vessel had reached China by that route, but had been wrecked off the Palau Islands on the return voyage.

8. Apart from the small enclave on an island off Nagasaki, where the Dutch were permitted to reside and trade.

9. R. O'Connor, *Pacific Destiny* (Boston and Toronto, 1969), p. 10.

10. Stanley P. Wright, *Hart and the Chinese Customs* (Belfast, 1950), pp. 74–5 and 207–08; and A. J. Sargent, *Anglo-Chinese Commerce and Diplomacy* (Oxford, 1907), pp. 14–5, 130–33.

11. W. C. Costin, *Great Britain and China 1833–60* (Oxford, 1937), pp. 149–50.

12. Vladimir, *Russia on the Pacific: the Siberian Railway* (London, 1899), pp. 100 *et seq.*, 170 *et seq.*; John K. Fairbank and Edwin O. Reischauer, *China: Tradition and Transformation* (Boston, Sydney and London, 1979), p. 302.

13. His empire embraced all of Vietnam.

14. Modern DaNang.

15. Being at the head of navigation on the Irrawaddy River and in close proximity to the Chinese Empire, Rhamo was the traditional terminus for commerce passing from Yunnan province to Burma. See Hall *op. cit.*, pp. 660–62; A. Redford, *Manchester Merchants and Foreign Trade*, 2 vols. (Manchester, 1960), vol. II, pp. 85–9. For eighteenth-century interest in the same question and regarding 'Prammoo,' see Howard T. Fry, *Alexander Dalrymple and the Expansion of British Trade* (London and Toronto, 1970), p. 11.

16. A. Michie *The Englishman in China during the Victorian era: The Career of Sir Rutherford Alcock*, 2 vols., vol. I (Edinburgh and London, 1900), pp. 163–64 *et passim*.

17. Ibid., vol. I, pp. 227–30.

18. In 1861 Captain Charles Wilkes, without authorization, intercepted the British steamer *Trent* in order to arrest two Confederate Government commissioners who were on their way to England and France.

19. Quoted by Helen Irving (ed.), in *The Centenary Companion to Australian Federation* (Cambridge University Press, 1999), p. 5.

Chapter Nine

1. Germany, Russia and Austria-Hungary.

2. Friedrich List (trans. G. A. Matile) *The National System of Political Economy* (Philadelphia, 1856), pp. 2–3, 79.

3. N. Tarling, *Britain, the Brookes and Brunei* (Kuala Lumpur, etc.: Oxford University Press, 1971), p. 198.

4. Taylor *op. cit.*, p. 68.

5. Charles W. Boyd (ed.), *The Speeches of Mr. Chamberlain*, 2 vols., vol. I (London, 1914), pp. 135–36.

6. Including the Admiralty Islands, New Hanover, New Ireland and New Britain.

7. Bourke Island, Choiseul Island and Ysabel Island.

8. Taylor, *op. cit.*, pp. 65 and 80.

9. List, *op. cit.*, pp. 474–75.

10. P. E. Roberts, *A Historical Geography of the British Dependencies*, vol. VII India (Oxford, 1916), pp. 314–15.

11. Hall, *op. cit.*, pp. 677–78.

12. Ibid., pp. 679 et *seq.*

13. *Annual Register for the Year 1884* p. 229.

14. *The New Cambridge Modern History*, vol. XI, pp. 223–24.

15. *Annual Register for 1888* Speech made on 24 April, pp. 103 *et seq.* and 113–15.

16. Ibid., pp. 300–01.

17. Crowley, *op. cit.*, vol. III, pp. 279–80.

18. E. Eyck, *Bismarck and the German Empire* (London and New York. 1950, repr. 1966). Pp. 294–96.

19. Pakenham, *op. cit.*, p. 456.

20. *Annual Register for 1893*, pp. 288–89, 330–31.

21. Ibid., pp. 2286–89.

22. *Annual Register for 1892*, pp. 232ff. *Annual Register for 1893*, pp. 345–47.

23. C. Wilcox. *Australia's Boer War* (Melbourne: Oxford University Press, 2002), p. 13.

24. Approximately 370 miles.

25. Percy H. Kent, *Railway Enterprise in China: An Account of Its Origin and Development* (London, 1907), pp. 28–9.

26. Ibid., p. 403.

27. Kent, *op. cit.*, p. 158.

28. T. S. Hoffman, *Britain and the German Trade Rivalry 1875–1914* (London, 1933, repr. New York, 1964), pp. 232 *et seq.*

29. See the next chapter.

30. Paul M. Kennedy, *The Rise of Anglo-German Antagonism, 1860–1914* (5th impression London, 1990), pp. 223–27.

31. Lord Charles Beresford, *The Break-up of China* (London and New York, 1899), pp. 237–38, 262, 323, 447–48.

32. Hitler absorbed these concepts as a schoolboy in Linz. In 1926 he met the elderly H. S. Chamberlain who declared that the encounter had set his soul at rest. See Joachim C. Fest (trans.R. and C. Winston Penguin Books, Harmondsworth, 1974), pp. 55, 181.

33. His dispatch to the Governors of the six Australian colonies, 34 March 1897, recorded in the *SMH,* 18 June 1898.

35. F. List, *National System of Political Economy* (Trans.G. Matell Philadelphia, 1856), p. 474.

36. *SMH,* 11 November 1899, p. 9.

Chapter Ten

1. See H. Irving (ed.), *The Centenary Companion to Australian Federation* (Cambridge. 1999); and F. Crowley, *A Documentary History of Australia,* vol. III (Melbourne, 1980), pp. 130–31. The Convention also adopted a draft Bill for a Federal Council, prepared by Samuel Griffith of Queensland, who would also draft the very influential Constitution Bill at the 1891 Federation Convention.

2. Friedrich List (translated G. A. Matile) *The National System of Political Economy* (Philadelphia, 1856), pp. 474–75.

3. Crowley *op. cit.,* pp. 279–80.

4. Ibid., pp. 280–82.

5. Ibid.

6. Ibid., pp. 95–6, 100–03.

7. Irving *op. cit.,* pp. 337–38.

8. Samuel Eliot Morison and Henry Steele Commager, *The Growth of the American Republic,* vol. II (New York etc., 1942), pp. 320–21.

9. *Annual Register for 1896* p. 1. Morison and Commager mention that it was only because the British had their hands very full in other quarters of the globe that the Salisbury government was in absolute need of American friendship, 'let this challenge lie.'

10. Governor-General Doumer of French Indo-China planned a trunk line connecting the port of Haiphong with the capital of Szechuanvia Hanoi and Yunnas-fu.

11. *SMH* 11 June 1898, p. 4.

12. Thomas Packenham, *The Scramble for Africa* (London, 1992), pp. 456–58.

13. *Foreign and Colonial Speeches by the Rt. Hon J Chamberlain* (London, 1897) p.87

BIBLIOGRAPHY

Chapter 1
Primary sources
Pocock Papers, Maritime Museum, Greenwich
Admiral Kempenfelt to Admiral Pocock 1 April 1762
Dutch Records A, vol xvii, India Office Library (in British Library)
Secret Committee to Earl Halifax, 14 January 1764

Secondary sources
Barnes, G. R. and J. H. Owen (eds), *The Sandwich Papers* (London 1932)
Brosses, C. de, *Histoire des Navigations aux Terres Australes*, 2 vols. (Paris 1756), translated into English by J.Callender as *Terra Australis Cognita* (London and Edinburgh 1766)
Cotton, Sir H. E. A., (ed. Sir C.G.H. Fawcett), *East Indiamen: the East India Company's Maritime Service* (London 1949)
Crowhurst, P., 'The voyage of the Pitt: a turning-point in the East Indian navigation', *Mariner's Mirror* vol.55 (1969) pp 43-56
Dalrymple, Alexander, *An Historical Collection of the Several Voyages and Discoveries in the South Pacific Ocean*, 2 vols. (London 1770-71)
Fry, Howard T., *Alexander Dalrymple and the expansion of British Trade* (London and Toronto 1970)
'Alexander Dalrymple and Captain Cook: the creative interplay of two careers' in Fisher, Robin and Hugh Johnston, *Captain James Cook and his Times* (Vancouver and London 1979), a selection from the proceedings of the conference held at Simon Fraser University, 1978
'The Eastern Passage and its impact on Spanish policy in the Philippines 1758-1790', *Philippine Studies* vol.33 (Ateneo de Manila, 1985) pp 3-21
Furber, Holden, *Rival Empires of Trade in the Orient* (Minneapolis 1976)
Harlow, V. T., *The Founding of the Second British Empire* vol.1 (London 1952)
Harris, John (ed. J. Campbell), *Navigantium atque Itinerantium Bibliotheca, or a Complete Collection of Voyages and Travels* 2 vols. (London 1744-48)
Marcus, G. J., *A Naval History of England* vol.1 (London 1961)
Parkinson, C. N., War in the Eastern Seas 1793-1815 (London 1954)
Richmond, Admiral Sir Herbert W., *The Navy in India 1763-83* (London 1931)

Vlekke, Bernard M., *Nusantara: a history of the East Indian Archipelago* (Cambridge, Mass. 1943)

Chapter Two
Primary sources
Annual Register for the years 1784–86
Diaries and correspondence of James Harris, first Earl of Malmesbury, 2 vols. (London 1844)
British Library:
   Add. Mss. 28060, 28061, 38,409
   Egerton Mss. 3498, 3505
Public Record Office
   FO 7/8, 7/9, 26/6, 27/16, 37/6, 37/10, 37/11, 37/12, 37/13, 37/14.
   PRO 30/8/157

Secondary sources
Fry, H. T., 'The Eastern Passage and its impact on Spanish policy in the Philippines', *Philippine Studies* (Ateneo de Manila Press, 1985) vol.33
Frost, Alan, *Convicts and Empire* (OUP Melbourne etc, 1980)
Tarling, Nicholas, *Anglo-Dutch rivalry in the Malay World 1793–1824* (Cambridge & St Lucia 1961)
The New Cambridge Modern History Vol. VIII (Cambridge 1971)

Chapter Three
Primary sources
British Library:
   Add. Mss. 38,346
   Egerton Mss. 3499, 3501.
   Log of the Antelope, L/MAR/B57A (India Office Library).
Public Record Office:
   FO 27/16, 37/5, 37/9, 38/6
   PRO 30/8/36

Secondary sources
Eden, Rt. Hon. W., *The history of New Holland from its first discovery in 1616 to the present time* (2nd ed. London 1787)
Ehrman, John, *The Younger Pitt* (London 1969)
Frost, Alan, *Convicts and Empire* (Melbourne 1984)
Fry, Howard T., *Alexander Dalrymple and the expansion of British trade* (London & Toronto 1970)
   'Alexander Dalrymple and New Guinea', *The Journal of Pacific History* vol.4 (1969)
Gibbin, R. W., *The Early history of Tasmania 1642–1804* (London 1928)
Hall, D. G. E., *A History of South-East Asia* (4th ed. London 1981)
Howe, Sonia E., *In Quest of Spices* (London 1939)
Hulot, E., *Baron, D'Entrecasteaux* (Paris 1894)

King, Robert H., 'The territorial boundaries of New South Wales in 1788', *The Great Circle* vol.3 no.2 (1981)
Tate, D. J. M., *The making of modern South-East* Asia 2 vols (OUP Kuala Lumpur etc. 1971)

Chapter Four
Primary sources
Board's Collections, India Office Library, British Library
The Melville Papers, National Library of Scotland, Ms 1069

Secondary sources
Cronin, Vincent, *Napoleon* (London 1971)
Dunmore, John, *French explorers in the Pacific* 2 vols. (Oxford 1965–69)
Ennis, Thomas, *French policy and development in Indo-China* (Chicago 1936.
Ingram, E., (ed.) *Two views on British India* (Bath 1970)
Moon, Sir Penderel, *The British Conquest and Dominion of India* (London 1989)
Parkinson, C. N, *War in the Eastern Seas 1793–1815* (London 1956)
Rainbow, S. G., 'English expeditions to the Dutch East Indies during the Revolutionary and Napoleonic wars' (London University MA thesis, May 1933)
Rose, J. H., *Life of Napoleon I* (London 1904)
Schama, Simon, *Citizens: a Chronicle of the French Revolution* (London 1989)
Sloane, W. M., *Life of Napoleon Bonaparte*, 4 vols. (New York and London 1896)
The Cambridge Modern History vol.IX (Cambridge 1906)

Chapter Five
Primary sources
Annual Register for 1800
India Office Library (in the British Library):
  Board's Collections F/4/159
  Bengal Foreign Consultations 165/80
National Library of Scotland:
The Melville Papers Ms. 1069

Secondary sources
Compton, H., *Particular account of European military adventurers of Hindustan, 1784–1803* (London 1889)
Fry, H. T., *Alexander Dalrymple and the expansion of British trade* (London and Toronto 1970)
Mack, James D., *Matthew Flinders* (Melbourne 1966)
Marlowe, J., *Perfidious Albion: the origins of Anglo-French rivalry in the Levant* (London 1971)
O'Meara, B. E., *Napoleon in Exile* (London 1822)

Pratt Sir John T., *The Expansion of Europe into the Far East* (London 1947)
Rose, J. H., *The Life of Napoleon I* (London 1904)
Scott, E., *The Life of Matthew Flinders* (Sydney 1914)
Tarling, Nicholas, *Anglo-Dutch rivalry in the Malay world 1780–1824* (St Lucia 1962)
The Cambridge Modern History vol.IX (Cambridge 1906)
The New Cambridge Modern History vol.IX (Cambridge 1969)

Chapter Six
Primary sources
India Office Library (in the British Library):
    Board's Collections F/4/159
    Bengal Foreign Consultations 165/80
O'Meara, B. E., *Napoleon in Exile* (London 1822)
National Library of Scotland:
The Melville Papers Ms. 1069

Secondary sources
Compton, H., *Particular account of European military adventurers of Hindustan 1784–1803* (London 1889–93)
Fry, Howard T., *Alexander Dalrymple and the expansion of British trade* (London 1970)
Mack, James D. *Matthew Flinders* 2 vols. (Melbourne 1964)
Marlowe, John, *Perfidious Albion: the origins of Anglo-French rivalry in the Levant* (London 1971)
Pratt, Sir John T., *The expansion of Europe into the Far East* (London 1947)
Rose, J. H., *The life of Napoleon I* (London 1904)
Scott, E., *The life of Captain Matthew Flinders* (Sydney 1914)
Tarling, Nicholas, *Anglo-Dutch rivalry in the Malay world 1780–1824* (Cambridge & St.Lucia 1962)
The Cambridge Modern History vol.IX (Cambridge 1906)
The New Cambridge Modern History vol.IX (Cambridge 1969)

Chapter Seven
Primary Sources
Public Record Office CO 201/146, 201/256, 201/264, 201/389, CO 202/34
FO 37/120
Historical Records of Australia: Series I vol.12, Series II vol.5, Series III vol.6

Secondary Sources
Austin, K. A., *The Voyage of the Investigator* (Adelaide 1968)
Cady, John F., *The roots of French imperialism in Eastern Asia* (Ithaca, N.Y., revised. ed. 1967)
Eyre, E. J., 'Considerations against the supposed existence of a great

sea in the interior of Australia', *Royal Geographical Society*, London, Journal vol.I, 1831

Howard, Dora, 'The English activities on the north coast of Australia in the first half of the nineteenth century' (London University MA thesis 1924)

Marchant, Leslie, *France Australe* (Perth 1982)

Spillett, Peter G., *Forgotten Settlement* (New South Wales 1972)

Tarling, Nicholas, *Anglo-Dutch rivalry in the Malay world 1793–1815* (Cambridge and St. Lucia 1962)

The New Cambridge Modern History vol IX (Cambridge 1969)

Chapter Eight
Primary sources
Oriental Herald vol. 3 1824

Secondary sources

Costin, W. C., *Great Britain and China 1833–1860* (Oxford 1937)

Dodge, Ernest S., *Beyond the Capes: Pacific exploration from Captain Cook to the Challenger 1776–1877* (London 1971)

Fairbank, John K. & Edwin O. Reischauer, *China: Tradition and Transformation* (Sydney, London and Boston 1971)

Fitzgerald, C. P., *A Concise History of East Asia* (3rd. ed., London 1961)

Fry, Howard T., *Alexander Dalrymple and the expansion of British trade* (London and Toronto 1970)

Michie, Alexander, *The Englishman in China during the Victorian era: the career of Sir Rutherford Alcock* (Edinburgh and London 1900)

O'Connor, Richard O., *Pacific Destiny* (Boston and Toronto 1969)

Pratt, Sir John T., *The expansion of Europe into the Far East* (London 1947)

Quiason, Serafin D., *English Country Trade with the Philippines 1644–1745* (Quezon City 1966)

Redford, A., *Manchester Merchants and Foreign Trade* 2 vols. (Manchester 1960)

Sargent, A. J., *Anglo-Chinese Commerce and Diplomacy* (Oxford 1907)

'Vladmir', *Russia on the Pacific: the Siberian Railway* (London 1899)

Wright, Stanley P., *Hart and the Chinese Customs* (Belfast 1950)

Chapter 9
Primary sources
Annual Register for the years 1884, 1886–7 & 1892–3

Secondary sources

Boyd, Charles W., *The speeches of Mr. Chamberlain*, 2 vols. (London 1914)

Crowley, Frank, *A Documentary History of Australia* vol.III (Melbourne 1980)

Eyck, Erich, *Bismarck and the German Empire* (London and New York 1950, repr. 1966)
Hall, D. G. E., *A History of South-East Asia* (4th. ed., London 1981)
Irving, Helen (ed), *The Centenary Companion to Australian Federation* (CUP Cambridge 1999)
List, Friedrich, (trans. G. A. Matile), *The National System of Political Economy* (Philadelphia 1856)
Pakenham, Thomas, *The Scramble for Africa 1876–1912* (London 1991)
Roberts, P. E., *A Historical Geography of the British Dependencies* vol. VII, India (Oxford 1916)
Sontag, R. J., *Germany and England: background of conflict 1848–1894* (New York 1969)
Tarling., Nicholas, *Britain, the Brookes and Brunei* (OUP Kuala Lumpur etc., 1971)
Taylor, A. J. P., *Germany's First Bid for Colonies, 1884-5* (New York 1970)
The New Cambridge Modern History vol. XI (CUP Cambridge 1970)
Wilcox, Craig, *Australia's Boer War* (OUP Melbourne 1992)

Chapter Ten
Primary sources
Annual Register for 1898
Beresford, Lord Charles, *The Breaking-up of China* (London and New York 1899)
Sydney Morning Herald, 29 March and 21 May 1898, 11 November 1899

Secondary sources
Clyde, Paul H. and Burton F. Beers, *The Far East: a History of the Western Impact and the Eastern Response, 1830–1965* (N.J. 1966)
Dallin, David J., *The Rise of Russia in Asia* (Yale UP 1971)
Garvin, J. L., *The Life of Joseph Chamberlain*, vol.III (London 1934)
Hoffman, T. S., *Britain and the German trade rivalry, 1873–1914* (London 1933, repr. New York 1964)
Irving, Helen (ed), *The Centenary Companion to Australian Federation* (Cambridge UP 1999)
Kennedy, Paul M., *The Rise of Anglo-German antagonism, 1860–1914* (London and N.J. 1987)
Kent, Percy H., *Railway Enterprise in China: Its Origin and Development* (London 1907)
Snyder, Louis L., *German Nationalism: The Tragedy of a People* (Harrisburg PA. 1954)
Taylor, A. J. P., *The struggle for mastery in Europe, 1848–1914* (OUP New York 1971)
Weale, B. L. P., *The re-shaping of the Far East* 2 vols. (London 1905)
Wilcox, Craig, *Australia's Boer War: The War in South Africa 1899–1902* (Melbourne 2002)